John McDonagh, EDITOR

Economy, Society and Peripherality
Experiences from the West of Ireland

Arlen House
2002

first published in October 2002 by

Arlen House
PO Box 222
Galway

and

42 Grange Abbey Road
Baldoyle
Dublin 13
Ireland

In association with GSI Special Publication No. 12

ISBN:

1-903631-25-4 paperback
1-903631-26-2 hardback

www.arlenhouse.ie
www.arlenacademic.com

Printed by ColourBooks, Baldoyle, Dublin 13
Typesetting: Arlen House

Cover design:
Front cover photograph of Connemara courtesy of Tommy Ó Fátharta and
Mary Redmond. Details from 1610 map and town plan of Galway courtesy of
the Map Collection, Department of Geography, NUI, Galway

CONTENTS

LIST OF FIGURES

LIST OF TABLES

ACKNOWLEDGEMENTS

The compilation of this book has involved the enthusiasm and dedication of a number of people. Firstly I would like to thank Alan Hayes of Arlen House for his initial support for the book, his advice throughout its compilation and the professional manner in which the book has been published. Secondly, I would like to extend special thanks to the individual contributors who made this book possible. Their interest, enthusiasm and excellent insight on the developments taking place in the Western Region of Ireland made my involvement all the more pleasurable and indeed educational. Further, may I also ask for the understanding of the contributors should I have misinterpreted their ideas in the process of editing their work. I would also like to thank the President of NUI, Galway Dr Iognáid Ó Muircheartaigh for his support and for providing the foreword to the book.

I would like to gratefully acknowledge the financial support provided by the Registrar's Office, NUI, Galway and Údarás na Gaeltachta toward publication costs. Their generous donations were instrumental in completing the book and ensuring a professional publication. Thanks to Ulf Strohmayer and the members of the Geography Department at NUI, Galway for their help throughout, and to the Geographical Society of Ireland for their support and involvement with the project, particularly Jim Walsh, Kevin Griffin and Des McCafferty. Thanks also to those copyright holders who allowed their materials to be used in the book and, while every effort was made to ensure accurate acknowledgements, I also take this opportunity to apologise to any copyright holders whose rights may have been unwittingly infringed and invite any corrections or additions for future editions of this book.

Finally, there are a number of people who contributed greatly to the successful completion of this book. As such I am greatly indebted to Siúbhan Comer for her cartographic assistance and to Kieran Hickey and Sheila Gaffey for their advice and comments. A special word of thanks also to Tommy Ó Fátharta and Mary Redmond for their help with the cover design and to Peadar Ó Fátharta and Donnchadha Ó Fátharta for keeping the pressure on to get the book finished! Last but by no means least, I would like to say a special word of thanks to Maria and Rachael. Thanks to Maria for her organisational skills, for the indexing and ensuring that the book ran smoothly from beginning to end. More importantly special thanks for her patience and her continued and unwavering support.

John McDonagh
August 2002

FOREWORD

Is mó forbairt agus athrú a tháinig ar Éirinn le deich mbliana anuas. Is faoin leabhar seo iniúchadh a dhéanamh ar an athrú a tháinig ar Éirinn trí úsáid a bhaint as Gaillimh agus as mórcheantar an iarthair mar mhiocracasm den tír ina hiomláine. The challenge for the recent development that has taken place in Ireland is to ensure that all areas benefit to the same degree. Despite this desire, and the aspatial world in which we live, there are still people and places left behind – those on the periphery. In fact current research indicates an uncertain future for much of rural Ireland and for those regions outside of Dublin. In terms of the Western Region we have witnessed unprecedented change over the last decade. This prosperity is clearly evident in many parts of the region, but equally there are still areas that display continued marginalisation and underdevelopment. Consequently, this book sets itself the target of addressing this complex debate and, while it is virtually impossible to deal with the myriad issues affecting society in the West of Ireland, this book does provide a questioning of many of the current debates ongoing in the region. The contextual setting for the book grows very much out of the emerging geographies that mould rural and urban space in Ireland. The themes of local and regional governance, the increased fragmentation of rural areas, the perceived deterioration of 'quality of life', poor infrastructure, challenges for rural youth, issues of social exclusion etc., are the focus of the book and are of major concern to individuals, communities and policy makers in our evolving Irish society.

As well as being an international centre of learning, NUI, Galway is committed to support national and regional development through teaching, research and service to the community. We attach great importance to serving our regional community, especially along the western seaboard of Ireland. As the only University in the Border Midlands and West (BMW) Region, NUI, Galway has a unique responsibility in regard to the development of the region. In fact, the NUI, Galway Strategic Plan 2006 declares, as part of its strategic thrust:

> to play a leading role in regional development, with due regard to its location on the Western seaboard and its relationship with the multiple communities of its regional environment, including the city and the Gaeltacht.

We are also fully cognisant of the importance for regional development of collaborative effort between all third-level institutions within the BMW Region. NUI, Galway is a founding member of Líonra (the Regional Higher Education Network), a unique partnership of all the Higher Education Institutions in the BMW Region, namely Athlone, Dundalk, GMIT, Letterkenny and Sligo Institutes of Technology, St. Angela's College Sligo and NUI, Galway. The most important ingredients of the Network are a commitment to the spirit of partnership, a mutual respect for our diverse institutional roles and strengths, and a determination to combine our respective resources in imaginative ways to the best educational advantage of our region.

As part of our contribution to the Region, significant research on issues of importance to the community is taking place across all faculties and departments in NUI, Galway on an ongoing basis. This book is an example of this commitment providing as it does a complementarity of expertise and resources from researchers within NUI, Galway and from those of other Universities, community groups, state and semi-state bodies and voluntary organisations. This is what is meant by NUI, Galway being recognised as a 'Community Resource'. Trí dhul i mbun comhpháirtíochtaí, is féidir le hOllscoil na hÉireann Gaillimh, trína cuid saineolais, a cuid acmhainní agus an mheastóireacht agus tráchtaireacht a dhéanann an Ollscoil ar gach gné den fhorbairt in Éirinn, ról ceannais a ghlacadh san fhorbairt réigiúnach sa tír. This book epitomises this role as it frames not only the academic and policy viewpoint, but also enhances these viewpoints through contributions from community experiences and pragmatism. Those of geographical, sociological, political and planning persuasions provide an interesting mosaic of the current process and practice of development in the West of Ireland and the challenge for future visions of economy, demography, society and environment in the region. This provides a healthy mix of views, all of which are underpinned by their commonality of a desire to ensure equitable development, progress across all aspects of life and the opportunity for all people to realise their full potential within the West Region. That the reader can experience contrasting arguments on similar issues, while also having the opportunity to evaluate how people of different professional backgrounds argue their particular perspective gives the book an important dimension.

This work will undoubtedly be of great interest to the general public, state and semi-state bodies, and of course, undergraduate and postgraduate students studying the social sciences. The important element is that the book will help community groups, individuals, those with an interest in the future of Galway and the West Region, and students, the future decision makers, to link contrasting perspectives in terms of theory and practice. Is é mo thuairim go gcuirfidh an leabhar seo tuiscintí nua ar fáil do na díospóireachtaí uile atá ar bun sa réigiún sin. That this can be achieved is very much due to the high calibre of the contributors to the book, all of whom are people of high distinction in academic, community and state organisations; all of whom should be congratulated on their excellent and thought provoking contributions.

Dr Iognáid Ó Muircheartaigh

Uachtarán/President
Ollscoil na hÉireann, Gaillimh/
National University of Ireland, Galway

chapter one

DIMENSIONS OF CHANGE IN WESTERN IRELAND

John McDonagh

Introduction

In recent years rural Europe has experienced a number of challenges. Issues of population decline, falling farm numbers, reductions in agricultural employment, emigration, rural industrialisation and counter-urbanisation have all had major impacts on the restructuring of rural areas. Regional development practice and policy is however striving to create new ways of thinking about rural areas with increased emphasis on:

> the unique combination of local characteristics and global socio-economic processes ... (and a) ... focusing on regional qualities and identities (Groote *et al.* 2000, p.1).

This focus on regional development and the emerging geographies that have begun to mould rural and urban space are nowhere more evident than in the regions of Ireland. Over the last ten years the population of Ireland has grown to almost four million – the highest since 1881; the economy has expanded rapidly while levels of unemployment have tumbled far beyond even the most optimistic political predictions. The tide of emigration has turned, levels of prosperity increased and there is accelerated growth in all areas of economic activity. Despite this reinvention of the Irish economy not all boats have been lifted on this economic tide. Falling farm incomes, decline and closure of rural services and the increasing social marginalisation felt by many rural dwellers has continued. Many rural communities, small towns and villages struggle to remain viable and are unable to compete with those areas endowed with good infrastructure, public transportation and communication networks. This fragmenting of Irish society is still visible between the East and West of the country and, despite the aspatial world in which we live, there are still people and places 'left behind' – those on the periphery. In fact current publications by government departments indicate an increasingly perilous future for rural Ireland and for those regions outside of Dublin. A recent Department of Agriculture report suggested that the quality of life in rural areas was falling and that rural populations were declining due to a lack of adequate infrastructure and a lack of access to other services (from quality water and waste disposal to those of post offices and hospitals). The government blueprint for a 20-year National Spatial Strategy *Indications for the Way Ahead* also proclaims an uncertain future socially and economically for much of rural Ireland. The general thrust is that if this is to be prevented, then development must be diverted from Dublin to the regions. But are the regions of Ireland equipped to undertake further development? What are the barriers to this happening? and what are the likely implications of developments that do take place? These are some of the fundamental challenges that are addressed in this book, the outcomes of which are likely to render the debates, insights and critical comments all the more significant.

The challenge to the Irish government then is one of initiating new and innovative ways of regenerating declining rural areas in a time of national prosperity. In this book these deep-reaching transformations are explored using Galway and the West Region as a microcosm of the larger Irish picture. The prosperity of the Celtic Tiger is clearly evident in Galway's increased population and economic success. The West Region also however displays the continued marginalisation of some areas and a lack of what the government allegedly strive for – balanced regional development. Consequently this book sets itself the target of addressing these complex dilemmas and, while it is virtually impossible to deal with the myriad issues affecting society in the West of Ireland, this book does provide an investigation of the many debates ongoing in the region.

The Structure of the Book

The diversity of material presented in this book is reflective of the variety of disciplines from which the authors hail. Those of geographical, sociological, political and planning persuasions provide an interesting mosaic of the current process and practice of development in the West of Ireland. This diversity of contributors also highlights a diversity of opinion and signifies the importance of interdisciplinary studies. Indeed selecting the topics for the book has been a case of not knowing where to begin or where to end. The result will inevitably be part of the criticism of the book in that some issues are included while others are not. There is cohesiveness however in the themes of local and regional governance and interlinked issues of economy, society and peripherality. Included under these are: the impacts of Objective One status on the region; aspects of spatial planning and the National Spatial Strategy; the fragmenting of rural areas by increased long distance commuting; the perceived deterioration of quality of life; poor levels of public transportation and infrastructure; rural youth and employment; the geographies of social exclusion; sustainability and issues of waste management and water quality. All of these themes are significant determinants in Ireland's evolving economy and society and are of major concern to individuals, communities and policy makers in the West Region of Ireland. This melange of topics enhances the extent to which debate can be generated by the book. The underlining coherence is also obvious in that the evolving economy, society and nature of peripherality in Western Ireland are all very much linked to 'planning for change'.

Providing the discussion with some formal structure the book is divided into three parts. The first contextualises the changing levels of governance and delves into spatial planning and the policy-practice interface; the second explores aspects of peripherality, spatial planning and poverty, while the third deals with planning for change through exploring aspects of demography, employment, economic development and environmental concerns.

In **Part I** the shift towards new forms of governance and some of the alternative channels between state and community in Ireland are explored. The first chapter of this section deals with a rethinking of regionalisation in Ireland. In this, **Chapter 2**, Gerry Finn details the impact of the Border, Midlands and West Regional Assembly, and the role to be played by this group in delivering the objectives of the National Development Plan 2000–2006 to the West Region. Padraig Ó hAoláin follows in **Chapter 3** with an assessment of a unique regional authority, namely, Údarás na Gaeltachta. The central focus of this chapter is on the need to address uneven patterns of economic growth in the Gaeltacht region and the need to ensure that the Gaeltacht is not second best in the distribution of wealth and resources regionally or in Ireland as a whole. The added challenge of maintaining the Irish language in the region is also addressed as Ó hAoláin attempts to 'balance the imbalances'. In **Chapter 4,** Des McCafferty raises broader questions in relation to balanced regional development, polycentrism and the urban system in the West of Ireland. The likely impact of the National Spatial Strategy and the desire for polycentric development is the central focus. The chapter begins with an examination of the nature of polarisation conducted through a review of sectoral and spatial aspects of recent growth in Ireland. Results are presented from an analysis of the Irish urban system and in particular those of the urban centres of the West Region. Further, using past and present regional policy as a benchmark, McCafferty makes some insightful comments on the potential problems in the pattern of urban development in the West. These regionally specific comments lead onto the increasingly important role that regional development and spatial planning has in the Irish public policy agenda dealt with by Jim Walsh in **Chapter 5**. In this chapter Walsh takes a critical view of the preparation of the National Spatial Strategy and the concept of achieving balanced regional development. He examines the issues that have been considered and the concepts underpinning this emerging strategy. What becomes clear within Walsh's chapter is that the concept of functional regions is central to combating rural decline. Michael Keane in **Chapter 6** further advances this discussion. Here the argument is focused on what Keane sees as a fundamental challenge facing spatial planning in Ireland namely the problem of defining the shape and form of functional regions. Keane, in an interesting addition to understandings of spatial planning, interrogates commuting data from the Census of Population using some exploratory data methods in an attempt to further the discussion and definition of functional regions.

Part II of the book continues on the themes of spatial planning and policy and explores the nebulous relationship between society, spatial planning and peripherality. Recognising that the notion of peripherality is central to rural policy making in Ireland, John McDonagh, in **Chapter 7**, begins this section by calling for a re-evaluation of peripherality and a greater recognition by policy makers and planners of aspatial peripherality. The argument of this chapter is that for too long Ireland has concentrated on addressing conventional peripherality, and while this should not be dismissed, McDonagh argues that there is now a need to view the greater impediment that is aspatial peripherality and the implications this has for many rural areas in Ireland. In **Chapter 8**, Barbara Walshe builds on this argument linking spatial planning and poverty in an attempt to determine how spatial policies in Ireland have led to a concentration of poverty in certain urban and rural areas. Making reference to the Border, Midlands and West Region and County Galway, this chapter makes recommendations which spatial planning policy at local, regional and national levels will need to address if there is any possibility of achieving sustainable communities in the future. Continuing with this theme, **Chapter 9** by Brendan Smith attempts to integrate a community perspective in to the planning process. Taking a community activist's viewpoint, this chapter provides an interesting insight to the development that has taken place in Galway City over the last three decades. Smith's commentary highlights not only the lack of consultation and community involvement in planning decisions during this period in Galway, but the need to change peoples' attitudes and the necessity for greater partnerships between community and local authorities in shaping the environment in which they live. In the final contribution to this section, **Chapter 10**, Patricia O'Hara moves from the local to the regional. The central focus here is on the need for specific economic and social targeting of the peripheral West Region. O'Hara takes a critical look at the limited progress achieved in the region at a time of record economic growth levels nationally. She further argues for more efficient and effective targeting of public and private investment in the provision of adequate access, communications and power, a strategy she argues, that should be paralleled with other social developments.

In the final section, **Part III**, some further significant challenges facing the West of Ireland are dealt with. Mary Cawley and Marie Mahon, in **Chapter 11**, provide the contextual setting for these challenges when they review the way in which the distribution of County Galway's urban and rural population has evolved since the early 1970s. By identifying the longer-term trends in population and distribution over this period Cawley and Mahon help inform, more fully, initiatives that may arise from the National Spatial Strategy and its attempts to achieve more balanced regional development. It becomes clear in this chapter also that the distribution of employment opportunities and service provision need to be linked more effectively to physical planning that hitherto seems not to have been the case. **Chapter 12** also explores the distribution of employment opportunities and their connection to the functionality of rural space. In this chapter John McDonagh attempts to determine the link, if any, between peripheral location, human resource deficits and the moulding of sustainable rural communities. Central to the argument of this chapter is the need for rural areas to attract and/or retain skilled personnel. For this to happen McDonagh argues that the aim of rural development should not only relate to issues of geographic location and job creation as seems to be the current policy strategy. He argues that rural development policy must also help determine the levels of functionality that can be created/expected within rural areas and thereby determine an area's ability to attract and retain human resources. Brian McGrath follows a similar theme, in **Chapter 13,** exploring the problematic of rural employment through the experiences of rural youth and the concept of labour market exclusion in North-West Connemara. In this chapter McGrath gives voice to young peoples' problematic experiences and encounters in employment in the Connemara region and highlights the types of social processes and encounters that serve to reinforce their labour market exclusion. The chapter also explores the different perspectives of young people toward economic development and policy and assesses how public and social policy can work towards labour market inclusion of young rural dwellers. The labour market theme continues in **Chapter 14,** when Seamus Grimes investigates the information economy. Information and communication technologies (ICTs) have made a major contribution to Irish economic development and employment opportunities in recent years. In this chapter Grimes contextualises Irelands ICT sector in an international perspective and specifically attempts to determine the extent to which Galway City and region have been successful in stimulating information economy activity both from foreign and indigenous investment. The chapter also attempts to identify some of the key barriers that appear to be preventing further growth in this activity in the West Region. Another major contributor to Irish economic development is explored by Sheila Gaffey in **Chapter 15**. The tourism industry is one of the mainstays of the Irish economy. Many western counties are particularly dependent on the revenues generated by tourists and tourism activities. As this is such a competitive industry great emphasis is placed on how an area is packaged or sold. In this chapter Gaffey attempts to 'unpack' some of the imagery that is used to sell the West of Ireland. In particular Gaffey focuses on the promotional materials of Small & Medium Enterprises (SMEs) in two regions in the West of Ireland and examines how they use imagery, particularly images of place, for the purpose of promotion and marketing of quality handcrafts and rural tourism.

Continuing with this theme of quality environments the final two contributors deal with two contentious issues, both of which play a determining role in future economic, social and environmental sustainability. In **Chapter 16**, Máire Ní Chíonna explores the whole area of sustainable waste management. She begins by questioning the conflict between waste and resource and argues for a greater emphasis on reduction, reuse and recycling of materials in terms of waste management. Ní Chíonna also outlines some of the local developments currently underway in terms of investment and raising environmental awareness in County Galway. Ultimately, she argues that if we wish to have a society in which waste is managed in a sustainable way then everybody has a part to play. Individuals, groups, communities, businesses, local authorities and central government have to engage with an integrated system of waste management that takes into account environmental, social and economic concerns. In the final contribution, **Chapter 17**, Kieran Hickey deals with another increasingly contentious issue, namely that of water quality, and the likely implications the lack of water quality will have on many parts of rural Ireland. Water in terms of domestic, industrial, agricultural and human consumption is one of the key economic resources of the State. There is however a growing concern within rural Ireland with regard to water contamination and pollution. Hickey examines some of the current problems through identifying changes in groundwater, river, lake and coastal water quality. This in turn is used to feed into discussion on two key issues facing the West of Ireland namely those of contaminated group water schemes and nitrate control zones.

In a final comment, it is perhaps necessary to mention how this collection will be an important addition to the future development of the West Region of Ireland. The necessity for this book has emerged from two directions. The first has come from observing my locale; experiencing change and so-called development while also recognising exclusion and the widening gap between the 'haves' and the 'have-nots'. The second is rooted in academic pursuits and specifically in my involvement with geography students at NUI, Galway and their pursuit of research topics in the West Region. From these experiences this book was initiated. A book that is sufficiently broad and with enough contrasting opinions that it should stimulate a questioning mind, further research in the region and increase levels of discussion on issues of concern in the local 'world' around us.

It is the intention of this book to provide a healthy mix of views underpinned by the commonality of a desire to ensure equitable development, progress across all aspects of life and the opportunity for all people to realise their full potential. This is displayed in the contributors' attempts to understand policy objectives and constraints and the practical desires of local communities. The book shows how academic debate and theory is enhanced by community experience and pragmatism and, how differentiation is often underpinned by common identities. That the reader can experience contrasting arguments on similar issues, while also having the opportunity to evaluate how people of different professional backgrounds argue their particular perspective, gives the book an added dimension.

The overriding concern is to draw together the multiple ideas that inform and mould our society in an effort to enhance the environment, development and quality of life experienced in the West Region of Ireland. It is hoped that this work will be of interest to undergraduate and postgraduate students studying the social sciences by helping them to link contrasting perspectives, theory and practice. It is also hoped that this book will be of use to practitioners, community groups and all those with an interest in the future of Galway and the West Region of Ireland.

chapter two

RETHINKING REGIONALISTION IN IRELAND
THE ROLE OF THE BORDER, MIDLAND AND WEST REGIONAL ASSEMBLY

Gerry Finn

Introduction

The way in which rural areas are governed has undergone a number of changes in recent years. Although Ireland has been dominated by a centralised administrative system, this is slowly changing:

> as the current political climate promotes the regional and local as important elements in forging paths for rural, economic and social development (McDonagh, 2001, p.162).

A significant step to a more devolved decision-making system has come about through the creation of two regions within Ireland, the Border, Midlands and West (BMW) region, which retains Objective 1 status to 2006, and the South and East (S&E) region, which moves to Objective 1 in Transition status for the same period. In this chapter the role played by the Regional Assembly in the BMW region will be explored in relation to its participation in delivering the objectives of the National Development Plan (NDP) 2000–2006 (Department of Finance, 1999).

The National Development Plan 2000–2006

The Irish National Development Plan 2000–2006 (Department of Finance, 1999) forms part of a series of National Development Plans implemented by the Irish Government since the mid 1980s. The Plan for the period 1987–1992 was essentially aimed at the consolidation of the public finances, which were in serious deficit at the start of that period. In this, it was eminently successful because the General Government Deficit was reduced from 10.6 per cent of GDP in 1986 to 2.4 per cent in 1992. Moreover, General Government Debt fell from nearly 120 per cent of GDP to just 92 per cent between these years. At the end of 2000 the General Government Deficit was in surplus to the tune of 4.5 per cent and General Government Debt was less than 39 per cent of GDP.

The 1993–1999 Plan was designed to address a different problem, namely, unemployment. Its main emphasis was on the development of industry and services and on the training and up-skilling of the labour force. Again, success was achieved, with employment rising by a total of 36 per cent over the Plan period and unemployment rate falling from over 15 per cent in 1993 to below 6 per cent in 1999. Unemployment is currently below 4 per cent. As a result of this sustained effort over more than a decade, Ireland's GDP per head of population rose from 67 per cent of the EU average in 1986 to 114 per cent in 1999, the EU's third highest. This success however, has created its own problems. In particular, the rapid economic growth of 9.5 per cent per year in the period 1995–1999 imposed very heavy strains on infrastructure and, indeed, exposed its inadequate nature. Moreover, there are disadvantaged groups in Irish society whom economic progress has more or less passed by (see also Walsh, Chapter 8).

The current NDP 2000–2006 (Department of Finance, 1999) is designed to underpin the development of a dynamic competitive economy over the planned period. It aims to build on the unprecedented economic progress of recent years and to strengthen the foundations for further strong and sustainable progress in the years ahead. Detailed analysis of the prevailing economic situation in Ireland preceded the formulation of the plan. Much of this analysis was undertaken by the Department of Finance in association with other key ministries and was also informed by major studies undertaken particularly by the ESRI in the *National Investment Priorities for the Period 2000–2006* (Fitzgerald *et al.* (1999) and, from a regional perspective, by the reports from Fitzpatrick & Associates (1999a; 1999b) outlining *Development Strategies for the period 2000–2006, in the BMW Region and the S&E Region* and the Western Development Commission's *Blueprint for Success: A Development Plan for the West of Ireland* (1999). Arising from this analysis the following key strengths of the Irish economy were identified:

> a macro economic stability reflected in a budget surplus,
> a declining debt ratio and low inflation;

> broadly based consensus on the key elements of economic and social policy as outlined through the national agreements between the social partners;

a growing and well educated workforce;

a favourable demographic structure particularly in terms of dependency ratios; and

a competitive and favourable environment for business, in particular, Foreign Direct Investment.

In addition, it was clearly identified that the Irish economy had a number of weaknesses that needed to be addressed and challenges that needed to be overcome if economic and social progress was to be maintained. These included:

significant infrastructure deficits especially in the transport and environmental services;

congestion in major urban areas and on main arterial routes;

a growing imbalance between and within regions;

housing shortages especially in urban areas;

labour capacity constraints and training requirements particularly in high skill areas;

an underdeveloped indigenous industrial sector lacking in innovative capacity and trading mainly with the UK; and

concentrations of deprivation and lack of opportunities in certain areas both urban and rural.

Following the identification of these issues four high level objectives were set out in the current NDP, namely:

continuing sustainable economic and employment growth;

consolidating and improving international competitiveness;

fostering balanced regional development, and

promoting social inclusion.

Funding for the National Development Plan 2000–2006

The NDP 2000–2006 comprises a total expenditure of 52 billion euro with approximately 6 billion euro being contributed by the EU under Structural and Cohesion Funds. The EU contribution represents 12 per cent of the total funding for the plan as compared to 40 per cent for the 1994–1999 period. A unique feature of the current NDP is the inclusion of a minimum target of

2.5 billion euro for Public/Private Partnership contributions to the funding of the Infrastructure Programme. The Plan itself is being implemented via three National or Inter-regional Programmes, two Regional Programmes, the PEACE Programme with Northern Ireland and the CAP Rural Development Plan. The breakdown of the investment is:

A   infrastructure was identified in the National Development Plan and all the major studies leading into the preparation of the Plan as one of the key deficiencies in the Irish economy. Consequently an investment of 22.4 billion euro in Economic and Social Infrastructure was provided with particular emphasis on roads, public transport, environmental services, housing and health.

B   the Employment and Human Resources Programme of over 12.6 billion euro reflects the priorities in the National Employment Action Plan and is organised under four sub-programmes to reflect the four pillars of the European Employment Strategy (EES.) i.e. employability, entrepreneurship, adaptability and equal opportunities. The main areas of expenditure in the plan are on employability, which combines the social inclusion measures in the education sector, and labour market integration. The adaptability pillar includes life long learning, skills development, apprenticeships, back to work schemes etc.

C   a total of 5.4 billion euro is being spent in the Productive Sector which will provide financial resources for Foreign Direct Investment particularly in the BMW Region and a major investment in Research and Development (R&D).

D   two Regional Programmes combining a total investment of approximately 9 billion euro and focusing exclusively on local infrastructure, local enterprise, agriculture and rural development and social inclusion.

E   the CAP accompanying measures concentrating on the REPS Scheme, Early Retirement Schemes, Compensatory Allowances and Forestry Measures which amount to a total expenditure of 4.3 billion euro.

Horizontal measures

All measures funded under the NDP 2000–2006 are proofed for their impact on:

The Environment;

Equality;

Rural Development, and

Poverty.

National Co-ordinating Committees have been established to oversee the implementation of the horizontal measures. In addition, there is a representative of each of the horizontal themes on the Monitoring Committees of each Operational Programme.

Regional issues

The NDP 2000–2006 identifies balanced regional development as a key objective to be achieved over the period of the Plan (see also McCafferty, Chapter 4; Walsh, Chapter 5). The rapid economic growth, which has manifested itself in increased urbanisation and clustering of economic activity, has raised a number of issues particularly in relation to balanced regional development and the distribution of national, economic and social progress. The key issues in this regard are:

> the growth and expansion of the greater Dublin area giving rise to problems of congestion and housing shortages;

> the rapid growth of major urban centres outside Dublin and their role in driving the development of their hinterlands and providing a counterbalanced Dublin;

> the implications of these trends for smaller towns and villages and rural areas;

> the economic, social and environmental consequences of these trends;

> the role of infrastructural provision in facilitating and promoting development at regional as well as national level;

> how the investment needed to underpin sustained economic progress at the national level might at the same time more effectively advance balanced regional development, and

> the relationship between economic and social planning, physical planning and land use policies.

The specific designation of two regions forms part of a process of achieving more balanced regional development in that it enables a clear focus on the key issues facing each of the regions and allows for a differentiation and targeting of policies in a manner which recognises their key attributes and needs. In particular it has highlighted the differentiation in the level and rate of development between the more prosperous S&E Region and the BMW Region and has thus emphasised the priority which needs to be afforded to the latter in terms of investment and development.

The BMW Region

The regionalisation arrangements negotiated by the Irish authorities in the context of the Agenda 2000 agreement resulted in the designation of Ireland into two NUTS II regions for Structural Funds purposes (see Figure 2.1). These regions are:

> the Border, Midland and Western Region (BMW Region) which has retained Objective 1 status for the purpose of Structural Funds for the full period to 2006. The headquarters of the BMW Regional Assembly is in Ballaghadereen, County Roscommon and the Region itself is made up of 13 Counties – Galway, Mayo, Sligo, Leitrim, Roscommon, Donegal, Cavan, Monaghan, Louth, Longford, Westmeath, Offaly and Laois.

> the South and East Region (S&E Region) will qualify for a six year phasing out regime for Objective 1 Structural Funding up to the end of 2005. The headquarters for the S&E Regional Assembly is in Waterford town and this Region is made up of the remaining 13 Counties - Meath, Dublin, Kildare, Wicklow, Carlow, Wexford, Kilkenny, Waterford, Tipperary, Cork, Limerick, Kerry and Clare.

A detailed analysis was carried out on the BMW Region, which identified its strengths and weaknesses, and the distinctive development challenge it faces. These included the need to increase the presence in the Region of the key drivers of sustainable economic growth, notably in the productive sector, and to improve the quality of the Region's economic and social infrastructure and human resources. Further, the need to build on the Region's natural resource base especially in the areas of agriculture, tourism, the seafood sector and rural enterprise was identified, as was the necessity of increasing the potential of the Region to act as a counterbalance to the S & E Region, especially Dublin. Moreover the pursuit of more balanced and sustainable growth within the Region was reflected, as was the desire to promote rural and urban social inclusion.

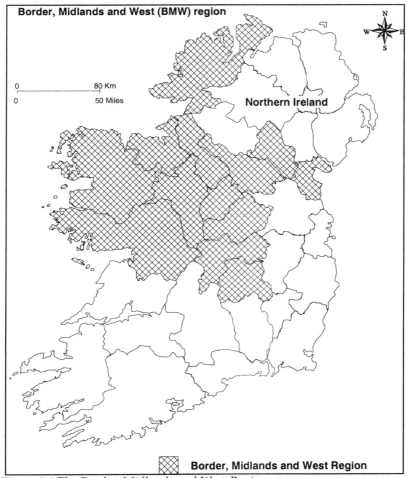

Figure 2.1 The Border, Midlands and West Region

In the government's approach to accelerating the development of the BMW Region, the central aim is to increase the presence in the Region of the key drivers for sustainable economic growth particularly in the productive sector. The key determinants of a sustained economic performance level are contained in:

the ease of access to domestic and foreign markets;

a modern telecommunications network;

back-up research and technology infrastructure which is accessible to enterprises in all sectors;

a well-developed educational system;

a highly qualified and skilled work force;

high quality physical infrastructure, including inter-urban transport and energy transmission systems;

an adequate supply of housing;

a good overall quality of life, and

a high quality and sustainable environment.

Success on all these fronts is essential if the drive to strengthen population structure; to promote development throughout the BMW Region, and to attract higher income earners to live and work in the Region, is to be successful. The measures in the BMW Regional Operational Programme (OP), which will complement the major projects in the Inter-Regional OPs, are designed to support the achievement of these ends.

The role of the BMW Regional Assembly

Following the designation of these two Regions, two Regional Assemblies were established and came into effect on 21 July 1999 under the Local Government Act, 1991 (Regional Authorities) Establishment Order, 1999. The Assemblies comprise a full time Director, a number of staff, and nominated elected representatives of the regional authorities within each region. The main role of the BMW Regional Assembly (and the S&E Assembly) is to:

manage the Regional Operational Programme under the National Development Plan;

monitor the general impact of all EU Programmes under the National Development Plan/ Community Support Framework in the BMW Region, and

promote the co-ordination of the provision of Public Services in the Region.

The BMW Regional Operational Programme complements the Inter-regional Operational Programmes and extends their impact at local level across the Region as a whole. The strategic objectives of the Operational Programme are to:

maintain and improve the transport infrastructure; to provide easier access to employment, training, social opportunities and to markets, for employers wishing to establish enterprises in more remote areas;

provide effective linkages to the National Road network and to the public transport system;

support the establishment of high value added information and services sector enterprises in the Region by providing access to advanced communications and e-commerce and digital infrastructure and services and promote an inclusive information society;

improve the quality of the environmental, cultural, social and recreational infrastructure so as to enhance the attractiveness of the Region, as a place to live, visit, work or establish an enterprise, and to contribute to sustainable development;

increase per capita of Gross Value Added (GVA) and support convergence with national averages by improving the quality of the labour supply, supporting the development of innovation systems at regional level and the establishment of high quality jobs within reasonable commuting distance;

support the regeneration of rural communities by providing alternative sources of income for farmers, rural dwellers, the underemployed and those engaged in marginal economic activity, through farm diversification measures, area-based rural development initiatives and by moving production up the value chain;

augment employment opportunities in the less developed and economically disadvantaged rural areas of the Region through the promotion of Tourism, Forestry, Fishery Harbours, Aquaculture Development and Gaeltacht/Islands;

provide structural aid and back-up support in rural areas, especially targeted at young farmers so as to support the production of commercially viable quality product at farm level and to promote the protection of the environment; and

provide support through a comprehensive programme of Measures for those seeking access to training, those wishing to enter or return to the workforce (especially women) and for family and community development.

These strategies will be implemented via four major Priorities (Sub-Programmes) namely, Local Infrastructure, Local Enterprise Development, Agriculture and Rural Development and Social Inclusion and Childcare. These sub-programmes will complement the major expenditure under the Inter-regional Programmes by focusing on the specific development needs of the Region.

Local infrastructure sub-programme

The objectives of the Local Infrastructure Priority (Sub-Programme) in the BMW Region are to primarily complement and reinforce the impact of investment under the Economic and Social Infrastructure OP and to contribute to the economic and social development of the Region (see Table 2.1). Further, this sub-programme will attempt to improve access, within the Region, to employment, training and social opportunities while also seeking to counteract those factors which restrict the potential of the Region as a place to live, work and visit, either for tourism, or for business. A key element to these objectives will lie in support for the retention of population in remote and rural communities. The Priority (Sub-Programme) will support these objectives through:

> improving the transport infrastructure to provide easier access to employment, training and social opportunities for the Region's inhabitants and, offering existing firms and potential investors in the Region better access to the national road network and, thus, to domestic and foreign markets, and

> supporting the establishment of high value-added information and services sector enterprises in the Region by providing access to advanced communications and e-commerce/digital infrastructure and services. Also by improving the quality of the environmental, cultural, social and recreational infrastructure so as to enhance the attractiveness of the Region as a place in which to live or work or establish an enterprise, or to visit.

Table 2.1 Local infrastructure sub-programme

Division	Euro millions
*Non-national Roads	1,075.47
*Rural Water	448.22
*Waste Management	370.76
*Urban and Village Renewal	50.79
*E-Commerce - Communications	352.99
Seaports	25.39
Regional Airports	11.43
Culture, Recreation and Sports	184.11
*Technical Assistance	2.54
Sub-total	**2,521.70**

* Co-financed by the EU.

Local enterprise sub-programme

The overriding objective for the BMW Region is to reduce the impact of peripherality, enhance the competitive position of the Region and promote inward investment. More specifically, the objectives of the Local Enterprise Development Priority (Sub-Programme) are to:

> enhance the quality and availability of employment within the Region;

> provide opportunities for alternative sources of income for the unemployed and under-employed, in particular, farmers and rural dwellers;

> upgrade and improve the capabilities and capacity of indigenous firms and their personnel;

> attract new inward investment and develop the base of non-indigenous industry in the Region, and

> build-up the marketing capabilities within firms to enable them to avail of opportunities in the global marketplace;

> enhance research and technological development within the Region generally, and

> enhance the contribution of the Region's natural resources to social and economic development particularly in the area of tourism, fisheries, forestry and aquaculture.

The Local Enterprise Development Priority will support the achievement of these objectives through the programme of funding outlined in Table 2.2.

Table 2.2 Local enterprise sub-programme

Division	Euro millions
*Tourism	154.91
*Micro-enterprise	121.89
*Regional Innovation Strategies	17.78
*Forestry	116.82
*Fishery Harbours, Aquaculture, Gaeltacht/Islands	144.75
Sub-total	556.15

*Co-financed by the EU.

Agriculture and rural development sub-programme

The overall objectives for agriculture and related rural development under the NDP 2000–2006 are to:

ensure that primary agriculture becomes more competitive and market oriented;

foster environmentally sustainable systems of production;

provide other sources of income for farmers through diversification of activities both on and off farm, and

promote rural development generally by harnessing voluntary and community effort at local level (see Table 2.3).

The implications of the recent reform of the CAP under Agenda 2000, especially the new Council Regulation (EC) No. 1257/1999 on Support for Rural Development *(Official Journal of the European Commission, L160/80 of 26/6/1999)*, were taken into account in drawing up the strategies to address the above broad objectives. In addition, the publication by the Government of the White Paper on Rural Development *Ensuring the Future – A Strategy for Rural Development in Ireland*, (Department of Agriculture and Food, 1999) commits Ireland to a specific framework for action in a number of areas to achieve a coherent rural development policy. It is also important to bear in mind that it is the CAP market measures which will have the major impact in determining the development of mainstream Irish agriculture over the coming period.

Table 2.3 Agriculture and rural development sub-programme

Division	Euro millions
*General Structural Improvement	435.52
Alternative Enterprises	60.95
*General Rural Development	101.58
Services for Agriculture & Rural Development	41.90
Sub-total	639.95

* Co-financed by the EU.

Social inclusion and childcare sub-programme

The objectives of the Social Inclusion and Childcare Priority (Sub-Programme) in the BMW Regional Assembly, Regional OP, are to:

alleviate poverty and social disadvantage in both urban and rural areas;

integrate/reintegrate the socially excluded into the community and the labour force;

reduce long-term unemployment and support the achievement of the NAPs targets;

support the development of vibrant and sustainable families and communities;

tackle the causes of social disadvantage amongst young people and communities at risk;

promote equality and, in particular, facilitate greater participation of women in the workplace and business and, more broadly, the achievement of equal opportunities generally, and

reduce the incidence of crime and re-offending.

These objectives will be achieved through investment in a range of targeted Measures that include:

significantly boosting childcare provision, thus enabling parents (particularly women), especially those from disadvantaged backgrounds, to combine family life with employment and education/training;

supporting initiatives aimed at increasing the participation of women in economic and social life and in decision-making;

supporting initiatives at local and community level, including a sustained effort to develop community leadership skills and capacity, designed to alleviate the causes and consequences of poverty and to promote greater social inclusion;

enhancing the capacity of the most disadvantaged families to improve their circumstances;

assisting the reintegration into the community of those who have been involved in crime;

directly addressing the needs and problems of young people, in particular young people at risk (diverting them from drifting into unemployment, crime and substance abuse);

supporting partnership approaches such as ADM Partnership companies and community groups and local drugs task forces in implementing local and community development action plans, and

providing an outreach service to the long-term unemployed (see Table 2.4).

Table 2.4 Social inclusion and childcare sub-programme

Division	Euro millions
*Childcare	119.36
Equality for Women	8.89
Community Development & Family Support	41.90
Crime Prevention	27.93
Youth Services	55.87
Local Development	124.43
Sub-total	**378.38**

*Co-funded by the EU.

Conclusion

The establishment of the Regional Assemblies represents a new departure in public administration in Ireland. The regional dimension of the NDP 2000–2006 is given effect in both the designation of the Regional Assemblies as Managing Authorities for the Regional Operational Programmes and the 'ring fencing' of allocations in each Operational Programme on a NUTS II Regional basis. The Regional Assemblies have also been given places on all Monitoring Committees and on the NDP/CSF horizontal co-ordinating committees. Clear objectives and strategies have been set out for each region. The achievement/realisation of these will be closely monitored and will be thoroughly reviewed as part of the mid-term review of the NDP.

References

Department of Agriculture & Food (1999) White Paper on Rural Development, *Ensuring the Future*, Stationery Office, Dublin.

Department of Finance (1999) *The National Development Plan 2000–2006*, Stationery Office, Dublin.

Fitzgerald, J., Kearney, I., Morgenroth, E. and Smyth, D., (eds.) (1999) *National Investment Priorities for the period 2000–2006*, ESRI Policy Research Series No. 33, Dublin.

Fitzpatrick Associates (1999a) *Southern and Eastern Region Development Strategy 2000–2006*, Dublin.

Fitzpatrick Associates (1999b) *Border Midland and Western Region Development Strategy 2000–2006*, Dublin.

McDonagh, J. (2001) *Renegotiating Rural Development in Ireland*, Ashgate, Aldershot.

Website: www.bmwassembly.ie

chapter three

REGIONAL DEVELOPMENT AND THE ROLE OF
ÚDARÁS NA GAELTACHTA

Pádraig Ó hAoláin

Introduction

The Gaeltacht covers extensive parts of counties Donegal, Mayo, Galway and Kerry and also parts of counties Cork, Meath and Waterford, including six offshore islands (Figure 3.1). Successive Governments since the foundation of the State have regarded the preservation and development of the Gaeltacht as an Irish-speaking community as of the utmost importance. The Gaeltacht areas are the main communities in Ireland where the language is spoken on a community basis. It is an important cornerstone in the building of a bilingual society in Ireland, and it provides an environment where the Irish language can evolve naturally in a modern community setting.

This chapter outlines the role Údarás na Gaeltachta plays in regional development. In particular, the major challenge of developing the economy of the Gaeltacht region and ensuring the preservation and extension of the Irish language is explored. The chapter also evaluates the future needs of the Gaeltacht region; determines the major obstacles and potential threats in terms of spatial discrimination, and ascertains how the internal economies of scale within the region constrain and challenge the development strategies for the Gaeltacht.

Údarás na Gaeltachta (The Gaeltacht Authority)

Údarás na Gaeltachta is unique among State development agencies in that it is the only such body in Ireland where the vast majority of the board members – seventeen of the twenty – are democratically elected by the Gaeltacht electorate. It is a unique regional development authority with a democratic dimension and wide ranging development functions. The Authority is representative of the various Gaeltacht areas and its devolved board structure, through three statutory regional/provincial committees, has effectively localised decision-making within the Gaeltacht communities. These regional committees in Donegal, Connacht and Munster, can approve grant-aid of up to 350,000 euro in respect of any one qualifying project.

In the 1996 Census the population of the Gaeltacht was a little in excess of 86,000 (including approximately 10,000 people who reside in new housing estates on the western, north western and eastern boundary of Galway city which have been built since 1990). The total labour force is 28,500. There are 8,250 people employed full-time and a further 4,000 part-time or seasonal workers in Údarás na Gaeltachta supported industries such as textiles, engineering, electronics, aquaculture and other natural resources, TV production companies and modern services. Other important economic activities within the Gaeltacht are, of course, farming, fishing and tourism. The statutory task of Údarás na Gaeltachta is to primarily develop the economy of the Gaeltacht in such a fashion as to facilitate the preservation and the extension of the Irish language as the principal language of the community. This brief determines the choice of development strategy whereby an appropriate balance must be struck between economic imperatives and social and cultural needs. To achieve this the Údarás promotes employment-generation through the development of local natural resources, skills and entrepreneurial abilities, the support of indigenous enterprises across a broad spectrum of business sectors and the attraction of mobile investment to the Gaeltacht. The Údarás also promotes and supports community development and pursues a range of focused language and cultural activities throughout the Gaeltacht.

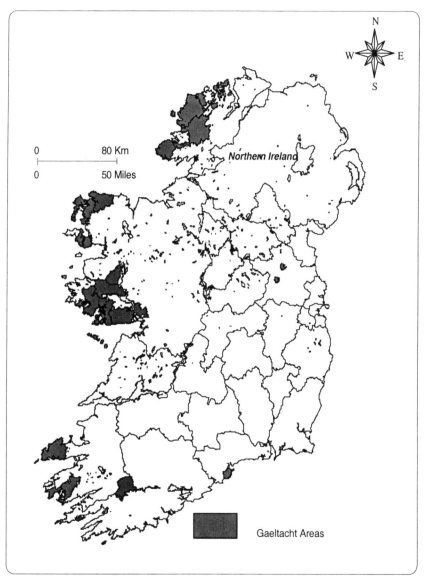

Figure 3.1 The Gaeltacht regions of Ireland

Strategic Initiatives

An important part of the Údarás' brief is to help remove impediments to progress and to take the initiative in kick-starting development in areas where the private sector may be reluctant to undertake the initial risks involved. One example was the decision to kick-start the TV/AV sector in the Gaeltacht in the early 1990s. This involved putting in place a series of audiovisual training programmes to develop a skills base and establish a production and postproduction studio to tackle a recognised facilities deficit in the region. This was critically important in order to ensure that the absence of these facilities could not be used as an argument against the setting up of an Irish language television station being lobbied for at that time. Another example was the development of the fishfarming industry on the west coast in the 1970s, which evolved through a Research and Development programme funded and managed through a subsidiary company of the Údarás. This sector is now a major source of employment, particularly in Galway and Donegal.

Commercial property market

There is no commercial property market *per se* in the Gaeltacht. The Údarás builds and manages all of its own commercial and non-commercial premises. As a consequence, the diversity of the property portfolio of the Údarás reflects its diverse role as a regional development agency. The property portfolio includes not only a substantial holding of industrial estates, factories and office premises but also three airstrips with ancillary services and a range of specifically commissioned properties. The latter include the Mara Beo aquarium in Dingle; specialised fish processing facilities in Kerry, Galway and Donegal; craft centres in Dingle, Co. Kerry, Spiddal, Co. Galway and Kilcar, Co. Donegal; television studios in Dingle; the Telegael facilities, TV training studios and the Ros na Rún soap opera set in Spiddal, Co. Galway. There are also a number of factories with state of the art cleanroom facilities. The Engineering Services Division of the Údarás builds all of the factories and office space required for client companies. Attempts have been made to design a range of incentives geared to attract property developers to build speculatively in the more attractive Gaeltacht locations but as this has proved unsuccessful, the Údarás have been left with no option but to 'go it alone' in the property sector.

Subsidiary companies

Údarás na Gaeltachta has established subsidiary companies where it is recognised that strategic initiatives are necessary to generate development in particular sectors and where the private sector is unwilling to take the initial risks. The objective in these instances has always been to develop prototype bridgehead enterprises that can attract private sector partners. These partners then have the opportunity of a buy out as the viability of the venture is demonstrated. This model has been successfully applied in strategic interventions by the Údarás in the aquaculture and audiovisual sectors. Risk-taking is an integral part of the development process and Údarás na Gaeltachta has not shied away from carrying an additional portion of the risk involved in initiatives that are necessary to drive forward development.

Balancing the Imbalances

In developing the Gaeltacht region there are two major regional development challenges that can be referred to as balancing imbalances. These challenges are:

the need to address uneven patterns of economic growth within the Gaeltacht, and

the need to ensure that the Gaeltacht overall is not neglected within the distribution of wealth and resources regionally and in Ireland as a whole.

Within the Gaeltacht there is an attempt to ensure an even spread of the benefits accrued during the national economic boom of the 1990s. In reality, this has met with mixed success. While the job creation targets set under the Operational Programme for Industry have been continually exceeded, employment in Údarás client companies, after reaching record levels, have reached a plateau within the past year or two. However, there is also an uneven spread of employment creation throughout the Gaeltacht. There are still areas that have not experienced the 'Celtic Tiger' phenomenon and communities in these areas feel they have been passive spectators of the 'improved prosperity' of their fellow citizens. The paradoxical position was that during the latter part of the 1990s the Údarás had to apply a 'brake' on job approvals in the more developed Gaeltacht locations because of an insufficient labour reserve to promote projects employing more than 50 people. On the other side of the coin, the less developed areas continued to suffer from unemployment and underemployment with underdeveloped infrastructure and a skills deficit being the main contributors to this situation.

The downturn in the US economy has compounded this position. Indeed it has created a situation where at least some of the employment gains in recent years may be lost in the short to medium term because of the dependence, directly or indirectly, of many client companies on the US market. More importantly, low-skilled manufacturing and sub-assembly operations are gravitating towards low-cost countries and the employment consequences are painful. This, in effect, means that Údarás na Gaeltachta will have to put a lot more time, energy and resources into retaining their gains and securing the plateau they have reached rather than expecting to attract the high levels of new investment experienced in these sectors in previous years.

Uneven development and poor infrastructure

Tackling the problem of uneven development is continually hampered by poor infrastructure in the Gaeltacht regions. This is particularly so in the more remote areas within the Gaeltacht – the real periphery of the periphery. The poor infrastructure encompasses not only substandard roads, but also the absence, in most areas, of an adequate telecommunications infrastructure and a diminishing social infrastructure. This is particularly so in the smaller and more remote communities and results in a drift of the younger population towards larger urban centres (see also O'Hara, Chapter 10). This has impacts on economic development within the region and also, quite significantly, on culture and the survival of the Irish language. For historical reasons, the Irish language is often strongest as a community language in the more peripheral areas, and so from a language maintenance and development viewpoint a strong economic base has a crucial role to play. However the poorly developed infrastructure of the region in sustaining these communities, has resulted in weakening the very communities that the language is dependent on for survival as a community language. In addressing this recognised disadvantage Údarás na Gaeltachta's response has not only included practical steps like grading factory rentals within areas and from area to area for inward and local investors but more strategically has culminated in the commissioning of two major reports on Gaeltacht infrastructural needs. These are now the basis on which Údarás na Gaeltachta is lobbying Government to vigorously and urgently address these issues.

Recognition of the Gaeltacht's special needs

A second challenge is to ensure that the Gaeltacht overall is not neglected in the distribution of wealth and resources in Ireland as a whole. One of the challenges facing the Údarás as a regional development agency is that the Gaeltacht areas are subsets of seven different counties, each with their own local authority and other state-agency administrative structures. Over the past ten years (in various submissions) Údarás has looked for more expanded structures. In particular there is a desire for a greater co-ordinating role, so that the broader mix of regional development interventions from roads, to housing development, to services, and not just job creation, could be addressed in an integrated way. This would ensure more cohesiveness, more effectiveness, and a clearer vision for the development of the Gaeltacht and the buttressing of the language. To date, no such formal arrangements have been put in place and the Údarás is now endeavouring to achieve the same objectives through alliances and partnerships. This includes developing high-quality collaboration with the local authorities to ensure the particular needs of the Gaeltacht are given high priority in County and Local Area Development Plans. Údarás is also working closely with the local authorities in formulating an agreed approach to the implementation of those provisions of the Planning and Development Act 2000 which require that due regard be given to language and culture. In the planning process for Gaeltacht areas there is also a dilemma. Local area plans are normally drawn up for towns with a population of at least 5,000 people, but there is no town anywhere in the Gaeltacht with a population of more than 1,000 people. In fact only two or three Gaeltacht villages come near that population figure. Understanding the question of resources and how local authorities have to set their own priorities on a county-wide basis, Údarás na Gaeltachta has employed its own planning consultants in some areas and shared the cost with the County Councils in others (Carraroe and An Tulach in County Galway and Iorras in County Mayo, for example). In addition Údarás is working collaboratively with Donegal County Council in relation to an initiative in the Derrybeg-Bunbeg/Dungloe area relating to the National Spatial Strategy (NSS). Indeed, the National Spatial Strategy itself poses a major challenge to Údarás na Gaeltachta in terms of fitting the concept of development 'Poles', 'Gateways' and 'Hubs' (see McCafferty, Chapter 4; Walsh, Chapter 5) to the particular needs and circumstances of the Gaeltacht areas.

Hubs, Gateways and spatial discrimination

Some of the major obstacles to the development of Gaeltacht areas arise from the absence of economic concentration and thus the inability to achieve internal economies of scale. One of the suggestions in the NSS discussion paper is the development of Growth Poles, Gateways and Hubs. Údarás na Gaeltachta has actively pursued this strategy and has provided investment on a 'planning region' basis over a number of years. Údarás na Gaeltachta's' planning regions are made up of spatially contiguous districts with up to 10,000 population. The Údarás argument is that similar strategies should be initiated at sub-functional area level throughout Ireland, particularly in areas that do not fall within the defined range of Poles, Gateways and Hubs and their hinterlands. This would, in respect of Gaeltacht areas, lead to a small number of peripheral centres being identified as development nodes and would prevent the general area they serve being precluded from the impact of the NSS. These development nodes or 'sub-hubs' should be considered in locations such as; Na Doirí Beaga/An Clochan Liath (Derrybeg/Dungloe), Cill Charthaigh (Kilcar), Béal an Mhuirthead (Belmullet), An Cheathrú Rua (Carraroe), Carna/Cill Chiaráin, An Daingean (Dingle) and Baile Mhic Íre/Baile Bhuirne (Ballymakeera/Ballyvourney).

As a state agency with a broad development brief for dispersed rural communities, Údarás na Gaeltachta has a particular interest in the debate about the relative underdevelopment of the Border, Midlands and West (BMW) Region compared to the rest of the country. The geographic and regional dispersal of major industries highlights the greater levels of disadvantage found in rural areas compared to urban centres. In pursuit of a sustainable national strategy at a sub-functional area level, Údarás na Gaeltachta recommends that policy makers adapt the strategies already put in place by the Údarás which focus on planning districts of up to 10,000 people incorporating villages and their hinterlands. Such a strategy would encompass the core principals of regional development research, namely, greater integration, improved public and private body linkages and increased community participation both laterally and vertically. Important within this would be the clear identification, in the report of the NSS to Government, of the economic role of Gaeltacht regions in functional areas where they exist and the role of the 'sub-hubs'.

Homogenisation of Incentives

The Gaeltacht's position as a subset of county structures was also presented with a further challenge with the division of the country into two regions for European Union and National Development Plan purposes. The Gaeltacht areas of Galway, Mayo and Donegal are located in the BMW region which has Objective 1 status, while the Gaeltacht areas in Kerry, Cork, Waterford and Meath are in the Southern and Eastern region which is in Transition status. So not only is there a two-tier Gaeltacht, but the homogenisation of the incentive packages across regions, while desirable in principal, gives rise to further major challenges in attempting to entice investors into the more remote Gaeltacht areas where the infrastructure is inadequately or seriously underdeveloped.

A legitimate question that can be asked by investors is why they should invest in Belmullet and not in Ballina if the incentives are more or less the same? Indeed why pass through Westport to Achill? through Killybegs to Kilcar? through Galway to Spiddal, or Spiddal to Carna? The lack of sufficiently effective state intervention to counter infrastructural imbalances is leading to an exacerbation of development as well as increasing the challenge of language maintenance faced by Údarás na Gaeltachta. The Gaeltacht, wrongly perceived to be mollycoddled by grants and subventions higher than elsewhere in the region or in the country, is dealt with within the same broad incentive parameters as any other part of the region. Údarás has no problem with this in principle, but disagree with those who preach that 'market forces' should prevail throughout the State and that the highest 'economic and social' return should be the core determining criterion for exchequer expenditure. Expenditure on the necessary social, physical and telecommunications infrastructure should not always have to be justified on the basis of 'the best economic' return. Such a strict approach will inevitably condemn large tracts of rural Ireland to continued underdevelopment and, in some cases, stagnation. There is a need to take a more holistic view of investment, such as the 'social payback' or in the case of our particular objective, language and social payback. Vigorous state intervention is vital if the Gaeltacht and other underdeveloped regions are to share fairly in Ireland's prosperity.

Job Creation Challenges, Education and Training

The two major challenges facing Údarás na Gaeltachta in relation to its job creation programme over the next few years are clearly bound up in the realm of providing quality education, training and technological skills.

Education and training

In terms of education and training Údarás has outlined their objective of continuing to strengthen the existing industrial base by supporting inputs into R&D, marketing, human resource development and strategy development in companies. Much of this activity is directly within the control of Údarás na Gaeltachta as we work closely with assisted companies. This strategy of 'capacity building' within the existing employment base is already bearing fruit. In 2001 the indigenous sector was again the major source of new jobs with over 50 per cent of the new jobs created attributed to expansions in the existing industrial base. This strategy must now be brought to a higher level. This will require substantial investment in a wide range of education and training programmes at company and community level in collaboration with Third Level Institutions which will allow for a localised delivery of courses to ensure greater access for as many people as possible.

Technology

While sectors such as aquaculture and seafood processing, cultural tourism, engineering, electronics sub-assembly and indigenous service-type enterprises continue to form a core part of the employment base in the Gaeltacht, it is vitally necessary that the Gaeltacht be equipped to get its fair share of the new technology-based investment. There is a need to attract new-economy type projects that will reduce the outflow of graduates and educated young people from the Gaeltacht areas and attract back some of those who have left in recent years. Here lies the dilemma – how can this be done without adequate telecommunications infrastructure? There is intense competition for this type of investment from all parts of the country and other parts of the West Region. Many of these areas have much more advanced telecommunication infrastructures than the Gaeltacht areas. Without further investment in this area, the Gaeltacht region, particularly in the more peripheral locations, will be unable to compete for such investment.

Government Funding and Local Authority Plans

In the planned improvement of the telecommunication infrastructure, the strategic thrust of the Government's decision to supply 90 per cent of the funding to public bodies to assist them in building a telecom infrastructure in the regions, with particular priority being given to the BMW region, is welcome. However, there is no part of a Gaeltacht region included in any of the proposals submitted to date by local authorities. The gravitational pull of the 'larger' centres of population has again militated against the more 'peripheral' western areas of Donegal, Mayo and Galway. While this may not be a deliberate policy to neglect the Gaeltacht when developing infrastructure, the net result is the same. In view of this situation Údarás na Gaeltachta has submitted its own proposals, two of which have been successful – one to install a fibre-optic cable between Letterkenny and Gaoth Dobhair in County Donegal and a second to install telecommunications duct rings at the Industrial Estate in Gaoth Dobhair.

High speed Internet access

Companies requiring high speed internet access need to lease lines from the nearest POP (point of presence) server which is paid on a per kilometre basis. There is only one POP in the West of Ireland, in Athlone. So what hope does a company in Spiddal, not to mention Carna or Belmullet, have when trying to compete with a similar company based in Galway or indeed Ballinasloe? This is a particular problem for Údarás na Gaeltachta as we try to entice companies to a Gaeltacht area particularly when, as already outlined, our ability to grant aid at a level commensurate to the infrastructural challenge has been eliminated (paradoxically the original concept of grants was to compensate for some locational or infrastructural disadvantage).

Submissions to Government

Although they are theoretically location-independent, modern service-based industries are almost exclusively attracted to urban areas. As such, there are major structural deficiencies that have to be addressed before the Gaeltacht can begin to benefit from the job-creation opportunities associated with these enterprises. Effectively, many parts of the Gaeltacht are currently excluded from the employment benefits that flow from the modern services economy. Here, however, lies a challenge not only for Údarás na Gaeltachta but also for the Government. To facilitate the Government in addressing this problem in a focused and planned way two major studies were commissioned by the Údarás in 2000/2001.

The first report prepared by Norcontel, assessed not only the baseline but also the upgrading and funding requirements in relation to telecommunications infrastructure in the Gaeltacht. The overall expenditure required was estimated at 15.25m euro (£12m). There is, however, continued uncertainty surrounding the Government-funded programme to provide fibre optics and Digital Subscriber Line (DSL) technologies to the BMW region. This is particularly so with regard to the extent of the distribution of these technologies within the region itself. Delays or inequities in the provision of an adequate telecommunications infrastructure will further impede the investment-promotion efforts of Údarás na Gaeltachta and of development agencies in the rest of the region. This in turn constrains job-creation efforts, particularly in the provision of the much needed employment opportunities to curtail the outflow of graduates and educated young people.

The second study involved a comprehensive examination of the state of the physical, social and transport infrastructure and the estimated cost of upgrading these to national standards. The main conclusion from this report, produced by Fitzpatrick and Associates, were that:

> while Údarás na Gaeltachta's vision for the Gaeltacht is the creation of the vibrant high quality and knowledge-based economy and society which will provide Gaeltacht residents with an attractive quality of life at least comparable to any other part of Ireland, this vision cannot be achieved without a base of infrastructure of commensurate quality. Major investment in this infrastructure over time is thus a pre-condition for achievement of Údarás objectives.

Further, Fitzpatrick and Associates estimated that investment in economic and social infrastructure in the region of 766.4m euro (£603.6m) was required throughout the Gaeltacht and the range and scale of infrastructure required meant the investment challenge goes far beyond the resources and remit of Údarás na Gaeltachta and the Department of Arts, Heritage, Gaeltacht and the Islands. In fact it was argued that this investment would require the commitment of a range of other sectoral Departments and state agencies and respective local authorities.

Fitzpatrick and Associates also recognised that less than 30 per cent of the estimated requirements were already explicitly earmarked in the *National Development Plan 2000–2006* (Department of Finance, 1999) for the Gaeltacht. Much of the required investment would therefore still have to be 'won' from the various responsible departments/agencies on a case-by-case basis. This, they argue, will require systematic, targeted and justified project level submissions to the many relevant bodies with a re-allocation of resources within the region rather than the provision of extra resources being required.

Conclusion

These studies by Norcontel and Fitzpatrick Associates are being used by Údarás na Gaeltachta to demonstrate to the Government that a range of infrastructural constraints in the Gaeltacht region are hindering job creation efforts and the development of the type of business environment demanded by a modern economy. These studies also highlight the fact that there is an urgent need to develop the social infrastructure where the young, the old and the working population can avail of the social services that are essential to maintaining a high quality of life. The future of Irish as a community language in the Gaeltacht depends in no small degree on a vigorous response to addressing these needs. Nowhere is the inappropriateness of the 'one size fits all' approach more obvious than in the context of the Gaeltacht and that is why Údarás na Gaeltachta continues to vigorously challenge it.

References

Department of Finance (1999) *The National Development Plan 2000–2006*, Government Publications, Stationery Office, Dublin.

Fitzpatrick Associates (2001) *Infrastructure Requirements in the Gaeltacht*, Unpublished Údarás na Gaeltachta Report.

Norcontel Telecommunications Consultancy (2000) *Broadband Telecommunications in the Gaeltacht and Islands*, Unpublished Údarás na Gaeltachta Report.

chapter four

Balanced Regional Development, Polycentrism, and the Urban System of the West of Ireland

Des McCafferty

Introduction

Largely because of the pressures exerted by rapid economic growth, a renewed concern for the spatial dimension of development has emerged in Irish public policy in the last few years. This has been signalled most clearly in the National Development Plan 2000–06 (NDP) which sets four objectives for economic and social development in the current programming period: improved competitiveness, sustainable development, social inclusion and balanced regional development (Government of Ireland, 1999). In addition, the government has mandated the Department of the Environment and Local Government (DoELG) to produce a National Spatial Strategy (NSS), the purpose of which is to establish a spatial framework for the development of the state over the next 20 years. It is intended that this strategy will allow the goal of balanced regional development to be met along with the other goals of the NDP. Specifically the NSS is to:

> set down indicative policies on the location of industrial development, residential development, rural development and tourism and heritage, and develop and present a dynamic conception of the Irish urban system (Department of the Environment & Local Government, 2000, p.7; see also Walsh, Chapter 5).

Even in an era of rapid growth, when the efficiency case for regional policy has been stronger than at any time heretofore, there are potential conflicts among the goals of the NDP. There are several aspects to this, but one of the most significant derives from the fact that, following the re-orientation of Irish industrial policy towards the high technology sectors in the 1980s, employment growth in the 1990s has shown a pronounced bias towards the larger centres of population. In a context of spatially uneven urbanisation this trend has inevitably entailed a growing spatial polarisation in economic development and employment growth. Polarisation is evident among, as well as within, regions, and its effects are felt most acutely in the West of Ireland, where the urban system is particularly weak. This structural weakness presents one of the more intractable problems facing policy makers as they attempt to delineate a framework that will allow a greater balance to be achieved in development, at both the inter-regional and intra-regional scales.

The purpose of this chapter is to examine this issue in more detail, based on a consideration of patterns of urban development in the West of Ireland. The chapter begins with an examination of the nature of polarisation, conducted through a review of sectoral and spatial aspects of recent growth in the Irish economy. Following this, results are presented from an analysis of the Irish urban system, focusing in particular on urban centres in the seven counties of Donegal, Leitrim, Sligo, Roscommon, Mayo, Galway and Clare that fall under the remit of the Western Development Commission (WDC). The analysis identifies a number of potential problems in the pattern of urban development, and describes past and current attempts to frame regional policy in the context of these problems. This leads into a discussion of one of the main concepts likely to underpin the NSS, that of polycentric development, and the chapter concludes with an appraisal of the difficulties in operationalising a policy approach based on this concept, again with particular reference to the West.

Sectoral and Spatial Trends in Recent Employment Growth

After a prolonged period of stagnation lasting from the 1970s to the late 1980s, the Irish economy showed remarkable growth in the 1990s. Initially, employment growth lagged somewhat behind the growth in output (NESC, 1992), giving rise to fears about 'jobless growth', but these proved to be unfounded as the long boom continued. Between 1995 and 2000 the average annual growth rate of GDP was almost 10 per cent (compound), and GDP per worker grew at just under half this rate (CSO, 2001a), indicating that, while there was a significant gain in productivity, employment also increased substantially. The number at work is estimated to have increased by 388,900 (or 5.4 per cent per annum, compound) in this period, with particularly high rates of growth between 1997 and 2000 (CSO, 2001b).

In an open economy such as Ireland's, output and employment growth is largely driven by manufacturing and the internationally traded services sectors. Permanent employment in these sectors, in companies under the remit of the State's development agencies, increased by some 34 per cent (net increase of 80,784) between 1995 and 2000 (Forfás, 2001). The fastest growing sector was internationally traded services, including financial services: with a three-fold increase in employment (albeit from a comparatively low base) this sector accounted for over half of the net change in employment. Within the manufacturing sector, the highest growth rate (37.9 per cent), and by far the largest net increase in employment (+30,523), was accounted for by the engineering and metals industrial group. The growth of this industrial group in turn is largely attributable to rapid expansion of employment in the electronics industry. In contrast, the clothing industry experienced a decline in employment of 51.2 per cent (-5,371), and textiles manufacturing a drop of 37.4 per cent (-3,823). Clearly, the growth in this period was associated with substantial restructuring of employment towards high technology activities (see also Grimes, Chapter 14).

The sectoral concentration of employment growth is paralleled by a pronounced spatial polarisation of growth in the late 1990s. This is evident at regional level, where the rate of jobs growth ranged from 62 per cent in the Dublin Region to just 1.5 per cent in the Border Region (Table 4.1). The capital city region, which contained under one-third of the country's labour force in 1996, accounted for close to one-half of the total increase in employment in the period. The regional concentration of employment growth in foreign owned firms was even greater, and growth rates ranged from 87 per cent in Dublin to -8 per cent in the Border Region. The West Region performed relatively well, and with the third highest growth rate of employment, recorded a small increase in its share of agency-assisted jobs over the period. However, the wider seven county Region did not fare so well: with an employment growth rate well below the national average, the Region's share of agency assisted employment decreased in this period.

The contrast between the performance of the seven counties under the remit of the WDC and that of Counties Galway, Mayo and Roscommon, is due to Galway City's comparatively more dominant role as a focus of employment growth in the latter. More generally, it points up the fact that the fundamental dynamic underlying the spatial pattern of recent economic growth is related primarily to differences in levels of urbanisation: the recent economic boom has been urban-led (Fitzpatrick Associates, 1999, p. 61).

Table 4.1 Employment Growth in State-Supported Companies, 1995–2000

Region	Change in employment (%)	Share of total change	Change in % share
Dublin	61.61	49.05	5.55
Mid East	43.27	10.45	0.55
Mid West	30.02	9.43	−0.35
South West	34.97	14.92	0.07
South East	13.60	4.29	−1.67
West	38.68	10.07	0.29
Midlands	8.29	1.20	−0.96
Border	1.46	0.60	−3.47
State	34.35	100.00	0.00
Western Region	21.14	11.94	−1.91

Source: Calculated from data in Forfás (2001) and Western Development Commission (2001)

While data on the distribution of employment change by town size has not been published, indirect evidence of the importance of urbanisation can be obtained by analysing the relationship between employment growth rates and levels of urbanisation at various spatial scales. Results are presented below for such an analysis, conducted both at regional level (using the NUTS III regions), and also at county level within the Western Region (Table 4.2).

Table 4.2 Association between Employment Growth and Level of Urbanisation

	Rate of employment growth:		
NUTS III Regions (n = 8)	Irish Firms	Foreign Firms	Total
Percentage of population resident in:	Spearman's rank correlation		
centres over 5,000 population	0.55	0.88	0.79
centres over 10,000 population	0.40	0.79	0.67
Counties in Western Region (n = 7)			
Percentage of population resident in:			
centres over 3,000 population	0.75	0.11	0.54
centres over 5,000 population	0.68	0.09	0.50

Source: Author's calculations.

The results show that, at the inter-regional level, employment growth was strongly linked to level of urbanisation: regions with higher levels of urbanisation were more likely to show higher rates of employment growth in agency-assisted companies. This was particularly the case for employment in foreign owned firms. At the intra-regional (county) level it is employment growth in Irish firms that, somewhat surprisingly, shows the strongest correlation with urbanisation, with growth in foreign firms only weakly related to levels of urbanisation. This may be due to differences in the sectoral distribution of foreign firms in the Western Region (with more orientation towards declining sectors, such as clothing and textiles, than is the case nationally), or it may simply be due to effects related to relatively small numbers of foreign firms in some cases. In any event the correlation between urbanisation and total employment growth is again moderately strong at this scale of analysis. These results are consistent with the findings of Commins and McDonagh (2000) that employment gains in the Midlands region in the period 1993–98 showed a significant shift towards towns of 5,000 population and over.

Public policy in a number of realms has worked to produce the strong association between urbanisation and employment growth. One of the most important of these is the urban renewal schemes introduced in the late 1980s, which, *inter alia*, led to the establishment of the International Financial Services Centre (IFSC) in Dublin as the main component of a major redevelopment plan for the docklands area of the city. The development of the IFSC accounted for a significant proportion of the total expansion in internationally traded services in the 1990s. However, of greater significance has been the strong emphasis of industrial policy on high technology sectors in both manufacturing (e.g., electronics, pharmaceuticals, healthcare, and biotechnology) and traded services (such as software, financial services, shared services, and, more recently, e-commerce) (see also Grimes, Chapter 14). Firms in these sectors, particularly the larger foreign owned firms, have shown a strong preference for city locations, which results from locational requirements that prioritise access to sufficient quantities of skilled labour, and to advanced communications and transportation infrastructures.

Given the strong urban bias of the high technology sector, the spatial and functional structure of the urban system becomes a key mediator of the geographical distribution of economic activity and employment growth. The next section explores some of the characteristics of the Western urban system that are of particular relevance in this regard.

The Urban System of the Western Region

Several reports and policy documents in recent years have highlighted the comparatively weak urban system in the West of Ireland (NESC, 1997; Fitzpatrick Associates, 1999; Western Development Commission, 1999; Government of Ireland, 1999). There are several aspects to this, but the most obvious is the low density of centres of various sizes, in particular those at the upper end of the size distribution (Table 4.3). With a land area equal to 37 per cent of the total area of the state, the Western Region contains just 14 per cent of the towns with over 10,000 population and 16 per cent of those with over 5,000 population. Consequently, the spacing of centres on each level of the urban hierarchy is considerably greater than in other regions, so that average travel times and distances for commuting trips, as well as shopping and social travel focused on the urban centres, are greater than elsewhere.

Table 4.3 Comparative Size Distribution of Urban Centres

	Western Region			Rest of Ireland		
Size category	No.	%	Density per 1,000 km²	No.	Percent	Density per 1,000 km²
Over 10,000	4	16.0	0.15	24	22.4	0.54
5,000 – 10,000	5	20.0	0.19	24	22.4	0.54
3,000 – 5,000	5	20.0	0.19	22	20.6	0.50
1,500 – 3,000	11	44.0	0.42	37	34.6	0.84
Total	25	100.0	0.96	107	100.0	2.42

Source: Author's calculations

In total, almost two-thirds of the urban centres in the region are under 5,000 population. Hall (1999) suggests that, in Europe and elsewhere, centres below this population level have lost services through competition and mobility to higher levels of the urban hierarchy, and that places on the lowest levels of the central place hierarchy – Christaller's *Marktort* and *Amtsort* respectively – have ceased to perform any significant role as central places. Commins and McDonagh (2000) suggest that centres of this size are also finding it increasingly difficult to attract new manufacturing enterprises.

Against these weaknesses, the region's larger centres appear to be performing strongly in terms of population growth and service provision. Galway, Letterkenny, Castlebar and Ennis all had growth rates in excess of 10 per cent, and well above the national average, in the period 1991–96. Additionally, research conducted to underpin the NSS has shown that all of the region's centres over 5,000 population, with the exception of Shannon, had a ranking in terms of their services provision equal to, or in excess of, that based on population (larger centres, in population or services, are said to be of higher rank than smaller centres). In the cases of Letterkenny, Castlebar, Ballina, Tuam and Ballinasloe the divergence was considerable, and on this basis these centres have been identified as 'strong market towns' (Brady Shipman Martin, 2000).

The NSS research, however, was based solely on data relating to the service functions of urban areas, and several of the NSS documents acknowledge the existence of a major information gap in relation to both these and other urban functions. In order to supplement the NSS research, an analysis of urban employment profiles has been undertaken using unpublished data from the 1996 census of population. These give employment levels in 22 intermediate industrial groups (including nine different manufacturing groups as well as extractive activities and the services industries) for all centres over 5,000 population in the State. The first stage of this analysis consists of a functional classification of towns based on the identification of 'basic' employment in each industrial category, and this is followed by an examination of patterns of overall functional specialisation.

The results of the functional classification are illustrated in Figure 4.1. Each centre was allocated to the functional category corresponding to the industrial group in which it had the highest level of basic employment. Basic employment is identified on the basis of national norms, but preliminary investigations using the alternative 'minimum requirements' approach show little variation in results (see Blair (1991) for a discussion of methods of economic base analysis). For ease of reporting, results were aggregated up to broader industrial groupings. This analysis clearly reveals the strong orientation of larger urban centres in the Western Region towards the professional services: six of the nine centres in the region, including three of the four largest centres, have professional services as the dominant basic sector. Nationally, employment in this sector tends to be dominated by the large public sector services – health and education – and the present result is evidence of the importance in employment terms of facilities such as regional and county hospitals and third level education institutions in towns such as Sligo, Letterkenny, and Castlebar. Professional services employs almost one-third of the entire workforce in both Letterkenny and Castlebar, as well as in Ballinasloe.

While identification of towns' dominant functions can provide useful insights into the functioning of the urban system as a whole, functional classification in itself tends to oversimplify the complexity of individual functional profiles, as it looks only at one category of employment in each case. To extend the analysis, the overall degree of specialisation of each town's employment pattern was measured using the coefficient of specialisation (Blair, 1991). The minimum value of the coefficient is zero, which indicates that a town's employment profile exactly matches that of some specified norm, in this case the employment profile of the State as a whole. Values above this, up to a theoretical maximum value of one, are indicative of higher degrees of specialisation, that is, employment profiles that are more discordant with the norm. The coefficient can also be interpreted, inversely, as a measure of the diversity of the urban economic structure – lower values representing greater diversity.

The results (Table 4.4) reveal that Western towns are more specialised in their employment profiles than those in the rest of the country. Within the region, the towns with the highest values of the coefficient are, in descending order, Shannon, Letterkenny, Ballinasloe and Castlebar. While Shannon is a strongly specialised manufacturing centre, the other three towns depend on professional services, as noted above. When centres are ranked nationally from the least specialised (rank = 1) to the most specialised (rank = 57), the towns in the Western Region rank considerably higher, on average, than those in the remainder of the State (an indication of the degree of difference between the two regions is that the difference in mean ranks would be statistically significant at the 95% level under the two-tailed Mann-Whitney U Test). In part these differences are due to the smaller average size of urban centres in the Western Region. It has been generally observed that smaller centres tend to have more specialised employment profiles, with increasing diversity coming with growth in a centre's population. Nevertheless, the overall correlation between size and specialisation level for the Irish urban system as a whole is comparatively low ($r_s = -0.17$), so that the smaller size of the urban centres in the region cannot be taken as the full explanation for the high degree of specialisation observed.

Table 4.4 Functional Specialisation in centres over 5,000 population

	Western Region (n = 9)	Rest of Ireland (n = 48)
Mean value of coefficient of specialisation	0.237	0.194
Mean ranking of centres on coefficient of specialisation	39.333	27.063

Source: Author's calculations

In summary, the urban system of the Western Region shows a number of significant weaknesses. Besides the well-documented lack of medium to large sized towns, the larger centres show a strong dependence on employment in professional services, and a relatively high degree of specialisation. One of the disadvantages of specialisation is the greater exposure to risk of economic downturns affecting particular sectors. To some extent this is compensated for in the case of the Western Region by the fact that specialisation tends to be in the more sheltered public sector. However, while there remains considerable debate in the literature about the benefits and costs of functional specialisation, the general thrust of findings seems to be that diversity fosters urban employment growth by attracting new and innovative sectors of economic activity (Duranton and Puga, 2000). If this is the case, then clearly the major urban centres of the Western Region are at a disadvantage, with deleterious consequences for the development prospects of the region as a whole.

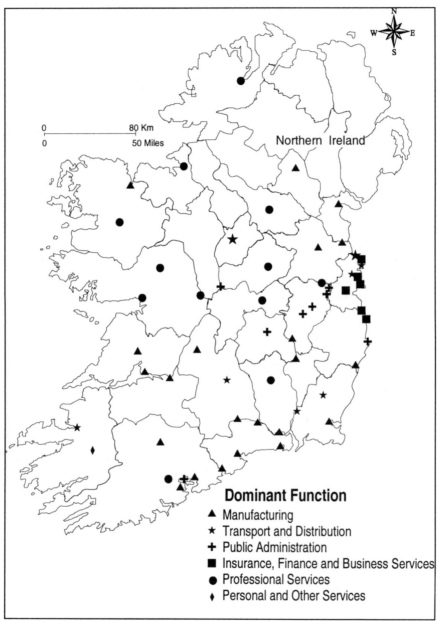

Figure 4.1 Functional classification of urban centres, 1996

Policy Responses: Past and Present

Lessons from the past

The weaknesses outlined above are of long standing. Essentially the same set of circumstances faced the last comprehensive attempt at spatial planning in Ireland: the Buchanan report of the late 1960s (Buchanan, 1968). Buchanan was asked to recommend on the spatial arrangement of population and economic activity that would best fit with macro-economic policy, as set out in the Second Programme for Economic Expansion, and the social goal of minimising internal population dislocation. In the spirit of 1960s spatial planning, he recommended the adoption of a growth centre approach to balancing the territorial development of the state, with growth centres identified at three main levels in the urban hierarchy. Such a policy was seen as offering the best prospects for securing greater balance between regions while at the same time exploiting scale and external economies in infrastructure and industrial development.

The Buchanan recommendations were never implemented, due to the considerable reservations expressed by a wide range of interests from academic commentators to political representatives. Given what appear to be a number of similarities between the regional situation and policy context in the late 1960s and the present, it is instructive to consider what these reservations were. Three main groups of issues can be identified as follows:

> (i) There were fundamental ambiguities in the growth centre concept itself. These related to two major issues. First, there were doubts concerning the very validity of the growth centre concept, which was seen by some commentators as a rather unconvincing attempt to develop a spatial analogue of Perroux's essentially aspatial concept of the growth pole (*pôle de croissance*). Second, it was never clear from the theoretical literature whether designation as a growth centre should be based on the past (spontaneous) growth performance of a centre, or its future prospects for growth, including policy-induced growth.

> (ii) International evidence suggested that the ability of growth centres to spread benefits into their surrounding regions was spatially quite restricted. Much of this is summarised in Moseley (1974). The latter's own primary research in Brittany (Moseley 1973a) and East Anglia (Moseley, 1973b) suggested that the spread effects of

growth centres were spatially confined to commuting hinterlands of no more than 20–25 kilometres radius. Growth centres were therefore seen as doing little for the development prospects of rural areas at greater distances from the designated centres, and potentially likely to decrease inter-regional disparities, if at all, only at the expense of increasing intra-regional disparities.

(iii) Specifically in an Irish context, there was the problem caused by the weak urban system of the West and North-Western parts of the country. This weakness was explicitly recognised in the 1972 Government Statement on regional policy and it was abundantly clear that a growth centre policy was likely to impact negatively on the West. Buchanan tried to overcome the difficulties in this respect by including his third tier of local growth centre, and four such towns were identified nationally, including Letterkenny and Castlebar. However, the inclusion of this tier never really convinced and was seen as no more than an afterthought, with O'Farrell (1971) pointing out, for example, that Buchanan failed to provide any analysis to justify the selection of these centres.

On the basis of the above it is clear that, as a minimum requirement, any new policy framework for spatial development will need to specify more clearly the links between economic growth and spatial structure. Further, it will need to be demonstrated how a spatially more inclusive growth dynamic can be established under which the development of larger centres need not be at the expense of smaller towns and rural areas. This is the challenge for the NSS.

Reconceptualising urban development under the National Spatial Strategy

The recently issued consultation paper *Indications for the Way Ahead* (Department of the Environment and Local Government, 2001) gives some insights into the NSS policy makers' thinking on how the tensions between industrial policy and regional development policy can be resolved (see also Walsh, Chapter 5). It would appear that the policy approach will involve a number of key elements. Of particular interest in the present context are two of these that relate to spatial structure, and more specifically to the urban system.

The first of these elements involves the promotion of new roles for selected larger centres of population as either 'Gateways' or 'development hubs'. The concept of Gateways emphasises the role of the main cities in attracting external investment and communicating the benefits of that and further induced investment to the wider regions in which they are located. The concept implies an acceptance that Ireland will continue, in the medium to long term, to depend on external investment as the major generator of employment. Recognising that Gateways need to possess a 'critical mass', it is indicated that there will be a limited number of such centres. In addition to the five largest cities already designated in the NDP, the consultation paper suggests that there will be at most three to four others. There will also be a relatively small number of development hubs, which are conceived of as medium-sized towns that are well linked to Gateways and that will act to diffuse growth from the Gateways to smaller towns and rural areas.

The second element of the strategy relating to spatial structure is the specification of a framework of functional areas within which the designation of centres as Gateways or development hubs is to take place. The country is divided into 12 functional areas or regions, based on commuting patterns and on catchments for shopping, social facilities, amenities or schools. Given that not every area possesses a centre that is large enough to be designated as a Gateway, the consultation paper suggests that development will take place within each functional area through the promotion of either a Gateway, one or more development hubs, or a Gateway plus a hub or hubs. It is also recognised that some of the new Gateways may need to be based on grouping together a number of neighbouring centres.

These elements of spatial structure, emphasising inter-urban and urban-rural linkages within a functional regions framework, reflect the influence on policy formation of the notion of polycentric development. This concept has attracted considerable attention in European spatial planning in recent years and is central to one of the three spatial development guidelines in the European Spatial Development Perspective (European Council, 1999). The next section examines the concept in more detail, and identifies a number of problems in applying it to the West Region.

Is Polycentric Development the Answer?

Polycentric development can take place at both the urban scale (giving rise to the polycentric city) and the regional scale (the polycentric urban region or PUR), but it is the latter that appears to be most relevant in the Irish context. A polycentric urban region is simply:

> a region having two or more separate cities, with no one centre dominant, in reasonable proximity and well connected (Bailey & Turok, 2001, p.698).

Several aspects of the PUR concept suggest it as an appropriate response to the spatial development problems found in Ireland. These include the promise of reconciling economic competitiveness with environmental sustainability by, for example, reducing urban sprawl. In addition, by allowing smaller urban centres to gain some of the competitive advantages of larger centres through co-operation based on complementarity, a policy of polycentric development would seem to hold out the best prospects for achieving balanced regional development. Finally, and perhaps most importantly, polycentric development offers a more inclusive vision of development than that provided by the outdated, monocentric, growth centre model. Consequently, it provides a better basis for consensus-building, and is politically a more palatable policy prescription.

There are however, several grounds for scepticism about the ability of this new spatial planning concept to deliver on the goals of the NDP. First, there is the problem that the concept of polycentric development has not yet been fully specified, and there continues to be a great deal of ambiguity surrounding it (Kloosterman and Musterd, 2001). Like clusters and related notions such as urban networks and industrial districts, the concept probably works most successfully as a description of spatial arrangements in successful regions of north western Europe, but it is yet unclear to what extent it can be used prescriptively to guide spatial development policy. In other words, polycentrism may be more accurately seen as the outcome rather than the cause of regional prosperity (Groth, 2000). The similarities in this respect with the older growth centre concept are obvious.

Second, there is the question of scale. In descriptive use of the concept, PURs are normally identified with regions containing two or more urban centres of a combined size considerably greater than that found in any of the 12 functional areas. This is especially the case for the northern part of the West Region, which is covered by three functional areas, the North Border, West Border, and North-Western functional areas. None of these has a single urban centre in excess of 20,000 population. It may be that there is, realistically, only one candidate polycentric urban region in Ireland: that defined along the Cork, Limerick, Galway axis. Development of such an axis would probably do most to counter-balance the Dublin region, or indeed the possible emergence of the Dublin-Belfast economic corridor, which has been advocated for some time (Coopers & Lybrand, Indecon, 1994). However, it would do little for the development prospects of the North-West.

Polycentric development is not just a matter of spatial form: much more fundamentally it is a matter of spatial function, and a crucial part of the construct is the notion of linkages and flows among urban centres. The problem is that in prescriptive application of the concept, the nature of these linkages has not yet been specified, so that it is not clear how policy is supposed to promote them, other than through investment in inter-urban transportation and communications networks. However, such networks merely facilitate: for interaction to actually take place there first has to be spatial complementarity. Given the patterns of urban functional specialisation in the West Region that were identified above, and specifically the common dependence on public sector services, the degree of inter-urban complementarity in the region is questionable, at least.

Finally, there is the fact that relationships between urban centres in Ireland are in many instances marked more by a spirit of competition than of co-operation. This in turn is linked to the weakness of regional government in Ireland. Though there has been a plethora of structural and institutional reforms in sub-national government in recent years, almost all of this has been at local (county and sub-county) level (McCafferty & Walsh, 2000). An exception has been the establishment of the Regional Assemblies for the two new NUTS II regions created in 1999. These Assemblies face considerable problems in developing their roles, stemming in part from the relatively large size and internal diversity (both in geographical and socio-economic terms) of the two regions in question. It is also relevant to note here that, while the older (but never properly resourced or empowered) Regional Authorities have as jurisdictions NUTS III regions which are closer in scale to the newly identified functional areas, the two sets of areas do not correspond; nor, according to the consultation paper, is there any intention of revising the NUTS III regions to achieve a better fit. While it can be argued that there is no need for functional and administrative units to correspond, this position does not fit easily with new concepts of governance based on greater devolution.

Summary and Conclusions

In the context of an industrial policy that has targeted high technology manufacturing and service firms, the Irish urban system represents a major constraint on the extent to which a greater balance can be brought to the spatial distribution of activity within the State. Early indications from the NSS suggest that policy makers are looking to the concept of polycentric development to help overcome this constraint. The attractions of the concept, especially *vis-à-vis* earlier spatial policy constructs, are obvious, and it may well be that the concept of polycentric development holds the best prospects for advancing the goal of balanced regional development during, and beyond, the programming period of the National Development Plan.

Considerable care in policy formulation will be needed to cultivate successfully functioning polycentric regions in Ireland. In the West Region certain structural and functional aspects of the urban system identified in this chapter mean that the challenge is all the greater. In the light of these, there are grounds for arguing that a re-examination of industrial policy is also needed. In this respect, the recently signaled switch to a cluster-based approach is timely, (IDA, 2001) since this would appear likely to support the emergence of polycentric spatial form. However more may be necessary, including the adoption of a regionally differentiated approach to industrial development, and a greater emphasis on indigenous, 'old-economy', sectors.

References

Bailey, N. & Turok, I. (2001) 'Central Scotland as a Polycentric Urban Region: Useful Planning Concept or Chimera?', *Urban Studies*, 38(4), pp.679–715.

Blair, J.P. (1991) *Urban and Regional Economics*, Irwin, Boston.

Brady Shipman Martin (2000) *The Irish Urban System and its Dynamics*, unpublished report to the Department of the

Environment and Local Government (Spatial Planning Unit), Dublin.

Buchanan, C. (1968) *Regional Studies in Ireland*, An Forás Forbartha, Dublin.

CSO (2001a) *National Income and Expenditure. First Results.* http://www.cso.ie/publications/demog/popmig.pdf, accessed 6 Nov 2001.

CSO (2001b) *Quarterly National Household Survey. Second Quarter 2001.* http://www.cso.ie/publications/labour/qnhs.pdf, accessed 6 Nov 2001

Commins, P. & McDonagh, P. (2000) 'Rural Areas and the Development of a National Spatial Strategy', paper presented to the Regional Studies Association (Irish Branch) National Conference, Tullamore, 6 April.

Coopers & Lybrand / Indecon (1994) *A Corridor of Opportunity. Study of the Feasibility of Developing a Dublin-Belfast Economic Corridor*, CBI (NI)/ IBEC, Belfast / Dublin.

Department of the Environment & Local Government (2000) *The National Spatial Strategy. Scope and Delivery*, Department of the Environment and Local Government, Dublin.

Department of the Environment & Local Government (2001) *The National Spatial Strategy. Indications for the Way Ahead*, Department of the Environment and Local Government, Dublin.

Duranton, G. & Puga, D. (2000) 'Diversity and Specialisation in Cities: Why, Where and When Does it Matter?', *Urban Studies*, 37 (3), pp.533–555.

European Council (1999) *European Spatial Development Perspective.* DG Regio, Brussels.

Fitzpatrick Associates (1999) *Border, Midland and Western Region. Development Strategy*, Fitzpatrick Associates, Dublin.

Forfás (2001) *Annual Employment Survey 2000*, Forfás, Dublin.

Government of Ireland (1999) *National Development Plan 2000–2006*, The Stationery Office, Dublin.

Groth, N. (2000) 'Urban Systems between Policy and Geography', *Regional Studies*, 34(6), pp.571–580.

Hall, P. (1999) 'The future of cities', *Computers, Environment and Urban Systems*, 23, pp.173–185.

IDA (2001) *Annual Report 2000*, IDA Ireland, Dublin.

Kloosterman, R.C. & Musterd, S. (2001) 'The Polycentric Urban Region: Towards a Research Agenda', *Urban Studies*, 38(4), pp.623–633.

McCafferty, D. & Walsh, J. (2000) 'Towards a New Local Governance in Ireland? Local Authorities, Partnerships and Local Development Policy'. Paper presented at the annual conference of the Political Studies Association of Ireland, Cork.

Moseley, M.J. (1973a) 'The Impact of Growth centres in Rural Regions. I. An Analysis of Spatial "Patterns" in Brittany', *Regional Studies*, 7, pp.57–75.

Moseley, M.J. (1973b) 'The Impact of Growth centres in Rural Regions. II. An Analysis of Spatial "Flows" in East Anglia', *Regional Studies*, 7, pp.77–94.

Moseley, M.J. (1974) *Growth Centres in Spatial Planning*, Pergamon, Oxford.

NESC (1992) *The Association between Economic Growth and Employment Growth in Ireland*, Report no. 94, National Economic and Social Council, Dublin.

NESC (1997) *Population Distribution and Economic Development: Trends and Policy Implications*, Report no.102, National Economic and Social Council, Dublin.

O'Farrell, P.N. (1971) 'The Regional Problem in Ireland: Some Reflections upon Development Strategy', *The Economic and Social Review*, 2(4), pp.474–486.

Western Development Commission (1999) *Blueprint for Success. A Development Plan for the West 2000–2006*, Western Development Commission, Ballaghaderreen.

Western Development Commission (2001) *The State of the West*, Western Development Commission, Ballaghaderreen.

chapter five

THE NATIONAL SPATIAL STRATEGY AS A FRAMEWORK FOR
ACHIEVING BALANCED REGIONAL DEVELOPMENT

Jim Walsh

Introduction

After a lengthy period during which regional analysis and spatial planning were neglected throughout many European countries there is now a renewed emphasis which has been inspired in part by the process leading to the publication of the *European Spatial Development Perspective* in 1999 (Eser and Konstadakopulos, 2000; Faludi, 2001) and the subsequent international *Study Programme on European Spatial Planning* (Nordregio, 2000). Many governments are also displaying a new interest in regional development and spatial planning. Regional development and spatial planning are back on the public policy agenda in Ireland. This chapter reviews the context for the preparation of a National Spatial Strategy (NSS), examines the issues that have been considered and assesses the concepts underpinning the emerging strategy (this chapter was completed prior to the finalisation of the National Spatial Strategy).

The Context for the National Spatial Strategy (NSS)

A new phase of economic restructuring has been underway in Ireland since the late 1980s which has, especially since 1993, resulted in an extraordinary transformation of the position of Ireland within the European Union (EU). The scale of the transformation is evident from the following aggregate statistical data. For most of the period between 1960 and 1989 the level of per capita GDP in Ireland was about 62 per cent of the average for the EU twelve member states. Only Portugal and Greece had lower levels in 1989. In the same year the unemployment rate in Ireland was 18.7 per cent compared to 11.3 per cent in the EU as a whole (NESC, 1989). Very high levels of emigration from both urban and rural areas were contributing to population decline (NESC, 1991; Walsh, 1992).

The Ireland of 2001 is very different. Annual economic growth rates in excess of 7 per cent have been experienced since the mid-1990s reaching a peak of over 11 per cent in 2000. The total at work increased by 40 per cent between 1991 and 1999 while the number unemployed declined by 52 per cent giving an unemployment rate of under 4 per cent. Per capita GDP levels had risen to the EU average by 1998. In 2000 the per capita GDP for Ireland was second highest, after Luxembourg, in the EU. Net emigration has been replaced by high levels of net in-migration including large numbers of return migrants and also many others from diverse ethnic backgrounds. The extraordinary turn-around since the early 1990s is the result of many interrelated factors that have been described in detail by others (see Bradley, *et al.* 1997; Barry, 1999; Walsh, 2000). The Irish 'success' story has attracted widespread international attention and has been applauded by many including the OECD which now regards Ireland as a model for many other developing regions and countries. The transformation that has occurred is all the more extraordinary given the openness of the economy. After Luxembourg Ireland is the second most open economy among the OECD members. Since the late 1950s successive governments have pursued policies aimed at integrating the Irish economy into the European and global arenas. While there has been a consistency in the broad policy over a period of four decades the supporting strategies have been subjected to revisions and modifications in order to take account of the changing external context. A significant aspect of the economic relationship between Ireland and the rest of the world has been a need for regular repositioning in order to take advantage of changes in the international organisation of production, new opportunities linked to EU membership, and new sources of comparative advantage in the area of human resources arising from investment in education.

Increased integration into the European and global markets has also impacted on the strategies for regional development adopted by governments. Throughout the 1960s and 1970s there was a strong emphasis on mechanisms to promote dispersal of mobile investments in order to promote balanced regional development. This was feasible in an era when there was a significant inflow of Fordist type branch plants into Ireland. In the context of a very difficult domestic macroeconomic situation in the 1980s the focus shifted towards a more targeted approach to inward investment and the primary 'regional' objective became the reduction of the differential in per capita GDP between Ireland and the EU average.

While the model that has underpinned the exceptional economic growth rates since the early 1990s is complex, there is general agreement upon the significance of the EU through both the single market and the Structural Funds, and also on the role of foreign direct investment as the principal driver (OECD, 1999). While these and other factors have significantly changed Ireland's position in the EU they have also contributed to the making of a new socio-economic geography within Ireland. Using a variety of indices it has been shown that outcomes from rapid development in the 1990s have been uneven between regions: see for example Boyle *et al.*, (1998/99) and Duffy *et al.*, (1999) and Walsh, (2000) on the regional trends in output and employment; O'Leary, (2001) on trends in living standards, and Commins and McDonagh (2000) for the impacts on rural areas. The exceptionally rapid growth since the mid 1990s took place against a background of serious infrastructural deficits arising from very limited capital investment in the 1980s. The very high reliance on foreign direct investment in selected manufacturing sectors and internationally traded services as the principal economic driver has resulted in a major shift in investment, employment and population towards Dublin and the other cities, especially Galway. The total population has increased by 250,000 since 1990 and the number at work by about 500,000. Additional numbers at work, higher incomes and an abundance of loan finance has resulted in an increase of 50 per cent in the number of cars on the roads leading to enormous problems of congestion, especially in and around Dublin. The concentration of employment has also contributed to a sharp rise in demand for housing which has resulted in spiralling house prices and also a rapid growth of new residential developments in towns, villages and the open countryside. This in turn has resulted in increased volumes of long distance commuting, mostly by private car. The increased levels of economic activity coupled with increased consumption levels have also lead to an increase of about 50 per cent in the volume of waste produced, resulting in serious waste management issues in many areas.

These pressures are not confined to the major urban areas. The general rise in affluence has resulted in increased demand for second homes and holiday accommodation, especially in coastal areas. There has been a proliferation of new house building in many rural areas, giving rise to concerns about the sustainability of this type of settlement in the future. At the same time there are some rural areas, largely remote inland areas, where there appears to have been relatively little new activity. Furthermore many of the previously strong farming areas are undergoing structural changes associated with the transition to post-productivist agriculture and experiencing decline in population and employment (McHugh and Walsh, 2000). These trends have emerged from a period during which the economic growth rates were much higher than anticipated; for which there was no overall spatial framework or appropriate administrative structures, to ensure co-ordination and integration of policies and actions. Serious concerns about the emerging spatial patterns of development have been articulated in relation to a number of policy areas. These include sustainable development (Department of the Environment, 1997), enterprise development (Forfas, 2000) and rural development (Department of Agriculture & Food, 1999) (for a more comprehensive overview see Walsh, 1999). The response to these concerns emerged in three very significant publications in 1999 by the Economic and Social Research Institute (Fitzgerald *et al.*, 1999), the National Economic and Social Council and the Government in its National Development Plan (NDP) 2000–2006 (Department of Finance, 1999). Each emphasised the need for a national spatial development strategy. The NDP 2000–2006 published in November 1999 includes fostering balanced regional development as a core objective. The Government's objective for regional policy in the NDP is:

> to achieve more balanced regional development in order to reduce the disparities between and within the two Regions and to develop the potential of both to contribute to the greatest possible extent to the continuing prosperity of the country. Policy to secure such development must be advanced in parallel with policies to ensure that this development is sustainable with full regard to the quality of life, social cohesion, and conservation of the environment and the natural and cultural heritage (para 3.19, p.43).

The NDP is by far the most ambitious ever involving a projected gross investment programme costing over 50 billion euro, almost two and half times the scale of investment projected under the previous NDP for 1994–1999. The NDP will be implemented through four Inter-regional Operational Programmes (covering Economic and Social Infrastructure; Employment and Human Resources; the Productive sectors; and CAP Rural Development measures) and two Regional Programmes which are expected to account for approximately 12 per cent of the total planned investment. In total, per capita expenditure in the Border Midland West (BMW) region will be about 38 per cent higher than in the other region and the region's share of total investment is set to increase from approximately 30 to 33 per cent (see also Finn, Chapter 3). Such an enormous increase in the scale of investment will undoubtedly have profound impacts on economy, society and the environment, especially on the landscape. The introduction of Regional Programmes with significant budgets to be administered by newly created Regional Assemblies (see Finn, Chapter 3) and the introduction of a more differentiated schedule of permissible levels of regional support through financial instruments makes it all the more important to have an overall spatial framework to guide investment decisions and to facilitate co-ordination and integration across programmes. The NDP includes a commitment from the government to prepare a strategy for spatial development in order to achieve the regional policy objectives within the guiding principles of maintaining economic competitiveness, enhancing social inclusion and promoting sustainable development. The proposed framework is intended to provide a blueprint for spatial development over a twenty year horizon. It is expected that the NSS will provide a basis for longer term co-ordination and co-operation in policy formulation and decision-making on major investment in infrastructure, including public and private transport infrastructure.

Preparation of the National Spatial Strategy (NSS)

The preparation of the NSS presented many challenges for a variety of reasons, not least the fact that the only previous attempt to undertake a broadly similar exercise was back in the mid 1960s (Buchanan and Partners, 1968). Typical of 1960s the preparation was very much a top-down exercise that resulted in proposals for a hierarchy of growth centres and major investment in the interurban roads network. The proposals proved to be too radical for the political system at the time and were quickly abandoned in favour of a more dispersed model that relied heavily on the attraction of inward investment (Breathnach, 1982). Preparation of the NSS commenced in Spring 2000. A Spatial Planning Unit (SPU) was established within the Department of the Environment and Local Government (DoELG). The objectives of the strategy were to provide a framework through which the following ideals could be achieved:

Continuing national economic and employment growth;

Continuing improvement in Ireland's international competitiveness;

Fostering balanced regional development;

Improving the quality of life for all sections of society;

Maintaining and enhancing the quality and diversity of the natural environment and cultural heritage;

Consolidating peace in the island of Ireland and developing political, economic and social interaction within the island (DoELG, 2000, 2001).

These will enable future patterns of development to be set within a context that will accord with the Government's overall aims on sustainable development which have been defined in a manner that encompasses:

Environmental Sustainability – living within the capacity of natural environmental systems;

Economic Sustainability – ensuring continued prosperity and employment opportunities, and

Social Sustainability – ensuring greater opportunities to participate in economic success in a way that adds to personal well-being and quality of life.

Following the preparation of the scoping report two processes were embarked upon. The first was an extensive research programme undertaken by members of the SPU and external consultants. The second was an elaborate programme of consultation. The latter involved mechanisms for consultation across government departments and also engaging many of the state agencies, presentations to the cabinet, and also to national fora that included representatives of all the social partners as well as the third sector. In addition a number of roadshows were organised throughout the country. An Expert Advisory Group that included representation from outside Ireland also guided the SPU. Before proceeding to consider some of the outcomes from the research programme it is useful to summarise the key issues arising from the public consultations. They can be grouped according to a number of themes (see DoELG, 2001):

(i) Quality of life
This is an overriding concern for many people in terms of its perceived deterioration.

(ii) Transport
Present systems of public transport are insufficient for the growing numbers of users;

A widespread perception of poor accessibility and availability of public transport in rural areas, and

The inadequate condition of many sections of the national roads.

(iii) Employment prospects
Job losses, particularly outside the main cities;

Limited range of employment options in rural areas, and

Reluctance of large companies to locate outside of Dublin due to poor infrastructure and scarcity of staff.

(iv) Declining populations in rural areas
Linked to poor job prospects, lack of public transport and absence of recreational facilities for young people, and

Long distance commuting from rural areas tending to fragment rural communities.

(v) Access to health/education facilities
Good access required to hospitals and universities via private or public transport.

(vi) Fitting the NSS in with other plans and programmes
Will the NSS fit in with county and city development plans and other strategic plans?

How will different programmes work along side each other and how will the objectives of the NSS be translated into results on the ground?

(vii) Scope of the NSS
Less developed areas may not be given as much priority as areas that are better developed economically, and

On the other hand, need to avoid becoming diverted from sustaining present growth in areas that are doing well.

A comprehensive analysis of the structure of rural areas was undertaken in order to identify the diversity of socio-economic conditions and adjustment patterns throughout the state (in all the research programme involved over twenty separate studies and it is beyond the scope of this chapter to review them all, and as such, only a limited number of key findings can be noted). Approximately 40 per cent of the total population resides in rural areas. A rural typology based on a multivariate statistical analysis of 30 indicators measuring over 2700 districts revealed the existence of six area types: two traditionally strong rural area types; two weak area types, and two types of areas where there are significant urban impacts. The latter category consists of on the one hand, areas on the fringe of urban centres, and on the other, remote areas that are mostly coastal and subject to changes related to tourism and other forms of consumption that emanate mainly from the larger urban centres (McHugh and Walsh, 2000).

Research on the urban system (see also McCafferty, Chapter 4) confirmed the increasing dominance of the capital city within the Irish urban system and also its pivotal role in linking Ireland to the international space economy and also to the sources of cultural, social and political change. The research identified a number of urban sub-systems including regional capitals, county towns, potential duo-centric and polycentric clusters and also extensive areas where the settlement pattern is particularly weak. An important conclusion from this research was that, apart from Dublin, none of the other cities on its own was likely to be large enough to become a significantly competitive location for economic development in the context of the European urban system. An analysis of urban functions revealed a lack of correspondence between population rank and functional rank in many cases leading to a trichotomous categorisation. The first consists of a number of strategically located towns that have a functional role in excess of what their population size might suggest (e.g. Letterkenny, Castlebar, Mullingar, Mallow, Thurles, Tuam, Athy, Cavan, Monaghan). A second grouping represents mainly dormitory settlements or towns with large numbers of commuters that have a relatively restricted functional base (Bray, Swords, Skerries, Maynooth, Greystones, Shannon, Carrigaline). The third category are those towns where there is a broad level of correspondence between population and functional ranks.

Linking with the rural analysis, the urban research noted that many urban centres in previously strong rural areas are now in decline. There was a striking difference in the performance of towns with populations either above or below 5000 persons. The majority of towns with more than 5000 population are growing and are the most likely locations for new manufacturing or service enterprises. Over half of the towns and villages with populations <1500, and 40 percent of those between 1500–3000, declined in population between 1991 and 1996. The analysis of recent trends in the geography of employment changes established a significant negative relationship between remoteness (measured in terms of distance to each of the 56 centres with more than 5,000 population, where the potential impact of each urban centre is weighted by its population total) and total employment change. Research on transportation pointed to the lack of coordination between investment in roads and rail services. The road investment programme planned under the NDP is likely to seriously erode the competitiveness of rail for long distance movements, even though the resultant movement patterns will be less environmentally sustainable. The small size of most urban centres is also likely to make it difficult to provide sustainable public transport systems.

The analysis of IT infrastructure provision revealed the existence of a major digital divide with the weaker rural areas particularly disadvantaged. While it is technically feasible to roll out the fibre optic cables across and within the regions and to establish connections through multiple mechanisms the main challenge lies in the fact that most of this activity is driven by the private sector which is most likely to concentrate its investments in areas of high population density where service demand is likely to be high. The lack of investment in electricity generation and also in the transmission network in the 1980s coupled with an enormous increase in demand to support a more energy intensive economy has resulted in serious bottlenecks over recent years. There are particularly serious constraints in extensive parts of the West and North-West which are likely to effect future industrial and service sector development over the short to medium term. The bulk of the research has analysed the contemporary socio-economic situation, in so far as it is possible to do so, within the constraints of very limited recent micro level spatial data. Population projections were prepared to identify future scenarios of population change. On the basis of the most reasonable set of assumptions the projections indicate that the total population could increase by about 900,000 (approx. 25 percent) between 1996 and 2021. In the absence of a spatial strategy it is expected that up to 80 percent of the increase will occur in Dublin and the three surrounding counties. More recently prepared projections by the Central Statistics Office (CSO) support this conclusion. They also suggest outside of the Dublin region the next highest levels of population growth are likely to be around Limerick and Galway cities. The prospects for the Midlands and the Southeast are the least encouraging (CSO, 2001).

New Perspectives on Regional Development

A very extensive body of international research on regional development has accumulated over the past forty years or more. Within the research traditions a broad distinction can be made between analyses that seek to enhance the competitive growth of weaker regions through external interventions and those analyses that seek to promote economic development from within by relying on place specific factors.

The first generation of regional development models of the 1950s and 1960s were associated with the so-called Fordist approach to production in which large international companies engaged in vertical disintegration strategies (creating branch plants) and favoured a geographically dispersed pattern of investment. At the same time national governments intervened to influence location decisions of corporate organisations through a variety of measures such as financial subsidies, public infrastructure investments (roads, industrial estates, etc.) and favourable tax concessions. The centralised top-down approach to regional development tended to produce short-term benefits such as additional employment but it did not lead to a dynamic self-sustaining growth model. In this approach there was an over-reliance on inward investment and insufficient support for strengthening the indigenous sectors of regional economies. There were a number of fundamental weaknesses such as a failure to encourage innovation, a tendency to foster a dependency culture, and an inability to understand the territorial dimension of productive systems. Attempts to promote regional growth centres generally failed for a variety of reasons including over reliance on inward investments, lack of integration mechanisms, and an absence of sufficient political will to take the decisions required to make the strategies work.

Since the late 1970s there have been number of major revisions in regional development theory leading to new policies and strategies that favour a more territorial based approach. Maillat (1997) contends that from the early 1980s a second generation of regional policies began to emerge. Changes in the overall context for economic development resulted in regionally differentiated responses leading to the further decline of some older industrial regions but also the simultaneous emergence of new dynamic regions in places as diverse as north-central Italy, southwest Germany, west Denmark, southwest Norway and parts of Austria. The strategies adopted in these regions have attracted much international attention which has resulted in attempts to identify the main factors that have contributed to their success (see for example reports prepared by Cooke (1996) for the National Economic and Social Council and by Dunford and Hudson (1996) for the Northern Ireland Economic Council). A key outcome from studies of these successful regions is that the development process is largely driven from within the regions. The distinguishing feature of this approach is that strategies are directed towards encouraging innovation, promoting networks and collaboration between all the main agents, and utilising the full potential of all of the regions resources rather than seeking to attract branches or subsidiaries of larger companies from outside the region. Towards the end of the 1980s the effects of globalisation on production systems and on regions or localities were becoming clearer. The impacts of information and communications technologies, and the adoption of more flexible forms of production, work and inter-firm relations have placed much greater emphasis on innovation and on the capacity of firms to incorporate new knowledge and to assimilate or develop new production technologies (Malecki, 1997). New types of relations between regions and the global economy were being formed.

The previous distinctions between exogenous and endogenous approaches to regional development had become less valid. The focus shifted in third generation models, to what have been described as intangible factors in the development process. These include a greater emphasis on improving the capacity for development at the level of the firm, the industry and the region. This especially involved supporting measures aimed at encouraging innovation, promoting information exchanges and adoption of best practices (in areas such as management, design and quality assurance, new technology, marketing) via networking, mobilising new financial sources, and fostering collaborative approaches based on principles of partnership to the design and implementation of regional programmes. The objective here was to ensure that there was a supportive local or regional milieu in which an additional form of capital, namely social capital, could be created and linked to the other forms of capital in a manner that resulted in added value for the region. The processes involved in creating social capital appear to work most successfully at the regional and local levels. They rely heavily on actions to encourage and facilitate information sharing and learning by all the key actors in the region – hence the term 'learning regions' has been applied to places where this strategy has been successfully pursued (Simmie, 1997). Learning regions do not emerge spontaneously, rather there is a need for an agency or authority to play an animation or catalytic role leading to a cultural change in relation to enterprise development (Morgan and Nauwelaers, 1999). Drawing on the findings of research undertaken by the OECD Maillat (1997) identified a number of measures that characterise third generation regional policies. These include:

> maintaining and developing specific and strategic non-material resources such as know-how, training and trust;
>
> selection and managing key information relating to the development of markets, technology and other competitor regions;

building up a critical mass through networks, and

forging new alliances in order to develop inter-regional forms of co-operation.

These changes in policy design indicate the need to interpret the level of development of regions not only according to quantitative criteria but that attention must also be given to the qualitative dimension of development. Thus while a regional strategy will seek to increase output and employment and reduce unemployment, the factors that are most likely to determine the capacity for productive restructuring and growth potential are the regional innovation rate, the level of skills in the labour force, the technological and managerial capacity of the firms, the flexibility of public and private organisations, and the integration of the firms, cities and regions within competitive and innovative networks (Cooke, 1996: Vazquez-Barquero, 1997). Regions that have supported social capital formation have remained vibrant or been revived. Since the mid 1990s there is a growing awareness that the impacts of increasing levels of competition between regions has implications for the global – local interplays encouraged by third generation regional development policies. Quevit (1991) and Malecki (1997) have emphasised the importance of medium-sized towns in mediating interactions between local/regional production systems and the global economy. The likelihood of mobilising the sources of competitive advantage identified in the new fourth generation regional development models, particularly the development of local linkages and networking, is greater in medium sized urban centres which have advantages as places of interaction and as locations for positive spillover effects based on proximity, variety and accessibility (Maillat, 1997).

Proximity is defined in terms of minimisation of geographic distance, which results from a spatial concentration of infrastructure, institutions, organisations and persons. It is also related to shared cultural values which increase the likelihood of formal and informal exchanges and interactions. Variety relates to the diversity of participants and activities associated with the multiple networks that are characteristic of successful regions. Urban centres offer greater possibilities of increasing the variety of actors and the range of opportunities for interactions to take place. These conditions are especially necessary in the context of economic development trajectories that are becoming more knowledge based and reliant on mobility within local labour markets as an important mechanism for the tacit knowledge transfers that are central to the adoption and diffusion of innovations. Another facet of new labour markets is the need to cater for the occupational aspirations of households where both partners are likely to be engaged in work outside the home. According to Maillat (*ibid.*) accessibility refers to the ability to exchange, transmit, communicate, understand and learn. It is promoted by physical networks and also by the existence of meeting places and opportunities for sociability.

Strategies to achieve a more balanced regional distribution of development opportunities will require a greater emphasis on fostering learning regions with a high innovation potential. A significant challenge for the current phase of regional development policies is to establish means of enhancing the competitiveness of medium size urban centres that can act as rivals to the dominant centre while at the same time providing a focus for production systems that are more diffuse than the more polarized systems associated with first generation growth centre approaches. Much of the recent literature on regional and local development emphasises the importance of fostering local entrepreneurship. The concept of entrepreneurship has several levels of meaning. At a most basic level it is used to describe small firms or enterprises frequently operating as part of the informal economy in sectors where there are few entry barriers and relatively low start-up costs. The second, and most common application of the concept is to describe new firm formation. Entrepreneurship linked to new small business formation is generally regarded as a significant component of local and regional development strategies and is likely to be influenced by factors such as the extent of accumulated local knowledge, values and experiences. At a higher level, entrepreneurship entails innovation and system-wide coordination of complex production strategies. At this level it involves new products, new production processes, new sources of inputs and new forms of organisation.

Research on regional variations in entrepreneurship has identified a number of relevant factors. Firstly, there is a substantial volume of evidence that regions, which become heavily reliant on branch plants, tend to have a low level of entrepreneurial activity. Secondly, regions where entrepreneurship has flourished tend to be distinguishable from others on the basis of two important criteria: the sectoral mix in the regions and the social mix. The sectoral profile is important because the barriers to entry and the levels of opportunities vary between sectors. In terms of the social mix of a place the key factor appears to be the quality of the educational system. The knowledge and skills imparted through the educational system have been shown to influence the rate of firm formation by enhancing the level of awareness about business opportunities and the willingness to take risks. Research on the factors contributing to the formation and sustainability of entrepreneurial environments has identified several factors including mechanisms to support R&D, innovation and technology transfer, actions to promote an enterprise culture, provision of appropriate hardware infrastructure in the form of business parks, incubator units, access to broadband tele-communications, and supports for networks and mentoring services (business angels). Others have emphasised the importance of concepts such as institutional thickness (Amin and Thrift, 1994) as well as social capital (Putnam, 1993) to describe the mesh of public and private sector interactions that foster and sustain economic and social activity.

Key Concepts in the National Spatial Strategy (NSS)

A number of key concepts have emerged in the discussions leading to the formulation of policy indications (DoELG, 2001). A central goal of the strategy is to facilitate the promotion of *balanced regional development*, while at the same time maintaining the competitiveness of the economy, improving the quality of life of all persons, and ensuring that the development model is sustainable. After much analysis it has been concluded that an approach to balanced regional development that is based on measures to ensure equity in distributions across regions is unrealistic and unlikely to succeed. Rather, an approach that seeks to optimise the utilisation of the specific and unique potential within definable areas is more realistic and more likely to succeed. The manner in which the concept of balanced regional development is defined and interpreted is a crucial issue in the formulation and ultimately the acceptability and viability of the strategy. The indications from the consultation process are that there is widespread support for a 'potential' rather than a 'redistribution' based approach to balanced regional development.

What is potential? The types of economic activity in an area, the nature of its urban and rural areas, its people, skills and resources, all comprise potential for economic and social progress and development. *Potential* might be defined therefore, as the capacity which an area possesses for development arising from its endowment of natural resources, population, labour, economic and social capital and location relative to markets (DoELG, 2001). Different areas have differing types and levels of potential. The NSS must explore how the level of potential that an area is capable of sustaining can be strengthened and built upon. Critical mass is an important concept in achieving this.

Critical mass has been defined as the size, concentration and characteristics of populations that enable a range of services and facilities to be supported and which, in turn, can attract and support higher levels of economic activity. This in turn tends to enlarge the population and so further support a strengthening of services and facilities. Once a threshold or critical level of development has been achieved it will permit the beginning of a chain reaction leading to further growth and development. The transformation that has occurred in Dublin since the early 1990s illustrates the importance of critical mass. Dublin's success has been assisted by its population size and structure, the levels of education, the availability of educational resources, the mix and clustering of different types of labour pools in niche sectors, transport links to other regions and countries, and informal networks of people and enterprise that provide the scale or critical mass to enable rapid economic progress to take place. Critical mass can be achieved in different ways. It will normally require a concerted effort to develop a single town or city to play a larger role and deliver benefits to its wider hinterland. Alternatively, in some areas it might involve providing a package of supports to enable a number of neighbouring towns to co-operate in order to collectively achieve a critical level of supporting infrastructures, facilities and services. The same level of critical mass cannot be achieved everywhere. Concentration of critical mass to achieve stronger centres and thereby the development of associated areas is a crucial dynamic in bringing about more balanced regional development. This will necessarily involve difficult choices of deciding how and where to concentrate efforts. However, concentrating on creating critical mass in particular places will achieve more benefits for their wider hinterlands and for the country as a whole in terms of enhancing the range of competitive locations for development, than would an approach that attempts to spread efforts too widely.

Maintaining an on-going dynamic of development is crucially dependent on the capacity to promote and sustain a high level of innovation within regions. The extensive literature on regional innovation systems points to the importance of supportive institutional structures to nurture an innovative milieu (Morgan and Nauwelaers, 1999). There is a very strong emphasis on communication structures to facilitate both formal and informal knowledge exchanges, and also on maximising the potential of local resources. Much of the international experience also suggests that local labour markets need to be large enough to cope with relatively high levels of staff turnover. These requirements support the emphasis placed in the approach to BRD on developing local potential and achieving critical mass. The foregoing analysis has implications for the choice of an appropriate spatial structure to fully realise the potential of the people and other resources throughout all parts of the country in a manner that will be sustainable, maintain overall competitiveness of the national economy and achieve balanced regional development. A number of alternative scenarios have been considered including:

continuing with present trends;

adjusting present trends by restricting growth of Dublin and expanding significantly the other four cities;

same as second scenario with the addition of a new city in the regions where the urban structure is weakest, and

restricting Dublin, no additional efforts targeted to other cities, and dispersal of supports to all towns with more than 1500 persons.

Each of these was considered and found to be deficient in relation to the goals that the NSS is seeking to achieve. The emphasis instead has shifted towards a *functional areas* approach.

The work completed to date for the NSS suggests that spatial trends and patterns of activity and development in Ireland can be seen in terms of twelve *functional areas* containing cities or towns and their hinterlands that are loosely defined in terms of boundaries. According to the DoELG (2001) these are areas that typically tend to share common characteristics and issues, where people live their working, schooling, shopping and leisure lives and with which many can identify. This sense of identification spans the urban/rural divide and frequently extends across county boundaries. Some of these areas, where there is a strongly dominant centre, such as the commuting catchment of a major city, are easier to identify than others. Another noteworthy feature is the merging of the various areas at their edges. Each of the areas contains an urban centre or a number of centres, which are central to the economic functioning of that area. There is also a recognised interdependence between the urban centre or centres and other parts of the overall area. Taking the concept of functional areas a stage further it is necessary to identify how such areas might be organised internally and how they might relate to each other and to places beyond Ireland. The NDP 2000–2006 (Department of Finance, 1999) used the concept of *Gateways* to describe centres that have a strategic location relative to a surrounding area. These centres possess good social and economic infrastructure and support services and have the ability to energise their surrounding zones of influence through, for example, good transport links and enabling other centres of various sizes and rural areas to play complementary roles. There are specific attributes common to these centres. Learning from their success and seeking to establish additional centres that could become competitive locations for investment at the national and international levels could have a vital role in promoting more balanced regional development. The NDP identified Dublin, Cork, Limerick/Shannon, Galway and Waterford as existing Gateways. The attributes that characterise these gateways include:

Civic vision and enthusiasm of key interest groups to act together in moving forward, combined with strategies for physical, economic and social development and environmental protection;

A large population in both the urban centre and its broader functional area;

Regional and/or national centres of learning;

Clustering of a large number of businesses and firms with a strong presence of larger firms and those involved in rapidly developing sectors;

Focal points for national, regional and public and private transport systems, with easy access to the national rail network, airports with daily scheduled flights and deepwater ports;

Public and private urban transport systems with improving facilities for pedestrians and cyclists;

Comprehensive facilities for healthcare and persons with special needs;

Regional cultural venues such as theatres, galleries, arts and sports centres;

Extensive zoned and serviced land banks for land uses including residential and industrial development, and

Water supply, wastewater disposal systems and a receiving environment capable of accommodating current water services requirements and major additional requirements into the future.

A key challenge for the NSS will be to facilitate further development of the existing Gateways in a manner that may over the longer term lead to the emergence of a strong counter attraction to the Greater Dublin Area. This may require a proactive infrastructural programme and some institutional initiatives to encourage greater linkages and facilitate the achievement of a higher level of critical mass through a network of the major urban centres between Galway and Cork. In addition to the Gateways referred to above, there are some strategically located relatively large urban centres, or clusters of centres, which may not at present have all the attributes referred to above, but which could, with appropriate supports, develop a capacity to raise the level of development within their respective areas. Centres such as these can play a key role in achieving more balanced regional development by offering locations for investment that are both nationally and internationally competitive. Developmental prospects for different areas must take account of current levels of potential, critical mass, and the capacity of the local environment to cope with substantial expansion. These factors suggest tailored solutions for different areas with most centres following a more organic rate of growth than the proposed Gateways. Taking into account the actual scale of population growth capable of being attracted to the new Gateways and the practicalities and investment involved in making new Gateways work, the indications are that only a small number of additional Gateways will be selected, possibly in the North-West, North-East, Midlands and South-East.

The Gateway approach will help create a dynamic that will also assist other towns and rural areas within the functional areas. As part of this process, medium sized towns, either individually or as part of local polycentric networks, will not only support and benefit from the national and international roles of the Gateways but, in turn, will relate in a similar reciprocal way to the smaller towns and rural areas within their own areas of influence. To underpin this 'hub' role, an integral part of the NSS will also be to set out how a limited number of different medium-sized towns, well linked to Gateways, could best support the development of smaller towns and rural areas in contributing to, and benefiting from, national economic development. The indications from the analysis suggest a relatively small number of hubs that might include individual towns such as Mallow or Tuam and local groupings such as Castlebar-Westport or Tralee-Killarney. Beyond the urban centres there will be a need for additional measures targeted specifically at rural areas. Some of these will emerge from local strategic planning undertaken by, for example, County Development Boards. A range of measures to support rural areas are being implemented as part of the programme outlined in the White Paper on Rural Development (Department of Agriculture & Food, 1999). Finally, the NSS attaches considerable importance to *linkages*. This relates to the means of moving people and goods, energy and information in order to access and develop the resources and potentials of areas. It enables the complementary strengths of places to be combined so as to develop critical mass, and to facilitate the development of a single island of Ireland economy. In order to redress the imbalances associated with the current patterns of development new types of linkages will need to be considered which may lessen the reliance on Dublin for some activities (e.g., seaport based cargo movement) and also strengthen the linkages between the Gateways and hubs.

Issues Arising from the Process

At this stage of the process it is useful to reflect, albeit very briefly, on some of the more general issues that have arisen. Throughout the process it has been important to remain focused on the each of the three key words in the title, National Spatial Strategy. The exercise is about creating a national framework that will be supported by more detailed plans at regional and local levels. It is not appropriate for a national strategy to become overly prescriptive about local development plans. Rather the strategy should be flexible enough to cope with unanticipated external shocks to the economic system and also to facilitate repositioning within a rapidly changing global context. The NSS is just one level in a hierarchy of spatial plans that also includes county and regional strategies. As a spatial strategy the primary orientation has to be on addressing spatial issues. There are many other public strategies to address issues that do not have explicit spatial dimensions. It is very important that the spatial strategy remains focused on providing a framework for solutions that are achievable through other strategies. As a strategy it is important to avoid becoming immersed in too much detail. Rather it should aim to provide a framework for addressing the bigger issues that are likely to impact on regional development over the longer term.

Achieving consensus

The previous attempt in the 1960s to devise a framework for regional development failed in part due to the inability to secure consensus around the main proposals. During the course of preparing this NSS considerable efforts have been made to secure the support of all of the main stakeholders. This has been time consuming and has at times required difficult negotiations and compromises. The achievement of widespread support in the political arena is perhaps the most difficult challenge as the strategy almost certainly requires making choices, some of which may not appear to be very attractive to politicians in some parts of the country. The challenge here is partly to devise a communications strategy that will convey the strategy as leading to win-win solutions (everybody and every place have an opportunity to win) rather than as a zero-sum game where there are some winners and losers.

Implementation

A key determinant of the ultimate impact of the strategy will be the structures put in place to ensure that it is implemented. It will be important to underpin the strategy with a legislative instrument. Responsibility for day-to-day implementation will need to be assigned to a unit in one government department, preferably the Department of the Environment and Local Government as it has overall responsibility for the implementation of planning legislation and also for local and regional governance structures. Because of the need for extensive coordination and integration across many policy areas the implementation should be supported by a committee of high level public servants and, at cabinet level, by a sub-committee consisting of the key ministers with responsibility for investments that are directly related to the strategy.

Quality of data

The background research for the strategy was hampered by the paucity of good data especially for sub-national level analyses. The Strategy will need to be supported by on-going research that will explore the underlying dynamics of adjustment in different areas. In addition to the need for sound theoretical foundations the research will require the development of integrated databases that can be linked within the framework of geographical information systems.

Conclusions

This chapter commenced with a reminder of the enormous changes that have occurred in Ireland over the past decade which have transformed the country from being a marginal region of Europe to a position where in 2001 it has a per capita level of income that is well above the EU average. Nevertheless, there are still wide disparities within and between regions that may become even greater if a comprehensive strategy for regional development is not adopted. The NSS will seek to address the needs of every part of the country through a framework that will seek to optimise local potential and also strive to achieve sufficient critical mass at strategically chosen locations. Through this approach it will seek to provide opportunities for investments leading to additional enterprise formation, employment and population growth, that will gradually lead to more balanced regional development.

The preparation of the strategy has raised a number of issues that have been discussed in the final section. Major challenges lie ahead in terms of securing agreement on the details of the strategy as well as in relation to implementation. However, the analysis indicates that it is essential for the government to adopt a strategy that will facilitate the achievement of the original goals set for the NSS. All the evidence points to the need for some radical proposals but these must be backed up by a level of political support at the highest level that will ensure a satisfactory balance between national and local interests. Ireland has been to the forefront in pioneering models for local development that have involved the establishment of local partnerships and the provision of support for a wide range of 'soft' interventions (OECD, 1996; Walsh, 1996; 1997; 1999). However, small-scale local development programmes have not been able to alter the balance in the regional distribution of development opportunities. The challenge for the years ahead is to implement a comprehensive strategy for spatial development that will lead to an improvement in the relative position of the marginal regions and simultaneously contribute to achieving a more sustainable model of development in all dimensions – economic, social, cultural and environmental. This is a challenge not only for the government but also for all stakeholders who will need to devise new structures for co-operative actions aimed at achieving balanced regional development.

References

Barry, F. (1999) *Understanding Ireland's Economic Growth*. Macmillan. London.
Boyle, G., McCarthy, T. and Walsh, J. A., (1998/99) 'Regional income differentials and the issue of regional income inequalities in Ireland', *Journal of Statistical. & Social Inquiry Society of Ireland*, 28, 1, pp.155–211.

Bradley, J., FitzGerald, J., Honahan, P. and Kearney, I., (1997) 'Interpreting the recent Irish growth experience', in D. Duffy, J. FitzGerald, I. Kearney, and F. Shortall, *Medium Term Review 1997–2003*, The Economic and Social Research Institute, Dublin.

Breathnach, P., (1982) 'The demise of growth centre policy: the case of the Republic of Ireland', in R. Hudson and J. Lewis (eds.) *Regional Planning in Europe*, Pion, London, pp.35–56.

Breathnach, P. and Walsh, J. A., (1994) 'Industrialisation and Regional Development in Ireland', *Acta Universitatis Carolinae Geographica XXIX*, pp.67–79.

Breathnach, P. (1998) 'Exploring the "Celtic Tiger" Phenomenon: causes and consequences of Ireland's economic miracle', *European Urban and Regional Studies*, 5, 4, pp.305–316.

Buchanan, C. and Partners (1968) *Regional Studies in Ireland*, An Forás Forbartha, Dublin.

Central Statistics Office (2001) *Regional Population Projections 2001–2031*, CSO, Dublin.

Commins, P. and McDonagh, P. (2000) 'Macroeconomic growth and rural development in Ireland'. Paper presented to conference on European Rural Economy at the Crossroads, University of Aberdeen, Scotland.

Commission of the European Communities (1999) *European Spatial Development Perspective*, Final Draft, Potsdam, EC.

Department of Agriculture & Food (1999) White Paper on Rural Development, *Ensuring the Future*, Stationery Office, Dublin.

Department of the Environment (1997), *Sustainable Development – A Strategy for Ireland*, Stationery Office, Dublin.

Department of Environment and Local Government (2000) *The National Spatial Strategy: scope and Delivery*, Department of Environment and Local Government, Dublin.

Department of Environment and Local Government (2001) *The National Spatial Strategy: Indications for the Way Ahead*, Department of Environment and Local Government, Dublin.

Department of Finance (1999) *Ireland National Development Plan 2000–2006*, Stationery Office, Dublin.

Duffy, D., Fitz Gerald, J., Kearney, I. and Smyth, D., 1999, *Medium Term Review 1999–2005*, ESRI, Dublin.

Eser, T. and Konstadakopulos, D. (2000) 'Power shifts in the European Union? The case of Spatial Planning', *European Planning Studies*, 8, 6, pp.783–798.

Faludi, A. (2001) 'The Application of the European Spatial Development Perspective: evidence from the North-West Metropolitan Area', *European Planning Studies*, 9, 5, pp.663–676.

Fitzgerald, J., Kearney, I., Morgenroth, E. and Smyth, D., (eds.) (1999) *National Investment Priorities for the period 2000–2006*, ESRI Policy Research Series No. 33, Dublin.

Fitzpatrick Associates (1999a) *Southern and Eastern Region Development Strategy 2000–2006*, Dublin.

Fitzpatrick Associates (1999b) *Border Midland and Western Region Development Strategy 2000–2006*, Dublin.

Fitzpatrick Associates (2000) *National Spatial Strategy study on Irish Rural Structure and Gaeltacht Areas*, Dublin.

Forfás (2000) Enterprise 2010 *A New Strategy for the promotion of Enterprise in Ireland in the 21st Century*, Dublin.

Goodbody Economic Consultants (2000) *The Role of Dublin in Europe*, Dublin.

Government of Ireland, (2000) *Planning and Development Act 2000*, Stationery Office, Dublin.

McCafferty, D. and Walsh, J. A. (1997) *Competitiveness, Innovation and Regional Development in Ireland*, Regional Studies Association (Irish Branch), Dublin.

McHugh, C. and Walsh, J. A. (2000) 'Developing an Irish Rural Typology', in Fitzpatrick Associates, *Study on Irish Rural Structure and Gaeltacht Areas*, Dublin.

National Economic and Social Council (1989) *Ireland in the European Community: Performance, Prospects and Strategy*, Report No. 88, Dublin.

National Economic and Social Council (1991) *The Economic and Social Implications of Emigration*, Report No. 90, Dublin.

National Economic and Social Council (1999) *Opportunities, Challenges and Capacities for Choice*, Report No. 104, Dublin.

Nordregio, I. (2000) *Study Programme on European Spatial Planning: Final Report*. Stockholm.

OECD (1996) Local *Partnerships and Social Innovation in Ireland*, Paris.

OECD (1999) *OECD Economic Surveys – Ireland*, OECD, Paris.

O'Leary, E. (2001) 'Convergence of living standards among Irish regions: the roles of productivity, profit outflows and demography, 1960–1996', *Regional Studies*, 35, 3, pp.197–205.

Walsh, J. A. (1989) 'Regional Development Strategies', in R. W. G. Carter and A. J. Parker, (eds.), *Ireland: Contemporary Perspectives on a Land and its People*, Routledge, London, pp.441–471.

Walsh, J. A. (1992) 'Economic Restructuring and Labour Migration in the European Union: the case of the Republic of Ireland', in M. Ó Cinnéide and S. Grimes, (eds.), *Planning and Development of Marginal Areas*, Galway, Centre for Development Studies, pp.23–36.

Walsh, J. A. (1996) 'Local development theory and practice: recent experience in Ireland', in J. Alden and P. Boland, (eds.), *Regional Development Strategies: A European Perspective*. London, Jessica Kingsley Publishers, pp.159–177.

Walsh, J. A. (1997) 'Development from below: an assessment of recent experience in rural Ireland', in R. Byron, J. Walsh and P. Breathnach, (eds.), *Sustainable Development on the North Atlantic Margin*, Ashgate, Aldershot, pp.17–33.

Walsh, J. A. (1998) 'Facing up to the challenges of regional development'. Paper presented to Conference of Irish Association of Regional Authorities on 'Effective Regional Policy for Ireland', Cork.

Walsh, J. A. (1998) 'Ireland 2000+ Towards a strategy for sustainable regional development'. Paper presented to Conference of Regional Studies Association (Irish Branch) on 'Ireland 2000+ Developing the Regions', Dublin.

Walsh, J. A. (1999) 'A Strategy for Sustainable Local Development', in R. Byron and J. Hutson, (eds.), *Local Enterprise on the North Atlantic Margin*, Ashgate, Aldershot, pp. 119–140.

Walsh, J. A. (1999) 'The path to a spatial development strategy', *Geonews*, 45, pp.24–33.

Walsh, J. A. 2000, 'Dynamic Regional Development in the EU Periphery: Ireland in the 1990s', in D. Shaw, P. Roberts, J. Walsh (eds.), *Regional Planning and Development in Europe*, Ashgate, pp.117–137.

Walsh, J. A., McHugh, C. and Craigie, H. (2000) 'The National Spatial Strategy: rationale and context'. Paper presented to Conference on Building the Framework for Development: the National Spatial Strategy, Regional Studies Association (Irish Branch), Tullamore.

Western Development Commission (1999) *Blueprint for Success: A Development plan for the West 2000–2006*. Ballaghaderreen, Roscommon.

chapter six

COMMUTING DATA AND THE DEFINITION
OF FUNCTIONAL REGIONS.

Michael J. Keane

Introduction

Strong national economic growth since the early 1990s has translated into significant geographical unevenness in prosperity and development. There are few specific insights however in to what are needed – institutions, skills, planning systems etc. – to improve the economic performance and quality of life in any given region. In this chapter the focus is on a fundamental challenge facing spatial planning in Ireland, namely that which concerns economic spaces and the shape and form of functional regions. Building on the previous debates on the challenges facing the Border Midlands and West (BMW) region; the Gaeltacht areas; the growth of the urban system; the National Spatial Strategy (NSS) and the whole concept of balanced regional development, this chapter determines how a deeper questioning of commuting-to-work patterns can help further our knowledge and understanding of functional regions. Further, while the form of the commuting data made available from the Census of Population has been considered deficient by most researchers, this chapter will show how this data might be interrogated through some exploratory data methods to help in the discussion and definition of these regions.

The Context

It is difficult to definitively document geographic unevenness in prosperity and development with up-to-date data or at spatial scales anywhere below the regional level. The share of the regions in national employment provides one useful summary measure of regional fortunes with regard to employment. The trend in these shares 1990–2001 (Figure 6.1) shows the cumulative percentage change in each region's employment share over the past 11 years. This is calculated as $\sum_{t}^{n} \Delta(\ell nE_{it} - \ell nE_{t})$ where E_{it} is employment in the ith region in year t and E_{t} is national employment in year t. Recent trends in the Dublin, Mid-East and South-East regions (Figure 6.1c) show the Mid-East with very impressive gains over the time period, rising by more than twenty per cent. Dublin just about keeps its share while the share of the South-East has declined. The employment shares of the Border, Midlands, West (BMW) region (Figure 6.1a) indicate this regions' share of national employment has declined with the most dramatic decline in the Midlands (-13.8 per cent) and the Border region (-8.0 per cent). The final set of data for the Mid-West and South-West (Figure 6.1b) show that the South-West region has seen its employment share consistently decline since 1994. The performance of the Mid-West is quite erratic, with very little overall change in employment share.

The picture that emerges from this analysis is one of significant redistribution of employment in favour of the Mid-East region. The shares of the Midlands, the Border and, interestingly enough, the South-East and South-West have declined significantly. The polarisation tendencies present in employment patterns in the economy can be detected right across the spectrum of economic activities. Tourism is a good example. Ireland, at least up until the events of September 11th 2001, has experienced rapid growth in its overseas tourism business, but this business growth has not been evenly spread. The huge growth in overseas bednights has occurred predominantly in Dublin. The success of Dublin in establishing itself as a city destination has been helped by improved access, more competitive fares and by the increase in global trends towards short holiday breaks. In contrast, the traditional holiday regions, the West and the South-West, have not kept pace (Western Development Commission, 2000).

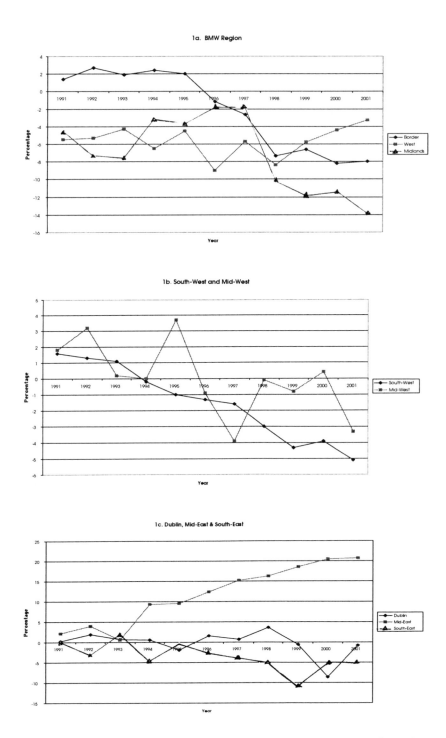

Figure 6.1: Regional Share of National Employment Cumulative Growth

This polarisation of growth is, of course, captured in the indicators of regional performance such as incomes or Gross Value Added (GVA). A useful exercise is to look at a decomposition of the variation in per capita income differences between the regions. Regional differences in per capita GVA can, for example, be decomposed into four terms – productivity (GVA per worker), the employment rate (inverse of the unemployment rate), the participation rate and the dependency ratio. While the four components of per capita production are interlinked we can explain the change in any of them by specific economic or institutional factors within each of the regions (Coulombe, 1997). For example, the dynamic process of neoclassical convergence assumes the gradual elimination of disparities in worker productivity though the interaction of the accumulation of physical capital and the law of diminishing returns. If major differences persist in worker productivity between the regions of the country they might be attributed to delayed development or to some barriers to capital accumulation in regions where capital is relatively scarce. Major inter-regional differences in the employment rate (unemployment) or the participation rate will be explained by considerations relating to labour market functioning and adjustments, the balance between work and leisure and household's choice of geographic location.

This decomposition can be expressed as

$$Y_{in} = \text{Prod}_{in} \, \text{ER}_{in} \, \text{PR}_{in} \, \text{DR}_{in}$$

Where i = region, n = the state and the subscript in denotes a regional relative, for example,

$$y_{in} = \frac{\text{Prod}_i}{\text{Prod}_n} \cdot \frac{ER_i}{ER_n} \cdot \frac{PR_i}{PR_n} \cdot \frac{DR_i}{DR_n}$$

or in logs

$$\log y_{in} = \log Prod_{in} + \log ER_{in} + \log PR_{in} + \log DR_{in}$$

This decomposition has been researched by Boyle $et\ al.$ (2000) and some of their results are presented in Table 6.1 in respect of GVA per capita measured at basic prices for 1991 and 1996. The results clearly point to productivity differentials as the dominant explanation for the inter-regional variation in per capita GVA.

Over the two years under examination, the variation in the other components; the employment rate, the participation rate and the dependency ratio, only ranges from 0 to about 6 per cent.

Table 6.1 Decomposition of Regional Variation in GVA per capita [ln y $_{in}$] 1991 and 1996

Region	GVA Per Capita	Employ. rate	Particip. rate	Depend. rate	Prod.
			1991		
Border	-18.09	-2.56	0.86	-4.82	-12.81
Dublin	28.06	-2.01	1.62	6.37	22.69
Midlands	-31.03	1.91	-3.01	-3.64	-22.51
West	-26.70	3.6	0.76	-5.41	-27.93
			1996		
Border	-26.16	-3.87	-0.15	-4.45	-21.93
Dublin	28.70	-1.12	3.17	4.65	23.65
Midlands	-40.14	2.88	0.49	-3.82	-30.00
West	-30.70	0.56	-1.15	-4.45	-34.02

Employ – Employment; Particip. – Participation; Depend – Dependency; Prod. – Productivity
Source: Boyle *et al.* (2000)

The substantial variation that is observed for productivity can be examined further in terms of 'within' and 'between' sector effects. The 'within' sector effects, suggest that specific sectors may experience different conditions in different regions (conditions which are (not) conducive to productivity), while the 'between' sector effects are suggesting that certain high productivity sectors may be strongly concentrated (localised) in some locations thereby giving these locations a high productivity reading. Some results of this analysis (Boyle, *et al.* 2000) are given in Table 6.2. The data show that the variation in sectoral employment shares is of minimal importance in accounting for inter-regional differences in productivity, and that the productivity differences are primarily due to 'within' sector effects. What this suggests is that there are features in the regions that give rise to the differences in productivity. The conclusions drawn (and this is very much the received wisdom) is that these significant productivity differences are closely related to the presence of urban agglomerations where there would appear to be opportunities to enjoy increasing returns and where, for example, multi-national corporations (MNCs) seem to prefer to locate their facilities.

Table 6.2 Decomposition of Regional Variation in GVA per Worker Productivity into 'Within' and 'Between' Sector Effects, 1991 and 1995

Region	'Within' Sector effect	'Between' Sector effect	Productivity
1991			
Border	-11.84	-0.94	-12.81
Dublin	19.23	-0.40	22.69
Midlands	-20.50	-2.10	-22.51
West	-20.80	-7.16	-27.93
1995			
Border	-23.15	2.12	-21.04
Dublin	29.67	-4.41	23.65
Midlands	-27.12	-1.82	-30.00
West	-24.10	-7.77	-34.02

Source; Boyle *et al.* (2000)

However, other than knowing that economic actors have strong incentives to agglomerate spatially we know very little else about the exact dynamic of this economic success. Explanations are somewhat tautological – urban growth centres can be identified by their success in development (Markusen, 1999). There are few specific insights about what it is that matters for success – is it institutions, skills, organisations or key actors – that can assist regional planners who wish to repeat this success so as to improve the economic performance and quality of life in their regions. The focus of this chapter is the debate about economic spaces and the shape and form of functional regions. This is a topic that is important in the context of the debate on national spatial planing. To define functional regions means that we must look at various forms of interaction including, most notably, patterns of commuting-to-work. The form of the commuting data made available from the Census of Population has been considered deficient by most researchers and consequently has not been used much. This chapter tries to show how this data might be interrogated through some exploratory data methods to help in the discussion and definition of functional regions.

Functional Regions

One implication of economic activity wanting to agglomerate spatially is to lengthen travel-to-work journeys. Garreau (1991) describes what he calls a long-standing law of commuting 'scholars have demonstrated for thousands of years, no matter what the transportation technology, the maximum desirable commute has been 45 minutes'. Taking this 'law' literally, it suggests that economic areas be limited to specific ranges of distance. The distance that will define a functional economic area (FEA) will be linked to two things; the degree to which growth disseminates geographically and to Garreau's law of commuting. Wheeler (2001) provides us with some evidence on the range for economic areas in the USA Metropolitan Statistical Areas (MSAs) with an average radius of 22 to 27 miles and Component Economic Areas (CEAs) extending up to 50 miles from a central node. The lack of suitable data sets makes this kind of geostatistical analysis difficult to do in Ireland. All we can do is offer very ad hoc notions about functional regions. A good example can be found in the ESRI's *National Investment Priorities for the Period 2000–2006* (Fitzgerald *et al.* 1999) which publishes a map of catchment areas for the main cities, defined in terms of 60 minute driving times. The most recent suggestions about economic areas are the functional areas outlined in the National Spatial Strategy (NSS) Public Consultation Paper (Department of the Environment and Local Government, 2001).

Acknowledging from the outset that these particular proposals are only indicative outlines, there is a striking lack of congruence between the ESRI's 60 minute travel-to-work areas and the functional area in the NSS. A good example is the 'functional' region that is defined around Galway City. In this context it is interesting to introduce some of the work undertaken by Buchanan and Partners (1999) on the Galway region as part of the *Galway Transportation and Planning Study*. Elements in the preferred strategy identified by the consultants are currently being re-examined in the light of current road planning in the study area. Thus, recommendations in this study have not yet been officially adopted by either of the local authorities. Buchanan and Partners took a pretty pragmatic approach to the notion of Galway and its economic hinterland by simply defining the Study Area as extending 30km from Galway city and including Rossaveel, Headford, Tuam, Athenry, Gort and Loughrea (Figure 6.2). The main plank of the recommended planning strategy is the adoption of the Oranmore corridor (Figure 6.2) as the location of the Study Area's primary development centre and the focus of public infrastructural investment.

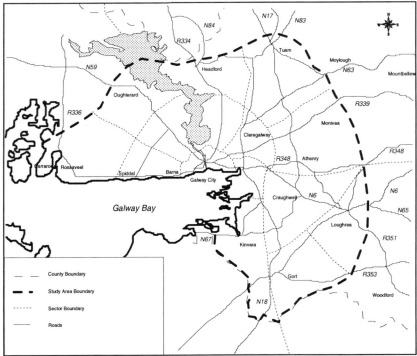

Figure 6.2 The study area

A case is also made for allocating a significant portion of growth to Tuam which, in the view of the consultants:

> an be distinguished from the other scheduled towns as a location which can not only absorb more development but which would benefit greatly from it.

It is useful to quote at length from the consultant's report (pp.4-13/4-14) as it helps to illustrate the kind of choices and issues which the NSS now seeks to frame through functional economic regions:

> Even if the consultants are right in suggesting that economic priorities favour the location of growth in Galway City east of the River Corrib, it does not follow that the development strategy should be based on this: there may be legitimate social factors which indicate that growth should be encouraged to locate elsewhere. The obvious candidates are the scheduled towns (and, to some extent, the Rossaveel area) where it is argued that

new employment opportunities are essential to reactivate communities suffering from depopulation and a lack of resources, and whose further development would take pressure off Galway City and the roads leading to it.

This is a persuasive scenario, and one put forward in the most recent report by the Western Development Commission (WDC, 2000). However, in the consultant's view, it has to be queried on a number of grounds. First, even if thought desirable, it is, in the consultant's opinion, unlikely to prove feasible. Little of the assumed incoming employment would be willing to by-pass Galway City in favour of an apparently peripheral location even if substantial additional (and expensive) incentives were to be offered. This view is supported by local experience: if the scheduled towns have not expanded during the past decade of unprecedented growth and subsidy, they are unlikely to do so now when both have probably peaked (see also Ó hAoláin, Chapter 3).

Second, it is possible to question the need for the diversion of new employment to outlying areas; to suggest, in fact, that such a strategy is perhaps rather unthinkingly aimed at returning those communities to their previous role rather than adapting them to a new role as dormitory towns to Galway City. Such a role could well be the natural successor in a situation in which economic forces are giving yet another change of direction to the physical structure of the Study Area. There are innumerable examples elsewhere of prosperous satellite communities enjoying a more peaceful existence in superior environmental conditions while exporting a high proportion of their citizens to work in less congested surroundings in the parent city. In a local context, it could be said that the inhabitants of the scheduled towns are lucky to have Galway City to turn to for employment and higher-level services: without it, they would be in a much less favourable position.

Third, it is possibly wrong to imagine that the importance of new employment is the only way to revitalise satellite communities. Both experience elsewhere and the surveys conducted locally by the consultants show that most people do not live close to where they work and that, increasingly, sub-regions such as the Study Area are becoming single social and labour markets in which a large number of travel networks, including home-to-work trips, overlap each other as people move in all directions to access a variety of services. What we see is not a number of inward-looking self-contained activity centres, but a highly mobile population looking for good access to whatever the area as whole can offer. It is therefore legitimate to envisage a situation in which new employment is allowed to settle down as it wishes, while housing and its associated uses are encouraged to locate in the scheduled towns, as is currently happening in places like Tuam where developers and buyers are seeking to benefit from the lower land costs, and where the simple accumulation of people can generate more services. The emphasis can then switch to providing a good transportation system to ensure ready access between the various centres of activity.

This lengthy extract is a good summary of the kind of choices that must be made if we embrace the functional area as a framework for economic and social planning. Some knowledge about the actual physiology of the functional region in terms of commuting patterns, the limits of labour market areas, service areas and spatial scale would be of help to planners in making strategic decisions for the different regions.

Boxplot and Batch Comparisons of Census Commuting Data

The factor that is most typically considered in defining functional economic areas is commuting patterns (Johnson, 1995). It is generally accepted that the commuting data available in the 1996 Census of Population is difficult to work with (for a discussion on some of the problems with the Census data see Horner, 1999). The significant shortcoming in the data is that it offers no insight into place of residence – place of work patterns. This is a basic piece of material needed for the definition of commuting zones and the delineation of local labour markets (Killian and Tolbert 1993, Fugitt, 1991). Both of these topics are profoundly important in understanding local economies and socio-economic conditions and for the formal delineation of FEAs. However, Census commuting data is useful to certain kinds of research questions and analytical approaches (see Keane 2001, 2002). In this section boxplots and batch comparison methods used in Exploratory Data Analysis (EDA) are applied to the Census data to see if it possible to tentatively identify patterns or structure in the data that might be useful in the debate about the definition of functional regions with a continued focus on the Galway City region.

EDA is concerned with resistant identification of data properties. Values are termed resistant in that they themselves are not affected by extreme or anomalous values (Emerson and Strenio, 2000). For example, as the middle or 'typical' value in a dataset, the median can be described as a resistant summary statistic, in contrast to the arithmetic mean (or average) which is not resistant because it can be affected by extreme values. The median is, of course, an average measure it represents, as was said already, the 'typical value' in the dataset. Additional useful measures are the upper and lower quartiles. These three measures can be used in a graphical display known as a boxplot which acts as a summary of a frequency distribution (Haining, 1989).

The salient features of boxplots are shown in Figure 6.3. The chief value of boxplots is in comparing several batches of data. A standard boxplot shows at a glance the location, spread skewness, tail length and outlying data points in a batch of data. In the examples shown in Figure 6.3a and 6.3b only location, spread and skewness are shown. Location is summarised by the median (M), the crossbar in the interior of the box (Figures 6.3a and 6.3b). The length of the box shows the spread (measured as the interquartile range). From the relative positions of the median, the third quartile, Q_3, and the first quartile, Q_1, we also see some of the skewness. In the example shown in Figure 6.3, commuting data for two DEDs are compared. In Figure 6.3a there is no skewness and the distance between Q_1 and Q_3 (a low quartile deviation) indicates that there is only a small variation in the distance travelled to work by the central 50 per cent of commuters. This could be interpreted further to read that there is a fairly coherent pattern in travel-to-work distances and all are close to the median. On the other hand, in Figure 6.3b the distribution is negatively skewed. There is a wide spread between Q_1 and Q_3 and the median is much closer to Q_3 suggesting that with this batch there is much variability and a tendency for longer distance commuting to be quite dominant.

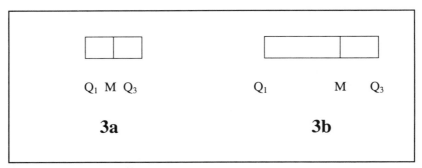

Q_1 M Q_3 Q_1 M Q_3

3a   **3b**

Figure 6.3 Examples of Boxplots

Figure 6.4 shows boxplots for three sets of DEDs in Co. Galway and a map showing the locations of these DEDs. The map identifies the three sets of DEDs as lying roughly along three radial paths leading away from Galway City: path 1 heads South-East past Loughrea [the first set of DEDs]; path 2 is south in the direction of Gort [set 2] and path 3 heads North-East south of Tuam and past Mountbellew [set 3]. There are two significant features suggested by the boxplots. The data values for the DEDs near to Galway City are the closest together while for distant DEDs the values are the most dispersed. There is also a strong relationship between spread and level. To understand this relationship it seems reasonable to plot the measure of spread ($Q_3 - Q_1$) against the measure of level (the median) (Figure 6.5).

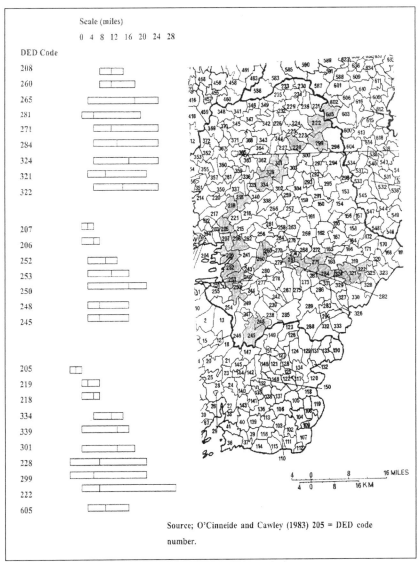

Figure 6.4 Boxplots and DEDs for part of County Galway

Looking at Figure 6.5 one can see two distinct groupings of DEDs; the first group is the set of observations which indicate a strong systematic relationship between level and spread, while the second is a set of observations where there is no such relationship present. This second set of DEDs is highlighted in Figure 6.5. It is possible to look more formally at these two groups shown in Figure 6.5 with discriminant analysis, a statistical technique which seeks to separate objects (DEDs) into two groups (G_1, G_2) on the basis of the observed values (Johnson and Wichern, 1998).

The objective is to derive a classification function where the chances, or probabilities, of misclassifying observations will be small. One useful approach to this classification problem is Lachenbruch's 'holdout' procedure where we have two groups with n_1 and n_2 observations in each. The procedure has the following steps: **1.** Start with the G_1 group of observations where we omit one observation from this group and develop a classification function based on the remaining $n_1 - 1$ observations. **2.** Classify the 'holdout' observation, using the function constructed in step I. **3.** Repeat steps 1 and 2 until all of the G_1 observations are classified. Let n_{1h} be the number of holdout (h) observations misclassified in this group. **4.** Repeat steps 1 through 3 for the G_2 observations. Let n_{2h} be the number of 'holdout' observations misclassified in this group. The total proportion misclassified, $(n_{1h} + n_{2h})/(n_1 + n_2)$, permits us to judge the performance of the classification exercise.

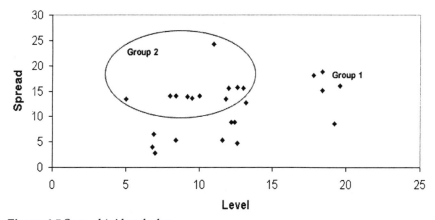

Figure 6.5 Spread 'v' level plot

The classification informally suggested in Figure 6.5 performs particularly well under Lachenbruch's procedure. A full discussion of the formal methodology and other aspects of classification can be found in Keane (2002). The results of the classification analysis can be interpreted within the framework of

Figure 6.4. Group 1 are part of a well-defined Galway City commuting zone while Group 2 (DEDs no. 219, 228, 222, 248, 246, 281, 271, 284, 324, 321, 325) appear to be delineating the edges of this commuting zone. For this second group of DEDs there is no systematic patterns in the commuting data, indicating that we are dealing with spaces where people are moving in a number of different directions and outside the sphere of influence of Galway City. Overall, the DED differences, as revealed with EDA methods, do give us fairly robust clues as to the geographic scale of commuting *vis-à-vis* Galway City. Obviously, the analysis can be extended to all DEDs to get a sense of how the general functional region might be defined. In addition, there is the interesting question about how the geographical scale of the functional region changes over time as the size and influence of Galway City itself changes. The EDA methods illustrated here are quite effective tools for looking at these sort of questions and for helping overcome some of the difficulties presented by the Census commuting data.

Conclusion

The geographic scope for growth in aggregate economic activity and employment appears to be restricted to urban agglomerations. From planning and policy perspectives it does make sense that we recognise these trends and begin to think, as is suggested in the NSS, in terms of FEAs. The challenge then is to provide the information about what may constitute a functional area. It is difficult to capture this concept precisely. By its very nature an FEA will not have definite boundaries. The dynamics and values of different activity spaces and relational networks are constantly jostling together so areas will be different, they can change and there is no constant definition. As Healey (1996) notes, all places are becoming increasingly fragmented into an amalgam of what she describes as 'bits and pieces' and 'niches and nodes'. The challenge for researchers is to try and make some sense out of these fragmented patterns.

An FEA consists of one or more economic nodes – metropolitan areas or large urban centres that serve as centres of economic activity – and the surrounding areas that are economically related to the nodes. The main factor used in determining the economic relationships amongst areas is commuting patterns, so each economic area includes, as far as possible, the place of work and the place of residence of its labour force. It is impossible to systematically operationalise this definition in the Irish context. The only comprehensive data set that is available, that is, Travel-to-Work Census data, is difficult to interpret along these lines and, consequently, this data has been largely ignored by researchers. The EDA techniques reported on in this chapter have produced a fairly robust and plausible indication of the nature of the commuting zone for Galway City. The systematic (albeit partial) interrogation of the commuting data, using the Galway City/Western FEA, as defined in the NSS Public Consultation Paper, suggests that the geographical range of the Western FEA is greatly exaggerated. If this conclusion also applies to other FEAs then we are left with a huge challenge for spatial planning as to how to address the future needs of the many areas that are realistically outside the commuting zone and the 'the warm glow' of the successful urban agglomerations.

Finally, if we take Garreau's 'law' of commuting as a benchmark that we might use in assessing quality of life and sustainability goals, then our current situation, in terms of roads infrastructure and public transport systems, is one where, for most rural commuters, travel times are considerably in excess of the 45 minutes. A strategic goal for functional area planning might be to guarantee that all that have to commute could get inside this time limit. This will be a huge challenge for all our systems.

References

Boyle, G., McCarthy, T. and Walsh, J. (1999) Regional Income Differentials and the Issue of Regional Equalisation in Ireland. Paper read to the Statistical and Social Inquiry Society of Ireland at University College Cork, April 15th.

Buchanan and Partners (1999) *Galway Transportation and Planning Study*, 4 Vols. Buchanan and Partners, London.

Coulombe, S. (1997) 'Regional Disparities in Canada: Characterisation, Trends and Lessons for Economic Policy'. *Working Paper No. 18*, Industry Canada, Ottawa.

Emerson, J. D., and Strenio, J. (2000) 'Boxplots and Batch Comparison', in D. C. Hoaglin, F. Mosteller and J. W. Tukey (eds.) *Understanding Robust and Exploratory Data Analysis*, Wiley, NY.

Fitzgerald, J., Kearney, J., Morgenroth, E. and Smyth, D. (eds.) (1999) 'National Investment Priorities for the Period 2000–2001',

Policy Research Series, No. 33, Economic and Social Research Institute, Dublin.

Garreau, J. (1981) *Edge City: Life on the New Frontier,* Doubleday, New York.

Horner, A. (1999) 'The Tiger Stirring: Aspects of Commuting in the Republic of Ireland 1981–1996', *Irish Geography,* Vol.32, pp.99–111.

Keane, M. J. (2002) Exploratory Data Analysis and Census Commuting Data. *Working Paper,* Department of Economics, National University of Ireland, Galway.

Keane, M. J. (2001) 'A Model of Commuting Distances: Some Preliminary Insights from a Spatial Model of Job Search', in D. Pitfield (ed.) *Transport Planning, Logistics and Spatial Mismatch,* European Research in Regional Science, No. 11, Pion, London.

Killian, M. S., and Tolbert, C. M. (1995) 'Mapping Social and Economic Space: The Delineation of Local Labour Markets in the United States', in J. Singelmann and F. A. Deseran (eds.) *Inequalities in Labor Market Areas,* Westview Press, Boulder, pp.69–79.

Healey, P. (1996) 'The Communicative Turn in Planning Theory and its Implications for Spatial Strategy Formation', *Environment and Planning B,* 23, pp.217–234.

Haining, R. (1990) *Spatial data analysis in the social and environmental sciences,* Cambridge University Press, Cambridge.

Johnson, K.P. (1995) *Redefinition of the BEA Economic Areas. Survey of Current Business.* Department of Commerce, Washington.

Johnson, R. A., and Wichern, D. W. (1998) *Applied Multivariate Statistical Analysis,* Prentice Hall, New Jersey.

Markusen, A. (1999) 'Fuzzy Concepts, Scanty Evidence, Policy Distance: The Case for Rigour and Policy Relevance in Critical Regional Studies', *Regional Studies,* Vol.33, pp.869–884.

O'Cinneide, M. and Cawley, M. (1983) *Development of Agriculture in the West of Ireland 1970–1980,* Council for Development in Agriculture, Dublin.

Western Development Commission (2000) *Blueprint for Tourism Development in the West, An Action Plan for Rural Areas,* Western Development Commission, Ballaghaderreen.

Wheeler, C. H. (2001) 'A Note on the Spatial Correlation Structure of County-Level Growth in the US', *Journal of Regional Science,* Vol.41, No.3, pp.433–449.

chapter seven

PERIPHERALITY AND THE WEST OF IRELAND:
THE NEED FOR RE-EVALUATION?

John McDonagh

Introduction

The notion of peripherality is central to rural policy-making. Indeed everybody knows what peripherality is until perhaps they are asked to explain it. The term peripherality instantly conjures images of geographic isolation, rurality, poor accessibility, sparse population, inadequate service provision and lack of investment. These are only some aspects of peripherality however. Peripherality is also dynamic and while many peripheral areas may be geographically isolated many others also have successful economies and high quality environments. This is where the difficulty arises. Promoting development in spatially peripheral areas must be achieved not only through reducing the sense of political or social isolation often felt by these communities but it must be achieved through reinforcing the intrinsic qualities that make these communities stand apart (culture, tradition, the imprint of their geographic space etc.). With particular emphasis on the attitudes to, and perceptions of, peripherality in the West of Ireland, this chapter explores peripherality from the traditional or conventional manner, that is, dealing with peripherality spatially in terms of geographic isolation; through policy targeting in relation to Objective 1 regions; and through investment in physical infrastructure; to more recent recognition of the part played by aspatial peripherality.

The Context

The 'global village' is here or is it? Undoubtedly we are now in an age of quicker, faster, better. We live in a time when we are just as likely to wear clothes or eat food manufactured in almost any part of the world. We are also in a time when people travel further and more often, where essentially a person in Sydney is no harder to contact by phone, fax or email than a person in Dublin, what Cloke and Goodwin (1992) refer to as 'time-space compression'. So why be concerned with peripherality and is there more to understanding this concept than we realise?

The restructuring of rural Europe is occurring at a variety of spatial scales (Nijkamp and van Geenhuizen, 1997) and the 'new geographies' that are being created (Hodge, 1997) provide an opportune time to rethink concept models, indicators and policy approaches (Copus, 2001) to peripherality. These new geographies have at their core not only the development of communications and transport technology networks that have the ability to

> redefin(e) patterns of accessibility (and) redefin(e) the possibilities of interaction between people, organisations and places (*ibid.*, p.33)

but the focus on 'polycentric development' will bring a redefining of peripherality.

In Ireland regional inequalities have undoubtedly increased as a result of spatial peripherality. The transformation of economic activity and changes in communication and information technology have however, made geographic location less significant. Instead, what is becoming increasingly important is 'aspatial' peripherality. While the argument here is not for the abandonment of peripherality, it is suggested that conventional peripherality be addressed in parallel with aspatial peripherality. Further, at a time of increasing 'time-space compression' and a move towards designing integrated spatial strategies, in the European Spatial Development Perspective (ESDP) and the Irish National Spatial Strategy (NSS) for example, it is crucial that policy makers be more aware of peripherality in an 'aspatial' context in order to ensure social and economic integration and the opportunity for all people to realise their full potential.

Some people and some places inevitably do better than others due to differing degrees of mobility, accessibility etc. There are also I would argue, different degrees of peripherality fostered by policies which are driven by the traditional approach of improving transport and communication costs at the expense of recognising other aspects of peripherality in such things as governance, social exclusion and deprivation. It is therefore crucial that in overcoming geographical remoteness or perceived isolation through road constructions, communication infrastructure, IT infrastructure at a European and national level, we do not create even greater peripherality at a local level through lack of access to these developments. Essentially we must avoid the 'tunnel effect' whereby there is greater concern with what is at either end rather than the areas traversed, or, where the areas traversed (by road, IT networks, gas pipelines etc.) are not connected.

Peripherality – Straightforward or Complex?

When we try to define peripherality we find that while it may be a term that trips easily off the tongue, and is used frequently in policy and lay discourse it can be notoriously vague and:

> a slippery notion … one of those common terms everyone uses until faced with the problem of defining and measuring it (Gould 1969, cited in Copus, 2001, p.540).

Ball (1996) suggested that peripherality has been:

> typically quantified by some variant of a market accessibility model (and) is generally interpreted as indicative of remoteness or inaccessibility (p.27).

In fact a key question is – peripheral to what? That is:

> what are the key factors that are not present in, or accessible to, a particular area (or population) that engender a sense of isolation or peripherality (DETR, 1999, p.21).

The typical definition of peripherality usually involves a description of activities, or the lack of activities, taking place on the margins, outside of the main core. It is associated with poor access, sparse populations, remoteness, inability to influence decision-making, economic and social exclusion, a predominance of small farms, unemployment, poor infrastructure in terms of road, rail or public transport, poorly developed or little industry, outmigration and decline. What must also be recognised is that the unattractiveness of remote or peripheral areas from a commercial or industrial sense can often lead to these areas becoming earmarked for uses as some form of national park or more worryingly as dumping grounds of one kind or another (see also Cloke and Goodwin, 1992).

Exploring earlier academic and policy literature, peripherality is primarily dealt with in the conventional geographic and economic sense rather than as an aspatial concept (aspatial peripherality takes into account those less tangible concepts of capacity building, access to knowledge, embeddedness and civil society, cultural diversity, local institutional capacities). There have been a number of significant contributions from authors such as: Keeble, Owens and Thompson (1981) Ó Cinnéide (1992, 1993); Grimes (1992); Copus (1992, 1997) Vickerman *et al.* (1999), (to name but a few) all of which have explored different aspects of peripherality and ways of developing what were largely geographically peripheral areas. From a wider policy angle the literature on peripherality has been no less forthcoming. Economic potential reports in the early 1980s on peripherality becoming a key theme within EC thinking was depicted in the seminal document on rural areas, *The Future of Rural Society* (EC, 1988). This document began much of what has been entrenched in policies of the last two decades and perhaps best underlined the conventional policy approach to peripherality through its recognition of three standard problem areas. The areas defined in this document were identified as: (a) areas suffering from the pressures of modern life, (modern agriculture and new residential areas); (b) areas suffering from rural decline (out-migration and marginal farming), and (c) very remote areas (geographically marginal, sparse population). These generalisations indicated that areas could in some way be categorised in an homogeneous way, and that they were not (such) complex entities. However it is easily argued that within an area of decline there may also be pockets of growth, and vice versa (for example Galway City in the West of Ireland). In fact such conventional generalisations focus on:

> space, not people, and thereby overlooks the obvious truism that it is people not places who have problems and that different people in the same place can have different problems (Cloke and Goodwin, 1993 p.23).

As such it is becoming increasingly apparent that it is no longer possible to deal with merely physical space; but a more appropriate model is to deal with a multiplicity of social spaces which overlap the same geographical area. Essentially becoming aware of a different type of peripherality, becoming aware of 'aspatial' peripherality.

In more recent times the strategic approach to peripherality has focused on the European Spatial Development Perspective (EC, 1999); Agenda 2000, and the more recent draft guidance for 2000–2006 on the Structural Funds. The Irish parallel has taken the form of the National Development Plan (NDP) 2000–2006, and the

National Spatial Strategy (NSS). It is the 'polycentric development' strategy inherent in these latter plans (the suggested growth centres of the NSS for example), that presents the greatest challenge to peripherality and should provide an opportunity for more 'balanced regional development' as seems the aspiration of current government policy. If however this balanced regional development overlooks the very real concept of aspatial peripherality as implicit in the ESRI Report *National Investment Priorities for the Period 2000–2006*, the *National Development Plan 2000–2006* and the *Medium-Term Review 2001–2007*, all of which concentrate, for the most part, on public infrastructure and how it constrains competitiveness, then the outcome may be debilitating. On a large scale, greater economic balance between countries within the EU may be generated, but on a smaller scale, greater social exclusion and indeed polarisation within countries may be the result. Examples documenting such possibilities can be seen in recent newspaper articles denoting 'the hastening of rural decline' (Anon, 2001) and 'the widening of the gap between the East and West of Ireland' (Coulter, 2001).

Peripherality – Asset or Constraint?

The issue of peripherality has never quite disappeared from the national policy agenda and the answer to whether peripherality is an asset or constraint in Ireland is a guarded yes to both. Ireland's geographic peripherality has been utilised to varying degrees over the last decade. Traditionally Ireland has been dealt with from a European perspective as geographically peripheral in terms of its island status. It has been deemed peripheral in terms of its rural economy and the 'problems' associated with such economies – problems of decline, emigration, unemployment, poor infrastructure etc. The West of Ireland for example was (and still is) seen as being peripheral within Ireland, with spatial constraints in terms of remoteness, isolation, sparse populations, dependence on small farms and continued outmigration to places like Dublin. Generally there is a perception of the 'unattractiveness' of the West losing out to the 'dynamic' and more 'sophisticated' East of the country.

Ireland has predominantly used peripherality in its conventional sense as it relates to spatial difference. This geographic or spatial 'marginalisation' has been marketed as the central influence on Irish economic success and failure. The Irish argument in the EU has been one of a desire for cohesion and integration and therefore a need for increased funds to improve infrastructure (among other things). Exploring the earlier literature penned on Ireland's economy, the issue of peripherality is very much to the fore, not only in explaining Ireland's poor economic performances, high unemployment rates and continued emigration of the 1970s, and 1980s, but also used as the central reason why Ireland deserved special consideration from the EU in terms of funding. Nationally the approach has been a case of using the rhetoric of regional policies and a desire to reduce regional disparities through the trickle-down effect. However, if Ireland is assessed as a whole, while there has been overall success, on a regional or county basis, the outcome is less impressive. Consequently it has been (and still is) argued by many community and voluntary organisations including Euradvice (1994) that it is inconsistent to claim special treatment for Ireland as a peripheral region if the same principle is not applied within Ireland.

The Irish government also use different and conflicting approaches in dealing with peripherality. Grimes (1992) reflected on how the National Development Plan of 1989–1993 placed considerable emphasis on the peripheral location of Ireland and the obstacle this was to economic development in relation to costs on production, access, infrastructure etc. Grimes (*ibid*.) also noted that there was a contradictory ethos within the Irish development agencies that often sought to promote the attractiveness of Ireland's peripheral location as a gateway to the European market. The *National Development Plan 1994–1999* also refers to Ireland's geographic peripherality but the emphasis in this plan is more closely related to the economic infrastructure (the development of key economic corridors for example and the linking to the Trans European Network) as a strategy to offset geographic and structural disadvantage. The most recent *National Development Plan 2000–2006*, the ESRI *Report on National Investment Priorities for the Period 2000–2006*, and the *Medium-Term Review 2001–2007* all refer to public infrastructure and the need for improvements in order to boost competitiveness. Groups such as the Western Development Commission also argue that the poor quality of road infrastructure in the West Region is one of the major barriers to investment and as a consequence a barrier to reducing peripherality within the region (Western Development Commission, 2001). Overall there is a strong connection between peripherality and the more tangible aspects of geographic location and its implications for economic development. While this is not disputed, is this strong connection overlooking the importance of aspatial peripherality?

So can peripherality be an asset? The quick answer is yes. In fact this provides another of the contradictions that exist with regard to peripherality. Geographic isolation, being cut off from the hustle and bustle of the European urban core, a place that is relaxing, old-fashioned, quiet, a step back in time (with not another person to be seen on the beach or on the roadways) is often used as a promotional tool for Irish tourism. This has undoubtedly been effective as a tourist attraction strategy. However it is also part of the paradox in that these 'attributes' are also seen as constraints in that they make it hard (or at least unattractive) for the indigenous population, especially the young to live in these quiet, old-fashioned areas. A further growing asset of peripherality is how it is increasingly being linked to quality of life issues. Geographic location seems to have become less important with the development of communication technologies and the new opportunities this has presented for residents and businesses in peripheral areas. A study by Keeble and Tyler (1995) on the geography of employment in Great Britain revealed a remarkable growth in employment in rural areas of Britain compared to London. The main factors underlying this urban-rural shift according to these authors was that rural settlements had been able to attract a relatively high proportion of actual or potential entrepreneurs, largely because of their desirable residential characteristics, the quality of life attributes and the high scenic amenity of the areas. Whether this could be replicated in Ireland is questionable however, with the issue of the functionality of rural areas a determining factor. In fact while it is true that:

> quality of the total environment in rural areas must be
> enhanced to the point where people with business ideas
> and urban-derived 'know-how' will choose to locate
> there (Ó Cinnéide, 1995, p.7),

the closing of post offices and rural garda stations, the lack of access to quality water, waste disposal systems and adequate health care facilities and the increasing disillusionment at community level at their lack of control and participation in the decision-making process are not positive indicators in this regard.

Peripherality – A View from the West of Ireland

The Ireland of 2001 emerged from a very different 'peripheral' economic environment to that of its predecessors. The background of budget deficits, unemployment and a poorly developed indigenous economy have given way to a much more prosperous

'Celtic Tiger' economy with low levels of unemployment and a generally high level of prosperity (McDonagh, 2001). In the last ten years the population of Ireland has grown to almost 4 million – the highest since 1881. The Celtic Tiger economy has expanded rapidly and the level of unemployment has declined. Conversely however, what is also important about this development is that not all areas have benefited to the same degree and, despite the aspatial world in which we live, there are still people and places left behind. There is still a divide economically and socially between the East and the West of the country. There are also divisions within the West with Galway being described as doing to the West of Ireland what Dublin does to the rest of Ireland. There is still peripherality, not only in the conventional sense, but also a growing peripherality in political and increasingly social terms. Slowly there is a developing awareness of aspatial peripherality. Recent publications by government departments indicate an increasingly perilous future for rural Ireland and for those regions outside of Dublin. A Department of Agriculture report suggests that the quality of life in rural areas is falling and that rural populations are declining due to a lack of adequate infrastructure and a lack of access to other services (access to quality water (see Hickey, Chapter 17) and waste disposal (see Ní Chíonna, Chapter 16) to those of post offices and hospitals). The government blueprint for a 20-year National Spatial Strategy *Indications for the Way Ahead* (DoELG, 2001) also proclaims an uncertain future socially and economically for much of rural Ireland if development is not diverted from Dublin to the regions. The fragmenting of rural areas by increased long distance commuting, the perceived deterioration of 'quality of life', poor levels of public transportation and infrastructure, growing levels of traffic congestion, shortage of skilled workers, demands for higher wage increases, increased house prices, and particularly the growing gap between rich and poor are but some of the major concerns facing individuals, communities and policy makers in the regions of Ireland. This gap is nowhere more evident than in peripheral rural areas exemplified in Galway and the West Region. This region is a microcosm of the larger Irish picture. The prosperity of the Celtic Tiger is clearly evident in the expanding urban area of Galway with its increased population and economic success, while the greater Western Region displays continued decline and marginalisation of some areas and a lack of what the government allegedly strive for, 'balanced regional development' (Department of Agriculture and Food, 1999).

So What is the Attitude Towards Peripherality in the West of Ireland?

In the West of Ireland there is a perception among many community groups of remoteness and a sense of being removed from the action (McDonagh, 2001). To explore whether this perception is still prevalent and indeed more widely felt across other sectors of society, a survey was carried out among community workers, development groups, voluntary bodies and some elected and appointed members of county councils to ascertain their understandings of peripherality. While the depth of analysis was inevitably constrained by the briefness of the study, it does provide a qualitative insight into the interpretation, perception and impact of peripherality as it is experienced, understood and addressed in the region. Further the study was also aware of the varying individual and spatial scales at which peripherality is expressed – individual, local, regional, national – and, rather than concentrate on any one aspect, the study took an over-arching view of the experiences of peripherality across these scales. The focus of the study area was on Counties Galway, Mayo and Roscommon. These counties form an interesting mix of prosperity and decline; of high technology and inadequate communication; of dispersed population and problems of traffic congestion, of escalating house prices and of derelict and abandoned buildings; of maintaining the Irish language and promoting development (industrial, economic, social etc.) through outside investment. Using the conventional indicators of peripherality – geographic location, sparse population, no major urban centre, high cost of service provision, poor infrastructural network, a lack of industrial development – these 3 counties (with the exception of Galway City) fit the standard peripherality indices. The population densities average 24.6 persons per sq. km (half that of the State (52) and one sixth of the EU) with Mayo's and Roscommon's density being 20 persons per sq. km, and Galway slightly higher at 31 persons per sq. km. Overall there have been population increases in the region (particularly in Galway) but there are still parts of Mayo and Roscommon that have experienced decline. At a superficial level the indicators of peripherality (coupled with Ireland's geographic position on the fringe of Europe) are very much present in this region. So what are the concerns of those living in the region and how do they view the constraints of peripherality? Two issues became apparent from the survey. The first was a concern for the lack of 'hard supports' to deal with peripherality, that is, infrastructure, public transport etc. (conventional peripherality) and the second was recognition of greater levels of social exclusion (aspatial peripherality).

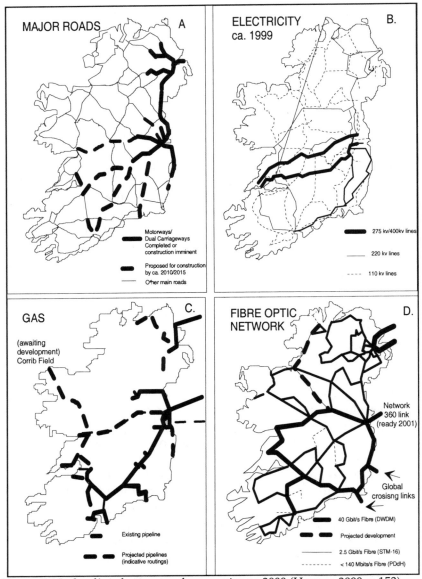

Figure 7.1 Ireland's infrastructural connections c.2000 (Horner, 2000, p.153).

The most prevalent aspects, at least initially, was that of geographic peripherality. This geographic marginalisation was seen to have been at the core of the weak economic performance within some parts of the region. Distances from markets, poor rural transportation networks and the lack of an adequate IT infrastructure were all referred to under this banner of peripherality. In counties Mayo and Roscommon there were also expressions of peripherality within the region itself whereby Galway City in particular was seen as attracting investment, infrastructure, industry and wealth to the demise of the other counties. Most respondents stated that access and transport were the main issues. The issue of what spatial level people felt peripheral to was more difficult to define as most respondents believed that there were varying levels of peripherality; people feeling peripheral to other regions and feeling peripheral within the region itself. People in the more rural areas felt peripheral to economic centres in the region that had concentrations of services and industry. Others, for example small companies, felt isolation from the market place and expressed concern on longer travel times with transport and communications infrastructure not being as well developed as in other regions. Overall there was a desire for a better dispersal of economic activity across the region, an improvement in infrastructure to achieve this and continued attention to the problems of the West from central government. What also began to emerge was a fear of greater social peripherality and an increase in the barriers to participation of individuals and groups and a lack of control or involvement in the decision-making process. Examples of this peripherality included incidences such as consultation processes taking place with regard to roads, waste, planning permissions etc. where there was a feeling that these consultations were mere window-dressing with the views of individuals or communities being ignored. As a result there was growing concern for the continued undermining of the fabric of rural communities and a move toward greater levels of exclusion.

Linking this exclusion from the decision-making process to the political arena, there was recognition that the Irish political system was very centralised and clientelist. It was also felt however that this was slowly changing particularly due to the emphasis of the EU on regional development. In this regard, the retaining of Objective 1 status by 13 counties in Ireland, including those in the study area, was deemed by many as a step toward greater decentralisation of power structures. The more sceptical observers suggested that this would not be the case and that power would remain in the grip of central government. This possibility was in some ways reinforced (some would argue pre-empted) by the moving of departmental offices to different regional locations. Essentially a decentralisation of 'buildings' but not of the power structures involved. Further it was suggested that while there was greater emphasis placed by government on the partnership approach this was merely a rubber-stamping of the decisions already taken by policy-makers and state agencies. The input of the community, while being valued in terms of government rhetoric, rarely instigated, led or controlled the direction in which development took place in any given community. In fact there was a suggestion that the whole nature of democracy in Ireland could be called in to question. What was given the title of 'consultation' between community and government was simply token gestures, merely informing communities of decisions that had already been taken. The concept of deprivation while tied in to this exclusion was deemed to be less recognisable – the hidden element within Irish society. There were a number of references to the relative deprivation that many people living in counties Galway, Mayo and Roscommon found themselves in. This deprivation was not only manifest in urban areas but there was also great concern expressed for the 'hidden' deprivation experienced in many of the more isolated rural areas (particularly as it related to the elderly population, the young, women, disabled and those without access to transport, communications etc.). This was supported by the Jackson and Haase (1996) study of the spatial extent of deprivation that indicated large pockets of deprivation not only in the main urban areas but significantly in many of the rural districts. Jackson and Haase's study revealed a definite spatial pattern between the east and west of the region with a higher degree of deprivation along the western seaboard in Galway and Mayo. Roscommon, while not as extensive, also showed some significant pockets of deprivation.

Aspatial Peripherality, Policy Implications and Conclusions

The argument of this chapter has been that Ireland has to a large degree concentrated on addressing conventional peripherality and for the most part ignored the other facets of peripherality. There is a need to emerge from this conventional use of the concept to one which re-evaluates peripherality in its 'aspatial' context. Issues of access, mobility and poor transportation structures have been among the main indicators and measures of peripherality. Improvements in the number and size of roadways, developments in transport, the exponential advances in communication and information technology suggest however that the traditional or conventional ways of viewing peripherality (in geographic terms) are no longer enough. Key features to more balanced development must include spatial and aspatial peripherality concepts. These range across social, structural, institutional and economic sectors. An improvement in road infrastructure, telecommunications and IT networks, or improvements in public transport provision and increased access to services, must be paralleled by improvements in access to knowledge and high education standards. Further, developing the human capacity, developing institutional capacity and re-building community (embeddedness and the civil society) are necessary components. Improving quality and access to IT infrastructure and cultural diversity must also continue apace. Further, there is a need to ensure that there are not only strong local networks but also strong European and global networks. In this regard the ESDP and the NSS can become key components in creating these networks, allowing for remote or spatially peripheral regions to be linked to the European and global market place. In recent years much has been made of the role of communities in rural development. Indeed in future years, the ability of communities to create and retain employment from within will become of even greater importance. Likewise the ability of communities to instigate, lead and control development will be significant. For this, education, research and training will be vital ingredients (Ó Cinnéide, 1996). Encouraging people to develop an idea, start up a business, instil a 'self-help' attitude, is a long and largely unmeasurable concept. This local value-added is an important asset in any community. This developing of the human capacity is very much linked to the institutional structures and the need for local control – essentially a reorganisation of systems of governance and power. There is also a need for strong local institutions and the development of an institutional capacity that has both strong vertical links between individuals, community groups and policy makers and also strong horizontal links within the communities themselves. Development must not be imposed from a centrally devised plan but must reflect widespread community participation and an opportunity for communities to influence the development taking place in their areas. The partnership groups are an example of this direction but there are still questions to be asked with regard to accountability, and legitimacy in this domain (see McDonagh, 2000).

Social relations are also very much bound up with economic transactions and the relative 'economic' success of any given area. It is essential therefore that the concept of social capital, that is, people supporting, encouraging, trusting, sharing ideas, knowledge, know-how, becomes more deeply entrenched in modern Irish society. Serageldin describes this concept as 'the glue that holds societies together and without which there can be no economic growth or human well-being', while Putnam (1994) has given examples of how regions with active community organisations, good voter turnout, large memberships and followings of clubs and societies etc. are all largely successful regions. In much of our rural communities today (taking community in its spatial sense) we are more likely to talk of commuters rather than community. People within these 'commuter zones' maintain links with their urban networks, through work, social events and in the education of their children, rather than becoming part of the communities in which they live and thereby undermine a very important fabric of rural society. A further part of this rapid change is in the IT sector. The changes that have taken place in the field of communication technologies are one of the main concepts that have helped negate geographic location and provide new opportunities for peripheral areas. The ESDP argues that:

> adequate access to telecommunications are a basic prerequisite for strengthening the competitive situation of peripheral and less favoured regions and hence for the social and economic cohesion of the EU (EC 1999, p.26).

Not only this, but the ESDP also recognises that:

> efficient ... telecommunication systems and services have a key role in strengthening the economic attractiveness of the different ... regional centres (ibid.).

As part of developing this network an important aspect will be the avoidance of what the ESDP refers to as the 'tunnel effect', that is areas being crossed with these networks but not being connected. In the Irish context it is clearly visible that the geographically peripheral areas (that is, the West and North-West) lag seriously behind in terms of the level of networks available to them (see Figure 7.1). In fact less than a quarter of the Irish population have easy access to internet facilities and with services being curtailed, as for example in banks with the introduction of on-line or telephone banking, this is going to further exclude certain parts of the population. The recent declaration by Eircom that it was withdrawing from the 37 billion euro communication investment in the Border, Midlands and West Region is also worrying in terms of development. The installation of fibre-optic and digital subscriber line technologies is essential in providing the region with high-speed internet access and multi-media connections. This would increase the region's potential to attract telecommunication-based industries and improve its employment and quality of life opportunities (see O'Hara, Chapter 10). Integrating these elements, combined with the coupling of conventional and aspatial peripheralities, and letting them become central to the future strategic planning of rural Ireland, will inevitably lead to greater social and economic integration and the opportunity for all people to realise their full potential.

References

Anon (2001) 'The hastening of Rural Decline', *Sunday Independent*, September.

Ball, (1996) 'Local sensitivities and the representation of peripherality', *Journal of Transport Geography*, Vol. 4, No.1 pp.27–36.

Cloke, P. and Goodwin, M. (1993) 'Rural Change: Structured Coherence or Unstructured Incoherence?' *Terra*, 105/3, pp.166–174.

Cloke, P. and Goodwin, M. (1992) 'The Changing Function and Position of Rural Areas in Europe', in P. Huigen *et al* (eds.) *The Changing Function and Position of Rural Areas in Europe*, Utrecht, pp.19–33.

Copus, A. (2001) 'From core-periphery to polycentric development: concepts of spatial and aspatial peripherality', *European Planning Studies*, 9, No. 4, pp.549–552.

Copus, A. (1997) *A New Peripherality Index for European NUTS II Regions*, Report for the Highlands and Islands European Partnership.

Copus, A. (1992) *An assessment of the Peripherality of the Scottish Islands*, Report for the Shetland, Orkney and Western Isles Island Councils. Scottish Agriculture College.

Coulter, C. (2001) 'Gap between the east and west growing, seminar told', *Irish Times*, 9 September.

Department of Agriculture & Food (1999) *Ensuring the Future – A Strategy for Rural Development In Ireland*, Stationery Office, Dublin.

DETR (1999) *Peripherality and Spatial Planning*, DETR Research Report CP0772.

DoELG (2001) *The National Spatial Strategy – Indications for the way ahead*, Dept of the Environment and Local Government, Dublin.

Euradvice (1994) *A Crusade for Survival*, Developing the West Together, Galway.

European Commission (1999) *ESDP – European Spatial Development Perspective*, Luxembourg, Office for Official Publications of the European Communities.

European Commission (1988) *The Future of Rural Society*, COM (88), 501, Brussels.

Grimes, S. (1992) 'Ireland: the Challenge of Development in the European Periphery', *Geography*, No. 334, Vol.77 (1). pp.22–32.

Hodge, D. (1997) 'Accessibility-related issues', *Journal of Transport Geography*, Vol. 5, No.1, pp.33–34.

Horner, A. (2000) 'Geographical regions in Ireland – Reflections at the Millennium', *Irish Geography*, Vol. 33 (2), pp.134–165.

Jackson, J. A. and Haase, T. (1996) 'Demography and the Distribution of Deprivation in Rural Ireland', in C. Curtin, T. Haase and H. Tovey, (eds.) *Poverty in Rural Ireland*, Oak Tree Press, pp.59–80.

Keeble, D. and Tyler, P. (1995) 'Enterprising behaviour and the urban-rural shift', *Urban Studies*, Vol. 6, pp.975–977.

Keeble, D., Owens, P.L. and Thompson, C. (1981) *The Influence of Peripheral and Central Locations on the Relative Development of Regions*, Cambridge University Department of Geography.

McDonagh, J. (2001) *Renegotiating Rural Development in Ireland*. Ashgate, Aldershot.

McDonagh, J. (2000) 'Partnership and Integrated Development in Rural Ireland', *Administration*, Vol. 48, No.1, pp.69–85.

Nijkamp, P. and van Geenhuizen, M. (1997) 'European Transport: challenges and opportunities for future research and policies', *Journal of Transport Geography*, Vol. 5, No.1, pp.4–11.

Ó Cinnéide, M. (1996) 'Rural Development – the Critical Issues'. Paper presented at the Conference on Rural Development – Striking a Proper Balance, 29–30 March, Kilfinane, Limerick.

Ó Cinnéide, M. (1995) 'Keynote Address'. Paper presented at the Conference of the West – The Economic Way Forward, Irish Management Institute, 9 June, Galway.

Ó Cinnéide, M. (1993) 'Ways to Develop the Competitiveness of the Periphery: The Example of Ireland', in L. Lundqvist *et al* (eds.) *Visions and Strategies in European Integration*, Springer-Verlag, Berlin, pp.209–224.

Ó Cinnéide, M. (1992) 'Approaches to the Development of Peripheral Rural Areas: Some Lessons from the Irish Experience', in M. Tykklainen (ed.) *Development Issues and Strategies in the New Europe*, Avebury, England, pp.77–88.

Putnam, (2000) *Bowling Alone: The collapse and revival of American community*, Simon &Schuster, New York.

Spiekermann, K. and Wegener, M. (1996) 'Trans European Networks and unequal accessibility in Europe', *European Journal of Regional Development*, No. 4, pp.35–42.

Vickerman, R., Spiekermann, K. and Wegener, M. (1999) 'Accessibility and Economic Development in Europe', *Regional Studies*, 33/1, 1–15.

chapter eight

SPATIAL PLANNING AND POVERTY

Barbara Walshe

Introduction

The National Spatial Strategy (NSS) is described as being:

> about people and places – the places where people live, the places where they work and how people move between one and the other (Department of Environment and Local Government, 2001).

It is, more crucially, about a:

> process concerned with managing the allocation, distribution and utilisation of those resources and assets that enable society to achieve goals related to environmental sustainability, competitive economic development, social inclusion, balanced distribution of population, employment and incomes within the regions (Walsh, 1999; see also McCafferty, Chapter 4; and Walsh, Chapter 5).

The development of a NSS is welcomed in that it offers a real opportunity to address the widely documented instances of spatially related disadvantage that exist in Ireland today. However, it can also be argued that the commitment of the NSS to the provision of a framework which will create greater equality for those who experience poverty is vague and ill-defined and is likely to lead people, who are already poor, to become even more marginalised. Furthermore, it could be argued, that the stated principle of 'improving the quality of life for all' is akin to the universal cry for world peace, worthy, but in the absence of concrete statements and realistic aims, is likely to remain in the realms of the aspirational. It is therefore increasingly recognised that specifically targeted measures are required if the 'quality of life' for those experiencing poverty and exclusion is to significantly change.

In this chapter, the national and local policy context within which the NSS exists will be outlined. Further, an attempt will be made to define poverty, explore its geographic extent and determine how spatial policies to date have led to the concentration of poverty within urban and rural areas. Making specific reference to the Border, Midlands and West (BMW) region and County Galway, the chapter will outline some recommendations that spatial planning policy at local, national and regional levels will need to address if sustainability is to be achieved.

The National Spatial Strategy, National Policy and Social Inclusion

The NSS is located within the framework of the *National Development Plan 2000–2006* and is being developed in accordance with the government's commitment to sustainable development as presented in *Sustainable Development – A Strategy for Ireland* (Department of the Environment, 1997). This includes a focus on social sustainability, equity and personal well being. This is interpreted as the careful location of residential, commercial and industrial planning and making effective use of existing developed urban areas and promoting integrated strategic, economic and social planning. The vision, contained in the latest and last public consultation document *Indications for the Way Ahead* (Department of Environment and Local Government, 2001) concerns the capacity to achieve economic, environmental and social sustainability through balanced regional development. This is to be achieved through the fulfillment of potential arising from a number of specific strategies. This will involve expansion of the existing five gateway cities, Limerick, Cork, Dublin, Waterford and Galway and the allocation of gateway status to an additional three or four strategically placed large towns that will have a role as internationally competitive drivers of a regional economy. Hubs (medium-sized towns) will play an important national role and will be linked to gateways. These hubs will also be linked or connected to smaller towns and villages. The development of a critical mass is seen as central to growth and economic stability on the one hand and to the maintenance of community viability on the other.

Social inclusion and balanced regional development have been recognised as key priorities within the *National Development Plan 2000–2006* (Department of Finance, 1999) because, despite strong economic growth, there has been an increase in relative poverty and the range of inequalities being experienced by specific groups within Irish society. Although the number of people living in consistent poverty in Ireland has almost halved from 15 percent to 8 percent, the recent *United Nations Development Report* has reported that Ireland has the second highest concentrations of poverty in the developed world after the United States and before Great Britain (Van Der Gaag, 1997). Furthermore although:

> the majority of people effected by poverty and social exclusion do not live in urban concentrations, it is clear that there are spatial concentrations of unemployment poverty and exclusion. It is also clear that this spatial concentration is not lessening but intensifying due to the consequences of long-term unemployment, poverty and past policy choices (NESC, 1999).

The NDP 2000–2006 has also stated that, in order to meet those objectives:

> a multi-faceted approach to the promotion of social inclusion would have to be adopted, including targeted interventions aimed at areas and groups affected by poverty and social exclusion through out the community (Department of Finance, 1999, p.8).

A step on this road is evident in the Planning and Development Act 2000, which lists sustainable development as one of its guiding principles. This view is also endorsed by the White Paper on Rural Development *Ensuring the Future - A Strategy for Rural Development in Ireland* (Department of Agriculture & Food, 1999). Further to this, the recent restructuring and reform of Local Government set out in *Better Local Government – A Programme for Change* (Department of Environment and Local Government, 1996) and the Report of the *Interdepartmental Task Force on Local Government and Local Development* (Department of Environment and Local Government, 1998) have also identified social inclusion as a key priority in the ten-year County/City social, economic and cultural strategic plans which are presently being undertaken by the County/City Development Boards.

Spatial planning at a local level

The concept of developing a NSS is new in Ireland. However, local authorities have had a statutory requirement to produce development or spatial plans at a County and City level since the introduction of the Planning and Development Act 1963. The Development Act emerged from the Lemass era and the economic stagnation of the fifties with high emigration and poverty levels.

This Act envisaged a dynamic role for local authorities as development corporations, which could respond to the economic, physical and social needs of people. However, in practice, the link between physical planning and social objectives became increasingly tenuous and planning became obsessively concerned with details of control and regulation (Bannon 1988).

The centralised nature of the Irish state, the lack of an independent source of income for local authorities, and the absence of political will to proceed with the necessary structural reforms to support the concept of development planning, has meant that planning departments in local authorities have become regulatory agents. One of the core reserved functions of local elected representatives is their role in 'adopting' the County/City Development Plan. The shape of the plan, and the designations within, are often mediated by the elected representatives on behalf of commercial, economic, residential or voter interests. Therefore, it is often not so much planning decisions as the underlying pressures associated with business, competition, markets and profits which determine the shape of towns and cities in modern market economies (Bartley, 1998). The marked absence of a regional dimension to spatial or development planning to date has also led to lack of coherence and co-ordination on strategic issues at all levels.

The Poverty Debate

The poverty debate has largely centred on the differences between relative and absolute poverty and how poverty is experienced in diverse ways both internationally and nationally. An absolute view of poverty assumes that it is possible to determine, in a scientific and measurable way, what counts as a minimum standard of living. Those who are defined as living in poverty live below that standard. Relative poverty is also increasingly linked to a range of inequalities that are experienced by certain groups of people within society. Relative poverty is something that varies and is usually described as a percentage of average national income. Income poverty however is just one indicator of deprivation. This is compounded by personal or collective powerlessness, alienation from decision-making processes, lack of opportunities and limited choices in where one lives, works or socialises. The cumulative effect of this exclusion can mean that people exist 'at a distance' from the benefits of mainstream society. Overall, when poverty is located and linked to inequality, the terms 'deprivation' 'marginalisation' and social exclusion can often accompany it. A useful definition is that used in *Partnership 2000* (Government of Ireland 1996) (Partnership 2000 was a National Agreement between 1997–2000) which defines:

> social exclusion as cumulative marginalisation from production (unemployment) from consumption (poverty) from social networks (community, family and neighbours), from decision making and from an adequate quality of life.

This increase in cumulative disadvantage in particular areas, whether in large urban housing estates, provincial towns or smaller rural communities is becoming increasingly identified as it slowly moves up the political agenda. Indeed it has become a key target area in such documents as the *National Anti-Poverty Strategy – Sharing in Progress* (National Anti-Poverty Strategy Ireland, 1997); the National Economic and Social Forum (NESF) *Rural Renewal – Combating Social Exclusion* (NESF, 1997), and the *National Investment Priorities for the period 2000–2006* (Fitzgerald *et al.*, 1999).

Where is poverty located?

There are similarities in where and how poverty appears, there are also differences in how it manifests itself and how poverty effects large numbers of Irish people in urban and rural settings. Cumulative disadvantage is not unique to Ireland. Great Britain contains some of the most disadvantaged neighbourhoods in Europe. Recently Britain developed their 'New Deal for Communities' initiative which targets disadvantaged communities for large-scale spending in service provision, infrastructure and social capital building. There is a growing acceptance that social inclusion for these communities will require a disproportionately higher allocation of per capita national spend due to the scale and extent of the disadvantage. In Britain, as in Ireland, it is in areas of public housing that people are most disadvantaged (Lloyd, 2000). The state as a provider of public sector housing, had not, until recently, taken responsibility for the invisibility of increasingly marginalised populations that have been relocated to the peripheries of towns, villages and cities, behind high walls, adjacent to local authority dumps or waste ground.

In Ireland there are a number of indicators that link disadvantage and public housing estates in large urban centres. These include the concentration of 50 per cent of all poor households in local authority estates; the high risk of poverty in these estates estimated at 42 per cent as compared to 9 per cent in other housing tenures (Nolan *et al.* 1998). This has occurred for a variety of reasons including the disappearance of traditional types of employment, changing family structures and a strong emphasis on home ownership. These changes have led to the development of socially segregated housing which in turn has led to the increased residualisation of the social housing sector. Public policy gave a further intensive push to this process following the introduction of surrender grant scheme in the 1980s. The Government in the 1980s initiated the House surrender grant in order to ease the housing crisis. It gave house purchase grants to people from public housing estates who wished to move into private accommodation. This resulted in the poorest and most vulnerable living in under-resourced urban housing schemes at spatial locations usually at the edges of cities with limited access to suitable employment, transport and diminished life choices.

Urban disadvantage has also become associated with multiple disadvantage and intergenerational unemployment. Due to these factors, other negative social effects are produced, such as crime, illicit drug use and neighbourhood insecurity. Other social problems such as isolation, poor health, family breakdown and lone parenthood have had an additional fragmentary effect on these neighbourhoods by further decreasing the capacity of communities to challenge their situation.

Low rates of participation in democratic structures and elections have further separated people who experience poverty from mainstream political, social and economic development. At a European level, the development of real participation and involvement of community/voluntary organisations is valued as an essential feature of all democracies. In Ireland a growing recognition exists of the need for local government to become participative as well as representative (Department of Environment and Local Government, 1998). This view is reinforced by the *White Paper Supporting Voluntary Activity 2000* (Department of Social, Community and Family Affairs, 2000) which sees participatory democracy as a vehicle for fostering active citizenship. Traditionally there has been little involvement by citizens in the planning and decision-making process of where and how they live and work. So-called 'experts' make these decisions. The consequences, both in planning and development, for those experiencing poverty, have been well documented and have now been recognised as examples of poor and ill-informed decision-making. At present a growing number of participatory planning models are being developed to enable communities to participate in decision-making at local level. This will require however, courage and vision from the local authorities and investment in the resources that will be necessary to support participatory planning models. The advantages of involving people in the planning and development of initiatives central to their lives means that local knowledge and expertise is valued as a mechanism which will inform and ensure good planning. It should also mean that the process of participation and consultation undertaken should enable people to take ownership and have a greater stake in their communities.

Recent negotiations by the Community Platform (the Community Platform consists of 24 organisations that have a specific focus on anti-poverty issues and have two seats on the Community/Voluntary Pillar (one of the social partners) on the Programme for Prosperity and Fairness) resulted in designating 25 of the most Irish disadvantaged urban areas for additional investment under the Revitalisation of Areas through Planning and Investment and Development (RAPID). A key element of this programme was to empower disadvantaged communities to be at the heart of decisions that affected their communities and their lives. A further 15 low density rural areas have been designated under the Clár programme (the Clár Programme is regarded as the rural equivalent of the RAPID Programme and is targeted at a number of rural areas that have experienced persistent depopulation decline since 1926); while a further 20 provincial towns, are being targeted under the Rapid II Programme. All of these initiatives are based on an ambitious programme of regeneration with recommendations that the participation of communities be at the heart of the regeneration process. These programmes however will only be as good as the understanding and commitment of those who are charged with their implementation.

Rural poverty and exclusion

The National Anti-Poverty Strategy in 1997 identified income, infrastructure, co-ordination and social capacity as the primary areas in which to develop new strategies around rural disadvantage (Lloyd, 2000). Within the Border, Midlands and West (BMW) Region there are areas of extreme deprivation, which suffer cumulative disadvantage. Sparsely populated and essentially rural in character (except for Galway City) the BMW Region covers 47 per cent of the state's landmass and contains 27 per cent of the population. Only 32 per cent of this population reside in concentrations of more than 1500 people, compared to the national average of 58 per cent. A combination of small town size, persistent lack of investment by successive governments in infrastructure and employment, and the continuing decline in agriculture as a main source of employment, have led to a vicious cycle of decline (see also O'Hara, Chapter 10). It is also evident that those living on or near the Border experience a double disadvantage due to both economic and political difficulties. Significant pockets of deprivation can be found in the larger urban centres especially in Dundalk and Drogheda. In both of these areas about 20 per cent of 'heads of households' are lone parents with the figure nationally at 14 per cent. In the region as a whole all areas have higher rates of unemployment and long-term unemployment compared to the national average. Moreover, areas of rural disadvantage, characterised by sustained outward migration, educational disadvantage and lack of employment opportunities are heavily concentrated in the region. These are principally located in the Donegal Gaeltacht, the Connemara Gaeltacht, Cavan, Mayo and Inishowen. Further compounded by aspects of demographic dependence, strong links are evident between the underdevelopment of services and socio-economic infrastructure in the towns and villages that comprise and service rural communities.

Social exclusion in rural areas exhibits distinct characteristics. These include high levels of invisibility, low levels of development activity and little acknowledgment of the existence of poverty. Access to land, property, education, employment, transport and services are key indicators of the social groups particularly at risk. These include low-income rural households, women, lone parents, single men over 45 years of age, people with a disability, travellers, the unemployed, the landless, the underemployed, those living in public housing and older people. Much of the poverty experienced in Ireland arises within town and villages of less than 3,000 people. Taking the 50 per cent of income poverty line for example, some 26 per cent of those classified as 'at risk of poverty' live in towns and villages of less than 3000 inhabitants. Furthermore those without land or resources are often ghettoised within public housing estates that are located outside villages and small towns (Jackson & Haase 1996). The spatial location of travellers halting sites, many of whom are located beside local authority dumps, railway tracks or waste ground also challenges our societies commitment to equality.

The Challenge for County Galway

Galway is recognised within the NSS as one of the country's main gateways and drivers in the Western Region. Recognised as one of the fastest growing cities in Europe it also contains some of the most sparsely populated peripheral areas in Europe. Galway City itself has experienced 12.6 per cent increase in population while Galway County excluding the City has experienced 3 per cent growth over the same period (CSO, 1996). The growth in Galway City has had a major impact on the entire county. The availability of services and employment opportunities draws people from the more remote areas, where these opportunities do not exist, into the city thereby undermining the population structure and sustainability of the more remote areas. Parts of north, west and southeast Galway have been identified as areas which have experienced persistent population decline and have been targeted under the Clár programme for additional investment by the Department of Agriculture and Rural Development.

Within the Gaeltacht areas the settlement patterns have had a number of diverse effects on the cultural and social life of the Gaeltacht. Culturally the arrival of large numbers of English-speaking homeowners can have a significant negative effect on the Irish language. Population decline has been experienced by Rosmuc/Camus (-5.6 per cent) while movement towards the city has resulted in the suburbanisation of Gaeltacht areas close to the city. Villages such as Moycullen (+9.3 per cent), Barna (+10.6 per cent) and Spiddal (+10.9 per cent) have all shown population increases which reflects the growing demand to live within an easy commuting distance of the city. This suburbanisation has inflated land and house prices and as a result places them beyond the reach of those on low incomes or those who are landless. It also drives those on low incomes to join an already over inflated public housing waiting list in Galway City.

In terms of transport, one of the overall objectives of current public transport policy is its commitment to social cohesion (Department of Public Enterprise, 2000). In a climate where privatisation, deregulation and the restructuring of public transport is presently being undertaken nationally it will be necessary to ensure transport routes that are regarded as being uneconomic but vital to the cohesion of both rural and urban areas are protected. Public transport in Galway City and County has also been described as 'a system of last resort rather than first choice' (Buchanan and Hanley, 1999, p.6). Furthermore poor public transport in County Galway has also been identified as a key barrier to participation in the labour force by 57 per cent long-term unemployed and 39 per cent short-term unemployed as highlighted in the recent survey of *Unemployed Customers and Employment Opportunities in Galway* (Department of Social, Community and Family Affairs, 2001, p.54). Key findings from the *Report of the Interdepartmental Working Group on Rural Transport 2001* (Fitzpatrick and Associates, 2001) indicate that many people in rural communities have no access to any scheduled public transport service. In three of the pilot areas, Kerry, Mayo and Westmeath, 40 per cent of the rural population live in District Electoral Division (DEDs) without any kind of scheduled stop (this refers to one which has a scheduled stop within the DED, not just passing through, or one which a 'hail and ride' type service such as the Bus Éireann local service). In Laois 60 per cent had no public transport service of any kind.

Challenges for the National Spatial Strategy

The consultation paper *Indications for the Way Ahead* (Department of the Environment and Local Government, 2001) concentrates on the problems of urban growth in centres such as Galway and Dublin more than the needs of rural Ireland. Developing the core areas does not sustain the periphery, rather it creates new peripheries, and in itself is not the answer to rural disadvantage. The development of these growth centres can be part of the solution, but such development must be done in balance with support from the periphery, and ensuring that there is minimal negative impact on the hinterland (Cumas Teo., 1999). The proposed development of corridors such as that planned for Belfast/Dublin has the potential to spread the benefits of development more evenly throughout Ireland rather than the creation of large growth centres (Bacon *et al.* 2001).

Transport

The public transport deficit points to the need to consider public transport as an integral part of any wider spatial planning strategies at national, regional and local level in terms of policy on location of housing, employment and public services. There is a need to address the options for a western/south western corridor as a counterbalance to the East, particularly having regard to the very strong future potential of the Belfast-Dublin corridor and its likely effect of further increasing the relative attraction of the East.

The proposal for a West of Ireland rail service, as part of a Western Corridor from Cork via Galway to Derry, is an important proposal in relation to the remedy of peripherality within Ireland. Furthermore since transport services are undergoing both restructuring and deregulation at national level, responsive public transport delivered in consultation with disadvantaged communities has an important role to play in the maintenance of social cohesion at both local regional and national level.

Housing

Current housing policy has shifted from the development of large urban housing estates to the creation of smaller developments, which will incorporate a combination of public, private and affordable housing. According to Section 5 of the Planning and Development Act 2000, up to 20 per cent of land for private development must be allocated to the provision of social and affordable housing. A recent declaration by the Irish Auctioneers and Valuers Institute stated that:

> you might say it is *(social housing)* socially desirably but that doesn't mean that it will have widespread acceptance (Brennan, 2001).

Therefore it is important that the Department of the Environment and Local Government and the local authorities have the political support which will ensure that these commitments to the provision of mixed housing are honoured.

Strengthening the social inclusion focus

An explicit commitment to social and cultural inclusion should be contained in the vision statement of the NSS. All government policies and programmes should be subjected to equality proofing, poverty-proofing and rural proofing in their design and implementation (NESF, 1997). The application of this principle to the design and implementation of policies and proposed measures is necessary in preventing the recurrence of spatial disadvantage problems including rural and urban social exclusion.

Public support and political will are needed if the NSS is to be accepted. The Strategy should be seen as a process and should have a permanent implementation team with suitable expertise across spatial, social, economic and environmental sectors. Flexibility and capacity for review and adjustment should be built into the NSS process due to the prolonged time period and the pace of change. Monitoring of the NSS and its impact on Irish society is essential. An independent monitoring committee should be established with social partner representation. Monitoring should clearly incorporate how the NSS impacts on other national strategies such as the National Anti-Poverty Strategy.

The issue of environmental quality is particularly important in the context of quality of life and should not be seen as secondary to growth requirements. Poor individuals and communities carry the burden of degraded and sterile environments, contributing to the stress and poor quality of life they experience. The rights-based approach of the National Sustainable Development Strategy should be incorporated into the NSS.

Travellers are particularly disadvantaged and marginalised communities in Ireland. They have particular requirements in relation to spatial planning. The NSS should address the fact that we have a nomadic tradition in our state and should ensure that this is catered for through a national system of transient halting sites as outlined in the Traveller Accommodation Act.

Finally while positive and concrete measures are suggested in relation to regional imbalance as for example in reducing the level of migration of young people towards the East Coast, by providing them with education and employment opportunities nearer the regions they come from it is inappropriate to apply one model to the entire country. Spatial/local difference must, and should, be acknowledged. Testing and piloting of new approaches should be considered as an option. Learning from international examples is also important as for example, in the Australian inter-agency one-stop service delivery; the Baltic States approach to social cohesion and the Curitiba integrated approach to public transport and land use (Plumpe, 2001). The NSS should also learn from local development models in Ireland that are successfully developing 'bottom up' integrated development strategies including those of the Local Development Programmes and the Integrated Area Plan concept.

Conclusion

The NSS will determine settlement patterns and policies beyond its stated 20-year timeframe. It is also anticipated that the NSS will acquire statutory status that will require all current and future sectoral strategies to adhere to its guiding framework. It is also hoped that the NSS will endorse the concept of integrated planning and the right to participation in decision-making by communities and particularly those who experience disadvantage. Ireland is being presented with an opportunity to acknowledge the negative effects of past spatial policies that have compounded poverty and inequality for specific groups of people in Ireland. We have the opportunity to learn from past mistakes and to take courageous and innovative steps to create a strategy that does not blindly copy a European model but acknowledges its potential while recognising the uniqueness of our settlement and cultural patterns.

References

Bacon & Associates and New Ground Ltd (2001) 'Social Exclusion and the National Spatial Strategy', Submission by the Community Workers Co-operative to the National Spatial Planning Unit, Unpublished.

Bannon, J.M. (1988) 'Development Planning and the Neglect of the Critical Regional Dimension' in Bannon *et al*, *Planning: The Irish Experience 1920–1988*, Wolfhound Press, Dublin.

Bartley, B. (1998) 'Social Exclusion and the neighbourhood in west Dublin', in Madanipour, A., *Social Exclusion in European Neighbourhoods Processes, Experiences and Responses*, Jessica Kingsley and the Regional Studies Association, London.

Brennan, C. (2001) 'Interview with CEO of the Irish Auctioneers & Valuers Institute', *Irish Times*.

Buchanan, C. and Hanley, R. (1999) *Galway Transportation and Planning Study*, Project No. 23781, Galway Corporation and Galway Council.

Central Statistics Office (1996) *Census of Population, 1996*, Government Publications, Stationery Office, Dublin.

Cumas Teo. (1999) *Pairtiocht Chonamara agus Arainn*. Strategic Action Plan 2000–2006, Unpublished.

Department of Agriculture & Food (1999) *Ensuring the Future: A Strategy for Rural Development in Ireland*, Government Publications, Dublin.

Department of Environment (1997) *Sustainable Development – A Strategy for Ireland*, Government Publications, Stationery Office, Dublin.

Department of Environment and Local Government (1996) *Better Local Government – A Programme for Change*, Government Publications, Dublin.

Department of Environment and Local Government (1998) *Interdepartmental Task Force Report on the Integration of Local Government and Local Development*, Dept of Environment and Local Government, Dublin.

Department of Environment and Local Government (2001) *Indications for the Way Ahead*, Public consultation document on the National Spatial Strategy, Department of Environment and Local Government, Dublin.

Department of Finance (1999) *The National Development Plan 2000–2006*, Government Publications, Stationery Office, Dublin.

Department of Public Enterprise (2000) *A New Institutional and Regulatory Framework for Public Transport*, Department of Public Enterprise, Government Publications, Stationery Office, Dublin.

Department of Social, Community and Family Affairs (2000) *Supporting Voluntary Activity – A White Paper on a Framework for Supporting Voluntary Activity and for Developing the Relationship between the State and the Community and Voluntary Sector*, Stationery Office, Dublin.

Department of Social, Community and Family Affairs (2001) *Survey of Unemployed Customers and Employment Opportunities in County Galway*, Department of Social, Community and Family Affairs, Dublin.

Fitzgerald, J., Kearney, I., Morgenroth, E. and Smyth, D. (1999) 'National Investment Priorities for the Period 2000–2006', *Policy Research Series, No. 33*, Economic and Social Research Institute, Dublin.

Fitzpatrick and Associates Economic Consultants, (2001*) Report of the Interdepartmental Working Group on Rural Transport*, Stationery Office, Dublin.

Government of Ireland (1996) *Partnership 2000 for Inclusion, Employment and Competitiveness*, National Agreement, Govt Publications, Dublin.

Jackson, J. A. and Haase, T. (1996) 'Demography and the Distribution of Deprivation in Rural Ireland' in C. Curtin *et al* (eds.) *Poverty in Rural Ireland – A Political Economy Perspective*, Oak Tree, Dublin, pp.59–85.

Lloyd, A. (2000) 'Targeted Investment in Disadvantaged areas: Promoting Social Inclusion by creating sustainable communities', *Developing a Strategy to Regenerate the most disadvantaged areas in the country*, Community Workers Co-operative, Galway.

National Anti-Poverty Strategy (1997) *Sharing in Progress – National Anti-Poverty Strategy*, Government Publications, Stationery Office, Dublin.

NESC (1999) *Opportunities, Challenges and Capacities for Choice*, National Economic and Social Council, Dublin.

NESF (1997) *Rural Renewal – Combating Social Exclusion*, Forum Report No. 12, The National Economic and Social Forum.

Nolan, B., Whelan, T. and Williams, J. (1998) *Where are the Poor Households? The Spatial Distribution of Poverty and Deprivation in Ireland*, Oak Tree Press, Dublin.

Van Der Gaag, N. (1997) 'Exploding the myths of Poverty', *New Internationalist*, Vol. 310, pp.18–19.

Walsh, J, (1999) 'Strategic Planning for the New Millennium – Spatial Planning at Regional Level'. Paper presented to the Irish Assembly of Regional Authorities Conference in Ennis.

chapter nine

CHANGING ATTITUDES TO PLANNING:
THE CASE OF GALWAY AND THE NEED FOR A COMMUNITY
PERSPECTIVE

Brendan Smith

Introduction

The concept of planning has become an important term in current development vocabulary. In this book there has been a lot of discussion about the concept of balanced regional development and the urban system, national spatial strategies, and indeed the link between spatial planning and poverty (see McCafferty, Chapter 4; Walsh, Chapter 5, and Walshe, Chapter 8). This chapter makes an additional contribution to this discussion, by way of a community activist's assessment. Essentially the chapter, using an applied, and indeed more personal, commentary will delve into some of the development that has taken place in Galway city over the last three decades in an attempt to highlight; the lack of planning that has taken place; the lack of consultation that has taken place and, significantly, the lack of community involvement in general. The chapter will argue for a more inclusive and integrated planning environment within Galway city and explore recent examples of how communities, in partnership with local authorities, can, do, and should play a determining role in shaping the environment in which they live.

The Example of Galway City

The 1960s in Ireland saw the beginning of massive changes across the country. Large-scale industrial development initiated by the arrival of multi-national corporations and the country's subsequent entry into the European Economic Community (EEC, now the European Union (EU)) all began to fashion the development of this newly emerging economy. With a modern economy, young educated workforce, a western European liberal democracy unburdened with the overcrowded centuries-old urban tenements of other European states, would our urban areas be designed to promote social comfort and harmony?

Unprecedented levels of growth, employment and economic prosperity have marked out Galway as one of the fastest growing urban areas in western Europe. This prosperity has however another side. Significant sections of society are excluded from the decision-making processes at work in the city. Added to this social exclusion the level of urban expansion/sprawl has begun to undermine the very fabric of local communities and threaten their long-term social sustainability.

The phenomenal change that Galway City has undergone in the last decade can be categorised under three components. These components are essentially:

the residential suburban developments,

the new road networks and avenues of travel, and

the new industrial, retail and institutional places of work.

The planning involved in these components has now been recognised as a contributory factor in undermining the community fabric traditionally associated with this part of the Western Region. In exploring some of the more recent developments in this relatively new city, it will become apparent that there is a need to re-evaluate the type and nature of the current planning and development environment in Galway and, there is a need/desire to re-introduce a more integrated community perspective.

Residential Suburban Developments

One of the first major residential developments of 1960s Galway was in Rahoon in the western part of the City. This development consisted of a series of high-rise apartment blocks populated by tenants of Galway Corporation. Described by many commentators as a social disaster, this residential block was totally unsuitable for the tenants, either young families or older residents, for whom it was built. The central reasons for this criticism included the fact that:

(a) the heating system was centralised allowing no flexibility for the differing heat needs of the apartments and their variant age occupants;

(b) residents occupying non-ground floor apartments often had extreme difficulties regarding access or when elevators broke down (which was all too often);

(c) the amenity land surrounding the high-rise blocks was open and unfenced thereby offering no protection and creating an unsafe environment for young children, and

(d) the children's playground surface was hard and unsafe to its users.

The vast majority of residents, while they waited to be re-housed in single or two storey dwellings regarded their residency in the so-called 'Rahoon Flats' as a 'Purgatory on Earth'. In the late 1990s rather unsurprisingly, the flats were demolished. The question is, were these dwellings a planning mistake? The answer however is not clear-cut. On the one hand they were a disaster for their target community, particularly for the reasons listed. On the other, perhaps not. The complex could have made an ideal living environment for occupants of the *same age group*. Research which I undertook in 1978 as a Student Union Officer at University College Galway (now the National University of Ireland, Galway (NUI, G)), evaluated the impact and alternative use of this complex and argued that they be converted into 'student accommodation units' similar to what existed in many parts of Europe. It was further argued that UCG should enter into negotiations with Galway Corporation over the ownership of the apartment complex and perhaps exchange a college-owned land bank further up the western side of the river Corrib. This proposal would have allowed the local authority to build houses for flat occupants (which is what the latter desperately wanted), and would have taken students out of competition with professionals looking for accommodation in the city, while providing them with a managed accommodation block in close proximity to the College. While the opportunity was ruled out by the authorities as being outside the remit of the College at that time, there are now a number of campus and off-campus student accommodation complexes across Ireland that seem to be an important profitable business for third level institutions.

In moving to the more typical residential developments, that is 'housing estates', one of the major developments on the western outskirts of the city occurred in the late 1970s with the construction of a large suburban development in Knocknacarra. In the 1970s this area was a typical rural landscape with a sparse population. In 2001 the population was approaching ten thousand. A second example of this type of housing development occurred on the north side of the Corrib river in the Ballinfoyle-Terryland area. In the 1970s this district consisted of a small Irish/Gaelic speaking rural community. Today, it has a population of approximately seven thousand people with little of the Irish language surviving.

These developments (to name two of many) can be defined as 'Urban Sprawl', that is, a mass of inter-connecting housing estates with no central focal point, no community centres, no pedestrian or cycling connections to places of work, of worship, of shopping or of education. It is only years after the completion of this kind of housing development and, in most cases quite recently, that proper outdoor recreational facilities have started to be put in place. This was the case despite the fact that the majority of the population in these areas comprised young couples and large numbers of children. A whole generation grew up and passed through these estates without the opportunity to enjoy a playground, a football field, a safe cycling excursion, a walk in the park. Any facilities that were built were done so in a complete vacuum with no established community-local government consultation structure. The roads into, and within, the estates lacked any type of protection for children at play or for non-motorised vehicle users. Any obstruction to cars was frowned upon by government or city officials be it road ramps (speed ramps could not be built on bus-routes), pedestrian crossings (allegedly there was not the volume of pedestrians to justify a pedestrian crossing) or street furniture. Furthermore, the failure of successive governments to introduce minimum standards of upkeep on private rented accommodation meant that many private estates were scarred by the blight of ramshackle rented houses and their overgrown jungle gardens.

This lack of integrated planning between local government and communities resulted in social decline. Outbreaks of joy-riding, burglaries and such like became more common place with older residents increasingly fearful for their safety. Safety fears also led to a movement away from using a bicycle as a mode of transport or by travelling on foot due to the vandalised nature of open spaces. In essence many estates had a sense of alienation born out of living in areas which negated any sense of belonging, community identity or cohesion.

The Road Networks and New Places of Work

The Galway city road infrastructure that was developed from the early 1980s onwards with its abundance of roundabout systems has, it can be argued, done much to destroy urban culture. When this road development was being initiated in the 1980s, local community activists pointed to its inherent flaws. Little or no heed was paid to these voices of concern.

The city transport system we now have is based around the new residential developments concentrated primarily west of the river Corrib, while the majority of work-places – the industrial estates and retail parks - are located east of the river. The main connecting artery between a worker's residence and his/her place of work is the Quincentennial Bridge, opened in 1984. Even at a cursory level the folly of this kind of development is evident. People living on one side of the city and working on the other side leads to massive traffic jams in the morning and evening rush hours (particularly on this bridge which takes the majority of traffic crossing the river Corrib). Worse still, the bridge has limited provision for public transport with the cycle lanes poorly designed with high kerbs at entrance/exit points and often large public signs being erected across the lanes providing either a barrier or obstacle to users.

The roundabout systems are also problematic, as they are by design and deed, anti-pedestrian, anti buggy/pram and anti-cyclist. In 1978, a UCG Department of Civil Engineering survey revealed that approximately 25 per cent of second-level pupils in Galway cycled to school. By 1996 this figure was down to 2.5 per cent. Today in primary schools the figure is likely to be less that one per cent. The reason for this dramatic decline seems to be strongly related to the inherent dangers associated with using the city's poorly planned road and travel networks. Roundabouts and their connecting motorways are built through densely populated areas and often curtail people's access to places of worship, education, shopping and social activity. Non-car users, children and senior citizens, seem to have limited rights of passage. This type of road infrastructure not only leads to a system that encourages aggression, impatience, selfishness and speeding, but I argue, it also has damaged the very fabric of urban communities. The ludicrous situation facing cyclists and pedestrians and the poor public transportation network has led to an over-reliance on car usage even though almost two thirds of the population of Galway live less than two miles from their place of work or education.

The majority of shopping and retail parks, the Galway-Mayo Institute of Technology (GMIT), most of NUI, Galway campus, and the industrial and business parks of Galway city were built from the 1970s onwards. With the possible exception of NUI, Galway, all of these constructions were very functional in design with little concern about aesthetics. There is little in many of these institutions by way of tree planting programmes, people parks, park benches, cycle facilities or public transport networks. GMIT for example, houses a Department of Forestry yet the grounds of this institution were until recently, almost devoid of trees or shrubs. Despite this gloomy picture however there are now serious attempts to develop a position where all sectors of the community have an input to the planning and design of their city:

> where the mistakes of the recent past are undone;

> where the green deserts that surround housing estates are being turned into living active amenity zones for all age groups;

> where concrete is broken up and turned into wildlife habitats;

> where people can move by foot, by wheelchair, by bicycle in safety and without hindrance, from one end of the city to the other, and

> where urban sprawls are being transformed into urban villages of concerned citizens.

This kind of progressive attitude and willingness to interact with the wider community is gathering pace. Promoted and demanded by the 1996 Local Government Act, this new approach is slowly starting to reap dividends. Its central tenet is the active involvement of all sectors of the local community in planning and shaping our local environment in all its aspects. Of course, the catalyst for this act, and other similar national legislation, are the new European directives on more openness and accountability in local government as well as the international legislation and protocols on environment and sustainability that the country has signed up for.

Galway City Development Board – The Hope of the Future?

In Galway City, the 1996 Local Government Act has resulted in the formation of the Galway City Development Board (GCDB). Set up in Spring 2000, it comprises all the major business, industrial, health, educational, community, social and tourism stakeholders of the city. These include the Industrial Development Authority (IDA); the Chamber of Commerce; Bord Fáilte; the Garda Siochána; Údarás na Gaeltachta; the Western Health Board; Galway Trades Council; Galway Corporation, and Galway Community Forum. The function of the GCDB is to prepare a strategy for the economic, social and cultural development of Galway City. For the first time in the history of the state, the overall planning of an area is being taken away from the sole jurisdiction of local and national government allowing all sectors of society to play a part in strategic development.

The GCDB has set itself the task of building an inclusive and people-centred City accessible to all, equitable, progressive and one that is environmentally, economically and community sustainable. Importantly, it is not just another bland aspirational plan. Rather it is a strategy with specific key result areas and definite target dates for completion. Some of the major proposals are to:

Promote public participation in decision-making at all levels;

Develop a city-wide pedestrian-friendly, cyclist-friendly and child-friendly infrastructure;

Promote the timely provision of an appropriate quantity and quality of recreation facilities as part of all housing developments;

Develop Galway as a disability-friendly city;

Protect and revitalise heritage streetscapes;

Prepare a plan for the city's waterway shores and bay areas which maximises their sustainable development for recreational, aesthetic and other purposes;

Celebrate multi-culturalism in the city;

Develop strategies to support Gaelic traditions within existing Gaeltacht city areas, and

Promote, preserve and enhance flora and fauna habitats.

An example of one of the latter goals - to promote, preserve and enhance flora and fauna habitats, and one of the most ambitious environmental programmes ever undertaken in Ireland, is the Terryland Forest Park project. This project has been taking place in Galway over the last twenty-one months. The Forest Park covers over 160 acres of prime city land where it is intended to plant 500,000 native trees in the next four years, making it Europe's largest urban forest park programme. This development has from its very inception, captured the popular imagination of Galwegians. Since last March, three major community tree-planting festivals have involved nearly 6,000 people of all ages planting 14,000 trees and 40,000 bulbs in the grounds of the new park (a major undertaking when one considers that in the Dublin Corporation conurbation the local authority planted 5,000 trees in total, last year).

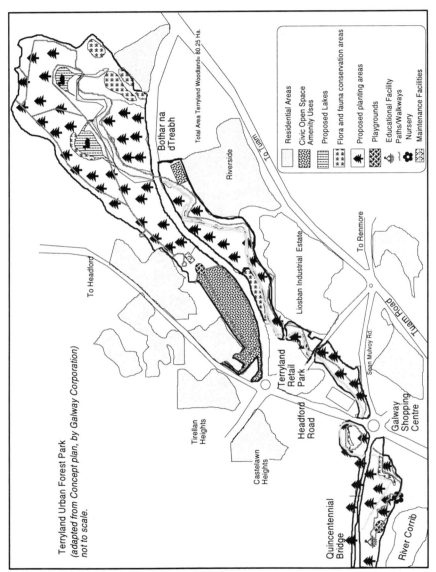

Figure 9.1 The Terryland Forest Park

The area selected in Galway was the Terryland River Valley, a unique geographical feature that stretches from the river Corrib through ever shrinking wetlands and threatened green pastures, past major new commercial and residential estates before disappearing underground in the rural Gaeltacht district of Castlegar. Refuse, building rubble and pollution were slowly strangling large sections of this major aquatic avenue. To counteract this, the innovative partnership of community and local authority coalesced to produce a 'greenprint' (Figure 9.1) for this 160-acre valley, the main elements of which are the:

development of a 500,000 tree forest;

re-introduction of wildlife such as otters and swans;

conservation of wetland and aquatic habitats/ sanctuaries;

preservation and re-construction of rural landscape human-made features such as dry-stone walls, hedgerows and natural stone gate pillars;

preservation of rural meadows;

construction of nature trails, forest walks, river walks, nature trails;

construction of a tree nursery;

construction of a woodland theme playground;

construction of an area for performing arts;

construction of sculptures and sculpture trails;

construction of an arboreal educational centre;

development of picnic areas, and

construction of aesthetic foot bridges.

The origins and management of this project was born out of an historic partnership between progressive local government officials, enthusiastic community organisers, supportive national politicians, skilled artists, visionary ecologists and environmentalists who joined forces in order to develop and nurture a vast green belt that would provide a harmonious blend of wildlife habitats and recreational facilities located a short distance from the city centre. It was seen by all parties involved that there was in existence a unique opportunity to create an urban forest that would serve as the 'Green Lungs' for a vast growing urban environment and become a green model for the rest of the country to follow.

Conclusions

Urban areas are changing rapidly. While this seems inevitable, we must also become more aware of the erosion of community involvement and the creation of a more overtly individualistic society. Using the example of the development and expansion of Galway City, this chapter has attempted to highlight the often poorly planned and designed development that has taken place. What it has also tried to show is that despite the poor history that the city has in terms of community involvement, this is changing. The introduction of the Local Government Act 1996, the creation of such integrated/inclusive bodies as the City Development Boards and the movement towards increased local government and community partnership, holds much hope for the future if both sides can overcome the historical antipathy that has defined their previous encounters. This much-needed progression, with the integration of community involvement in planning, is ably demonstrated in the Terryland Forest Park project. From the outset, the Terryland Forest Steering Committee emphasised the need for all sectors of local society to get involved in making this plan come to fruition. Special emphasis was placed on ensuring the active and consistent participation of schools, youth groups, senior citizens' associations, residents' committees and environmental organisations in a series of high profile tree planting festivals. The result displayed how a spontaneous spirit of individual and communal ownership was created by this newborn togetherness in creating this 'People's Park'. It also demonstrated what can be achieved with community involvement and why it is necessary for communities to play a determining role in shaping the environment in which they live.

References

GCDB (2001) *Galway City Development Board - Draft Strategy for Economic, Social & Cultural Development 2002–2012*, (Unpublished).

Walsh, S. (2001) *Terryland Forest Park*, Galway City Parks Section, (Unpublished).

chapter ten

Developing the Periphery – The State of the West

Patricia O'Hara

Introduction

The establishment of the Western Development Commission (WDC) on a statutory basis in 1999 to promote economic and social development in the seven western counties of Donegal, Sligo, Leitrim, Roscommon, Mayo, Galway and Clare, was part of the wider process of the re-emergence of regional development as a policy issue in the 1990s. As Ireland's newfound prosperity became apparent, it was clear that serious regional disparities persisted, and that addressing them would require significant diversion of resources to the more disadvantaged peripheral regions. The National Development Plan 2000–2006 (NDP) (Department of Finance, 1999) committed the state to 'fostering balanced regional development' as a fundamental objective. It also signalled the preparation of a National Spatial Strategy (NSS) to identify regional gateways to drive development and provide a framework for spatial planning over the next two decades (see also McCafferty, Chapter 4 and Walsh, Chapter 5).

The WDC's remit presents a difficult challenge, but also provides an unprecedented opportunity to seriously engage with the perennial 'problem' of Western development at a time when policy commitment and public resources are available to tackle it. Not surprisingly, much of the WDC's work to date has concentrated on analyses of the development needs of the region and the development of programmes of strategic action or 'blueprints' (see Western Development Commission, 1999a, 1999b, 2000, 2001a). The WDC's first policy document *Blueprint for Success: A Development Plan for the West 2000–2006* (WDC, 1999) contained a wide range of new information on the socio-economic performance of the Western Region and set out an integrated strategy that provided the basis for a radical improvement in economic performance. The NDP incorporated much of the broad strategic thrust of the *Blueprint* report and acknowledged its input to the development of a regional development strategy.

In 2001 the WDC published *The State of the West* (WDC, 2001b) in order, as the name implies, to establish how the West has fared in recent years. In this chapter the findings of this report are drawn on to examine socio-economic conditions in the Western Region; the nature and extent of the infrastructure problems; and the challenges posed by deregulation of the utilities markets. The chapter concludes with a discussion of the implications for development in the region in the light of the NDP and the NSS.

Recent Population and Employment Trends in the Western Region

Population

The Western Region is predominantly rural, having only four towns with populations in excess of 10,000, and a further five with more than 5,000 in 1996. More than 80 per cent of the population live outside of towns of greater than 5,000 population. A century and a half of population decline in the Western counties was finally arrested in the 1990s and the turn of the twenty-first century saw the population increase and its profile become younger. Between 1991 and 2000, the population grew by an estimated 5.2 per cent, and in 2000, 65 per cent of the population in the Western Region was of working age – up three per cent on 1996. Reversal of population decline due to retention and in-migration of population associated with employment growth is, most likely, concentrated in larger towns and their environs (see also Cawley and Mahon, Chapter 11). However, a more complete understanding of population dynamics in the region must await analysis of results from the 2002 Census of Population. One crude indicator of population growth is the trend in planning applications. The number of planning applications in the Western Region increased substantially during the 1990s, at a rate higher than the state average. Applications for domestic dwellings more than trebled between 1993 and 1999. In 1999 the number of new dwelling units for which planning permission was granted in the Western Region was 17,494 – representing 22.8 per cent of permissions in the state. These data are confirmed by the trend in housing completions, which rose by 66.7 per cent over the period 1996 to 2000. This compares with a national increase of 47.7 per cent over the same period. In Leitrim, the number of house completions trebled between 1996 and 2000. These increases probably also reflect the impact of tax incentives for the construction of residential accommodation in the Upper Shannon area. As already noted, it is likely that population growth is associated with the larger towns and their catchments, particularly Galway. However significant economic development elsewhere in the region would have a major impact on stabilising the population in those parts still experiencing decline.

Employment

The Western Region has garnered a relatively small proportion of employment growth in recent years, accounting for just 15.9 per cent of national employment growth in the period 1998–2000. Nearly three quarters (73.4 per cent) of national employment growth over the same period occurred in the Southern and Eastern region. As in other regions, two-thirds of the increase in the West was in female employment. Over 70 per cent of the increase in male jobs was in the construction industry.

Unemployment in the region has fallen considerably, but youth unemployment is still high (see also McGrath, Chapter 13). In 2000, among 15–19 year olds, the female rate was nearly twice the national average. Analysis of new entrants to the labour market in the Western Region reveals that they are disproportionately concentrated in construction work, with a lower than average concentration in white collar occupations.

Five of the seven counties are attracting a very small share of state-supported industrial employment (employment assisted by the IDA, Enterprise Ireland, Shannon Development and Údarás na Gaeltachta). Over the period 1995–2000 the number of assisted jobs in the Western Region increased by 9,649. However, 6,877 of these (71.3 per cent) went to Galway and a further 2,333 to Clare (24.2 per cent), leaving a net gain for the other five counties of just 439 jobs, or less than 5 per cent of the total to the region. These same five counties had a net gain of only 201 jobs over the years 1999–2000. Since 1999, the numbers employed in foreign-owned assisted companies in Ireland have exceeded those in indigenous assisted companies. However, in the Western Region the share of employment in foreign companies has declined consistently, from 22.0 per cent in 1995 to 18.7 per cent in 2000. Jobs in foreign-owned assisted companies are again concentrated in Galway and Clare. Between them, these two counties account for 61 per cent of all such employment in the Western Region.

Job gains are offset by losses and there was a net loss of 300 assisted jobs in manufacturing in six of the seven Western counties between 1999 and 2000. The greatest losses occurred in the 'traditional' industries of food, clothing and textiles. The greatest gains were in electrical and optical equipment, with an increase of 1,434 jobs in the Western Region of which 93 per cent were located in Galway. There was an increase of 1,128 jobs in international services between 1999 and 2000, of which over 40 per cent were located in Galway. The fact that five of the seven counties were losing ground at a time of unprecedented growth and prosperity in Ireland illustrates the magnitude of the challenge of attracting industrial investment to the Western Region. One of the consequences of this is a failure to retain, or to attract, third level graduates to the seven counties (see also McDonagh, Chapter 12).

Loss of human resources

Participation in third level education is particularly high in the Western Region and this is a reflection of the traditionally strong value placed on educational attainment among farm families in the West. However, much of this human capital is being lost through persistent immigration to better jobs outside the region. In 1999, only 6.6 per cent of all new graduates with primary degrees found work in Sligo, Leitrim and Donegal, whereas 60.5 per cent went to work in counties Dublin, Kildare, Meath and Wicklow. In 1998, 37.7 per cent of graduates originating from the Western Region found their first job in Dublin, whereas 18.3 per cent got their first job in Galway and only 15.9 per cent in the remaining six counties combined. The pattern is somewhat different for sub-degree award recipients, more of whom find jobs in their own region. However, there is still a high proportion (43.5 per cent) of all sub-degree award recipients gaining their first employment in the eastern counties.

The net effect of high educational participation and insufficient attractive employment opportunities is a brain drain from West to East whereby much of the human resource potential of the region is lost to other areas with more and better employment opportunities. This leaves a major human resource deficit (see also McDonagh, Chapter 12) and a significant gap in the knowledge infrastructure.

Productive Sectors – Manufacturing and Services

The key productive sectors of manufacturing and services have a weaker structure in the Western Region. There is a relatively high reliance on 'low tech/low value' industries so that wages, salaries and net output are much lower than in the more developed parts of the country, where growth can largely be attributed to 'high tech/high value' firms. In 1998, annual wages and salaries per employee in the seven Western counties averaged 19.503 euro (£15,357), compared to a national average of 22,994 euro (£18,106).

Nationally, net industrial output grew by 14.6 per cent per annum during the period 1991–98; the equivalent figure for the Western Region was just 4.5 per cent. In 1991, the Western Region accounted for 14.6 per cent of all industrial output in the state. By 1998, this had fallen to 7.6 per cent. All counties in the Western Region experienced a decline in their share of net national output between 1991 and 1998. At the same time the Southern and Eastern region increased its share from 69 per cent in 1991 to nearly 81.9 per cent in 1998. Some counties have particularly high sectoral concentrations, notably food and textiles in Donegal and food in Roscommon. Employment forecasts suggest that these sectors will be among the most vulnerable to employment losses in the future. This points to a real need to diversify and develop alternative employment opportunities there.

To date, the West has not attracted its share of higher value added growth sectors such as financial and international services with only 5.5 per cent of all employment in financial services, and just 9.3 per cent in international services. Indeed, Enterprise Ireland has pointed out that, among its client firms in the Border, Midland and West Region, international traded services is the smallest sector and that more than half of the 150 firms it supports in this region are trading out of Galway.

Productive Sectors – Agriculture, Marine and Tourism

Agriculture

Only minorities of farmers in the Western Region are at present generating an adequate income from full-time farming alone, and, even on these farms, incomes lag considerably behind the national average. Given the income prospects, and the alternative opportunities available, fewer farm children will opt for a career in full-time farming. At best, by the end of the decade, a small minority of farm families in the Western Region will generate an adequate income from full-time farming and the remainder will be heavily reliant on off-farm income. The future viability of family farming and of rural areas is therefore heavily dependent on the availability of off-farm employment.

Diversification within farming can provide a viable income on some farms and an important income supplement for those with off-farm jobs. Organic production, horticultural crops, farm forestry and on-farm enterprises are among the options with considerable potential that should be encouraged and facilitated. The WDC's *Blueprint for Organic Agri-Food Production in the West* (WDC, 2001a) contains detailed recommendations on the development of organic production, domestic and overseas market development, expansion of added value processing and development of distribution channels, research and development, education and training and information technology.

The marine sector

The national fisheries industry is concentrated along the western seaboard with approximately 40 per cent of employment located in the Western Region. While the tonnage has decreased, the value of Irish sea fish landings has increased over the last three years. The aquaculture sector is also concentrated along the western seaboard and production has grown significantly in the last decade. Forty three per cent of producers are located in the Western Region. There are further opportunities for expansion of this sector, but marketing and business development are urgently needed. More than half of the employment in the seafood processing industry is located in the Western Region and is concentrated in Donegal.

Tourism

Tourism has the potential to make a greater economic contribution to the West's rural areas but this requires the creation of a driving force for change which can give a clear strategic direction and provide integration of support to deliver it. In *Blueprint for Tourism Development in the West* (WDC, 2000), the WDC sets out a detailed strategic, spatial approach to dispersing tourism development in the Region. The strategy addresses the infrastructure requirements for tourism development in three distinct tourism development zones and sets out how to achieve a more co-ordinated approach to developing, marketing and managing the tourism potential of the Western Region. A particular feature of the approach is that the focus is on enabling local communities and the private sector to develop tourism projects which cover a larger local area and which have greater economies of scale. A Steering Group under the leadership of Bord Fáilte is already in the process of implementing the strategy.

Public Infrastructure

The ESRI report *National Investment Priorities for the Period 2000–2006* (Fitzgerald *et al.*, 1999), together with the National Development Plan 2000–2006 (Department of Finance, 1999) and the *Medium-Term Review 2001–2007* (Duffy *et al.*, 2001) have identified public infrastructure as a major determinant of competitiveness. The priority given to public infrastructure in the National Development Plan recognised that upgrading the level and quality of provision is also one of the keys to tackling regional disparities. The relatively poor performance of the Western Region over the past two years, and the implications of deregulation of the telecommunications and utility markets, underlines the need to give greater priority to infrastructure provision.

Transport infrastructure

As road transport is the predominant means of travel and movement of goods in the region, the quality of road linkages is of crucial importance to trade, investment, tourism and quality of life. Poor quality road infrastructure is consistently mentioned by development agencies and business interests as a major barrier to investment in the region. Poor roads increase operating costs by increasing travel time and transport costs to and from markets. Long travel times can also deter potential investors, senior executives or tourists from travelling to the region and consequently increase its peripherality. Moreover, residents of predominantly rural regions, such as the seven western counties, are more dependent on car transport and travel longer distances for services.

While the roads from Dublin to Sligo (N4), to Galway (N6), to Ennis (N7), Sligo to Letterkenny (N15) and Galway to Shannon (N17/18) are designated as major inter-urban routes and earmarked in the NDP for significant investment, other major primary road routes into and through the Western Region, notably the N2 to the Border and the N5 to Castlebar, are in need of major upgrading. Businesses in the region are constrained by the added cost due to inadequate road quality, especially in the case of the N5, which is the main primary route to the east coast from counties Mayo and Roscommon. There is ample evidence from businesses, and from development agencies, that poor road quality is a major deterrent to investment in the region.

Given the peripherality of the Western Region and the significance of road infrastructure in achieving balanced regional development, it is essential to substantially improve the links between the Western Region and the rest of Ireland and equally within the region in order to:

> facilitate existing and future economic activity;

> ensure speedy and efficient access to the airports;

> improve access to and between towns in the region; and

> improve the coastal routes to support tourism and marine development.

Air access is also very important for both tourism and business expansion in the Western Region. The WDC argues that Shannon and Knock should be designated as priority airports for international access because they are spatially well located and have international standard runway facilities. Consequently, they should be enabled to compete for commercial and tourism business. However, additional demand can only be fully capitalised on when access to airports is improved through upgrading the road network, particularly the N17/N18 routes to Shannon and Knock. It is important to recognise that transport infrastructure investment requires a different rationale in much of the Western Region. Such investment must drive development as well as alleviate congestion.

Energy infrastructure

The Western Region has some significant energy infrastructure problems. Adequate electricity supply is hampered by both generation and transmission weaknesses. Loss of a major generator during the winter peak period would give rise to severe difficulty in maintaining voltage levels in parts of the region (i.e. the West and North–West). While there is a relatively sparse 220kV network in the south and east of Ireland, there is no 220kV transmission link at all west or north of a line from Galway to Carrick on Shannon. The Western Region is served only by long 110kV lines, which in the case of a number of western 110kV stations are not meshed. This means that even one line outage can have a severe impact on system performance.

The electricity transmission system in the Western Region is, therefore, neither reliable nor robust, and there are large parts of the region experiencing low voltage, low capacity and the threat of voltage collapse. There is considerable risk of unplanned outages due to the weaknesses in the transmission system. This has immense implications for investment in the region and effectively precludes much of it from attracting industries that are particularly reliant on quality power supply.

The Western Region has no existing natural gas infrastructure and, until the discovery of the Corrib field, had no real prospect of a generally available gas supply to population centres in the region. Although there is government commitment to ensuring that Corrib gas reaches Ballina and Sligo, the inevitable result of the deregulation of the utilities markets is that the primary focus of profit-driven providers will be to serve only the larger population centres where profits are greatest.

Telecommunications infrastructure

A universally accessible broadband network is a basic requirement for the telecommunications and data transfer needs of modern technologically–sophisticated businesses. Ireland has very good international broadband telecommunications connectivity, but internally provision and competition are very uneven and mainly confined to the larger centres. Broadband access is underdeveloped, with locations outside of larger centres not having access to high capacity services. Rollout of appropriate technologies for widespread access such as Digital Subscriber Line (DSL or xDSL), Wireless Local Loop (WLL) and advanced digital, interactive TV services has been restricted due to the downturn in the telecommunications industry and associated decisions to confine rollout of new services to areas where there is high demand (essentially large urban centres).

The delays in unbundling the local loop (thereby ending the Eircom monopoly) mean that there is, as yet, little competition among providers for Small and Medium Enterprises (SMEs) and residential users. As the deregulation process is evolving, rollout is proceeding in areas with high-density business and residential usage and it is the free market that is largely determining supply and provision. If free market principles continue to determine rollout, then much of the Western Region will have extremely limited provision and capacity. This will hamper the efforts at enticing new investment into the region as well as limiting the development of existing businesses there. Eircom may continue to be a monopolistic provider in the Western Region, so that consumers have no choice of service or price. This will discourage and postpone private investment, which could prove detrimental to the region's ability to participate in e-commerce, thus further widening the gap between East and West.

Without adequate telecommunications, energy and transport infrastructure, the Western Region cannot compete for mobile investment and the growth potential of existing businesses may be hampered. A free market situation associated with deregulation is worsening the Western Region's weak position, as profit-driven investors concentrate on areas of greatest demand.

Developing the Western Region – Some Implications

This brief account of recent trends in the Western Region reveals the limited progress achieved even in a time of record national economic growth and prosperity and unprecedented public support through the National Development Plan. Apart from Galway, and to a lesser extent Clare, the region has been losing ground in recent years. Given the nature and scale of the infrastructure deficit, it is clear that the West's development prospects are dependent on an immediate and sustained attempt to address this shortfall. The provision of adequate access, communications and power in the Western Region is the only basis on which economic and social development can proceed. All other local or centrally driven initiatives to promote production in sectors such as tourism, fisheries, agriculture and industry will have limited success and little long-term impact unless these basic elements of infrastructure are put in place. This requires that public and private investment in infrastructure provision be targeted as effectively and efficiently as possible.

In *The State of the West*, the WDC sets out detailed recommendations for tackling the transport, power and telecommunications deficits and recommends the establishment of two high level working groups to co-ordinate a strategic response to the region's infrastructure problems. In a deregulated 'free' market, only government intervention can redress regional imbalances, and the WDC argues that the actions it proposes can ensure a more regionally centred approach to infrastructure policy planning as well as more acutely addressing the regional implications of the current regulatory, legislative and national planning framework.

In the context of the development of a National Spatial Strategy, it is clear that for the predominantly rural Western Region, a city-led approach to development based on gateways alone is not appropriate. Galway and the Ennis-Shannon axis are doing well, and their continued growth is essential for Western development. However, the challenges facing these centres are fundamentally different from those of less developed areas, and the nature of public support should reflect this. For regions like the West, it is also necessary to target smaller economic focal points for SME investment. Given the right conditions, it is possible to generate significant growth in smaller centres – the current investment 'boom' in Carrick on Shannon (pop. 1,868 in 1996) is a case in point. Moreover, in productive sectors such as tourism, fisheries and specialist agri-food production, smaller centres can become growth hubs and in *The State of the West* the WDC has proposed an 'Invest in the West Programme' aimed at making more locations in the Western Region investment-ready.

Finally, it is important to recognise that locally based development activity constitutes a considerable 'social capital' resource in the Western Region. It can be harnessed productively within the context of a well co-ordinated strategic approach to tackling Western development, particularly in relation to tourism, local infrastructure provision, social inclusion and quality of life.

References

Department of Finance (1999) *The National Development Plan 2000–2006*, Government Publications, Stationery Office, Dublin.

Duffy, D., Fitz Gerald, J., Kearney, I., Hore, J., MacCoille, C. (2001) *Mid-Term Review 2001–2007*, Economic and Social Research Institute, Dublin.

Fitzgerald, J., Kearney, I., Morgenroth, E. and Smyth, D (1999) *National Investment Priorities for the Period 2000–2006*, Policy Research Series Number 33, Economic and Social Research Institute, Dublin.

Western Development Commission (1999a) *Blueprint for Success: A Development Plan for the West*, WDC, Ballaghaderreen.

Western Development Commission (1999b) *Blueprint for Investing in the West: Promoting Foreign Direct Investment in the West*, WDC, Ballaghaderreen.

Western Development Commission (2000) *Blueprint for Tourism development in the West: An Action Plan for Rural Areas*, WDC, Ballaghaderreen.

Western Development Commission (2001a) *Blueprint for Organic Agri-Food Production in the West*, WDC, Ballaghaderreen.

Western Development Commission (2001b) *The State of the West: Recent Trends and Future Prospects*, WDC, Ballaghaderreen.

chapter eleven

GALWAY COUNTY AND CITY 1971–1996:
A DEMOGRAPHIC PERSPECTIVE

Mary Cawley and Marie Mahon

Introduction

This chapter reviews the way in which the distribution of County Galway's urban and rural population has evolved since the early 1970s. By identifying the longer-term trends in population size and distribution, it is hoped to inform more fully initiatives that may potentially arise from the National Spatial Strategy (NSS), and its attempts to achieve more balanced spatial development. The NSS under discussion since January 2000 aims *inter alia* to provide:

> an explicit overall national framework for dealing with spatial issues within a sustainable national economic and budgetary context (Department of the Environment and Local Government, 2001, p.4; see also Walsh, Chapter 5).

As part of this mission, balanced regional development is to be achieved through focused targeting on a small number of stronger urban centres (particularly the five largest cities, including Galway). These 'Gateways' are perceived as having an 'energising' role deriving from their functional links with broader areas and their potential to create a further beneficial critical mass. Medium sized towns (with less than 20,000 population) are viewed as benefiting from the national and international roles of Gateways and in turn:

> relating in a reciprocal way to the smaller towns and rural areas in their own areas of influence (Department of the Environment and Local Government, 2001, p.18).

In the NSS document all of County Galway forms a functional area with Galway City as a Gateway and Ballinasloe and Tuam being the only other named towns (both of which have a population of less than 10,000 people). Galway City was classified as a Municipal Borough until 1985 when the boundary was extended and the status of County Borough was conferred. Since January 2002, it has been designated a city. This change in area has implications for comparison of population change in the city and county between 1981 and 1986. To permit comparison, the Central Statistics Office has revised the 1981 census data to relate to the 1986 boundary area. Thus, in some tables, two sets of data are given for 1986 for Galway City. The area of Athenry, Ballinasloe and Tuam towns was revised in 1991 and revised data are presented from the 1986 census for the 1991 areas to permit comparison.

The choice of the early 1970s is deliberate in that it marked the beginning of a new phase of rapid and sustained growth in the population of the city and its adjoining hinterland (Ó Cearbhaill and Cawley, 1984; Cawley, 1996). The Census of Population for the four census periods 1971–1981, 1981–1986, 1986–1991, and 1991–1996 is the primary source of data used. Four issues are investigated: population growth and decline in Galway county and city; the relative distribution of population between towns more generally and the countryside; local geographical patterns of change at the level of the District Electoral Division (DED) and the city Ward; and the issues arising from the documented trends for strategic spatial planning.

Galway County and City Population Change 1971–1996

The early 1970s were years of marked growth in the Irish economy associated, in part, with the success of a policy of attracting overseas investment in manufacturing industry, through cash grants and tax incentives, and also influenced by broader economic trends in Ireland and in the wider European economy (Haughton, 2000). From approximately 1975 on, international recession contributed to the closure of old established, less competitive, industries and it became more difficult to attract internationally mobile investment (O'Farrell and Crouchley, 1983). Decline in agricultural employment accelerated following Ireland's accession to the then European Economic Community (EEC) in 1973, as restructuring and capitalisation took place (Matthews, 2000). The recency of much of its manufacturing base cushioned the West Region from the severe losses of employment experienced in the Dublin and East Regions (O'Farrell and Crouchley, 1983). The presence of a Gaeltacht in County Galway meant also that additional investment was available in the west of the county. The numbers employed in manufacturing industry increased by some 62 per cent in both county and city between 1973 and 1981 (Ó Cearbhaill and Cawley, 1984). Service sector employment grew by 42 per cent in the county and 67 per cent in the city, associated in part with industrial growth but also with the regionalisation of state agencies and the expansion of third level educational provision at the then University College Galway (now National University of Ireland, Galway) and at the new Regional Technical College (now Galway Mayo Institute of Technology).

Marked national population growth occurred between 1971 and 1979 in which Galway county and city took part to a greater extent than other western counties (Cawley, 1992). This was also a phase when the rates of population growth in the county began to lag behind those in the city, a circumstance that had implications for the relative distribution of population between the two areas (Table 11.1).

Table 11.1 County Galway and Galway City: population and annual % change 1971–1996

	Population (000)				
	1971	1981a (b)	1986	1991	1996
County	121.5	134.2 (128.8)	131.5	129.5	131.6
City	27.7	37.8 (43.2)	47.1	50.8	57.2
	% annual change				
	1971–'81	1981–'86*	1986–'91		1991–'96
County Galway	1.0	0.4	−0.3		0.3
Galway City	3.7	1.8	1.6		2.52
STATE	**1.56**	**0.56**	**−0.1**		**0.56**

Source: Central Statistics Office, *Volume 1*, Various years.
a 1981 boundary; b 1986 boundary; * 1986 boundary

Net inmigration and reduced outmigration together with a relatively high, although falling birth rate, were the main factors contributing to growth (Table 11.2). Net migration refers to the difference between the number of inmigrants and outmigrants over a census period. It is a net figure calculated by the Central Statistics Office when the effects of births and deaths on population numbers over a census period have been taken into account. The birth and death rates given here are crude rates calculated as the average number of births and deaths per 1000 average population over a census period.

Table 11.2 County Galway and Galway City. Births, deaths and net migration: annual average rates per 1000 of the average population for census years 1971–1996

	1971–81	1981–86	1986–91		1991–96	
	County*	County*	County excl City	City	County excl City	City
Births	21.1	19.0	16.8	13.0	14.0	13.3
Deaths	10.8	9.9	10.8	5.4	10.6	5.3
Net Migration	3.9	–1.7	–9.0	7.7	–0.2	15.6
State^	21.6	19.1	15 7		14	

Source: Central Statistics Office, *Volume 1*, various years; *Volume 4, 1997a.*
* CB Figures are non-applicable for periods of 1971–81 and 1981–86
^ crude birth rate per 1000

One-year change of residence, if any, over the previous year is recorded at each census and whilst limited in temporal coverage provides a useful perspective on trends. The early 1970s migration data indicate that limited inmigration took place from other counties in Ireland and from overseas and that more than 50 per cent of those returning were Irish born, attracted by the improved employment opportunities available (Table 11.3).

Table 11.3 County Galway and Galway City: one year migration, 1970–71, 1980–81, 1985–86, 1990–91, 1995–96 (as % of total population)

	70–71	80–81	85–86	85–85	90–91	90–91	95–96	95–96
	Co.	Co.	Co.	City	Co.	City	Co.	City
SA	96.3	93.6	96.6	84.2	96.5	83.94	95.4	81.0
Mig	5344	10629	4339	7308	4428	7943	5892	10586
SC	1.7	3.9	1.9	8.6	1.4	7.6	2.1	8.8
OC	1.1	1.6	1.1	6.2	1.1	6.1	1.5	7.3
FOS	0.9	0.8	0.4	0.9	0.9	2.3	0.9	2.9
IB	56.4	43.0	53.7	44.6	60.9	54.6	50.6	36.8

SA - Same address; **Mig** - Migrants (number); **SC** - Same county;
OC - Other county; **FOS** - From outside state; **IB** - Irish born as % of those who moved from outside the state.
Source: Central Statistics Office, *Volume 11, 1978; Volume 9, 1986a; Volume 8, 1993c, 1996; Volume 4, 1997c.*

By the late 1970s, net outmigration and growing unemployment were re-established at a national level and the 1980s were characterised by recurrent phases of recession and recovery (Cawley, 1992; Haughton, 2000). Unemployment exceeded 15.5 per cent between 1982 and 1989 and outmigration accelerated during the second half of the decade, as successive governments pursued a policy of strict control of public expenditure in order to control inflation and prepare for membership of European Monetary

Union (O'Hagan, 1995). County Galway and Galway City were again less affected by recession in the 1980s than older industrial locations and the numbers at work in both areas increased during the second half of the 1980s, with losses in agricultural and related employment being compensated by growth in manufacturing and services (Table 11.4).

Population growth moderated in County Galway during the first half of the 1980s but the city's rate of growth was three times that of the state average (Table 11.2). Birth rates fell during these years, as did death rates, and net outmigration took place from the county (i.e. more people left the county than entered it over the five years) (Table 11.2). Population movement increased both within the county and from other counties; overseas inmigration declined as a proportion of the total as did the component of Irish born returning, reflecting the weakening economy (Table 11.3).

Table 11.4 Galway County and City: % change in labour force by broad industrial groups, 1981–1996 and % at work by group in 1996

	% change in labour force					% at work by broad industrial group, 1996	
	1981–86	1986–91		1991–96			
	County	County ex. City	City	County ex City	City	County ex. City	City
AFF	–10.4	–13.7	–4.9	–18.1	–9.3	22.0	1.2
IND	–2.0	4.9	7.4	19.0	17.0	26.6	23.0
SER	9.1	18.0	15.8	24.9	28.0	51.4	75.8
TTL	55388	58816	17295	67497	21613		

AFF - Agriculture, Forestry, Fishing; **IND** - Industry (including mining, manufacturing, electricity, gas, water, building and construction; **SER** - Services and not stated; **TTL** - Total number at work in terminal census year.
Source: Central Statistics Office, *Volume 4*, 1985, 1995; *Volume 6*, 1993b; *Volume 5*, 1998.

Low population decline took place at a national level between 1986 and 1991 (Table 11.1). Loss occurred also in County Galway (of –0.3 per cent per annum) but growth in the city continued almost at the rate registered during the first half of the decade. Birth rates continued to fall and a marked disparity in death rates emerged between the county and city which reflected the increasing imbalance in the age structure in the two areas (County Galway's population was ageing whilst the city's population was becoming more youthful; deaths per 1000 in the former area therefore translated into a higher rate than in the latter) (Table 11.2). The net migration trends were equally imbalanced (the county experienced annual net outmigration of 9.0/1000 whilst the city recorded net inmigration of 7.7/1,000) (Table 11.2). People who moved to the city over the year 1985–86 came predominantly from County Galway and from other counties in Ireland. Out-of-state migrants and those of Irish birth fell as a proportion of those moving to the county but increased slightly among those moving to the city (Table 11.3).

The economic stringency of the 1980s laid the basis for economic recovery and, with the benefit of increased Structural Funding from the European Union (EU) from the late 1980s on, annual growth of GDP per capita accelerated (from an average of 4.8 per cent between 1987 and 1993 to 9.2 per cent between 1994 and 1998) (OECD, 1999). Growth in manufacturing and service employment also accelerated in Galway county and city between 1991 and 1996, although the city experienced a significant loss of employment in 1992–93 through the downsizing of the Digital computer assembly plant, as part of the international restructuring of the company (see Grimes, Chapter, 14). Data provided by Galway Chamber of Commerce (GCC) indicate that manufacturing employment continued to grow strongly in the city in the late 1990s, by 11 per cent between 1997 and 1998 (from 7923 to 8816 persons) (GCC, 1999). The corresponding increase for the county was 5 per cent (from 7075 to 7399 persons). Service sector employment also grew and tourism made an important contribution to this growth (GCC, 1999).

During the first half of the 1990s, national population growth became re-established at the levels registered during the first half of the 1980s (Table 11.1). Galway county and city took part in this recovery and notably the latter where annual population growth reached 2.52 per cent. The county continued to experience low net outmigration whilst the city registered high net inmigration (Table 11.2). County Galway and other counties in Ireland remained the main sources of migrants. Overseas migrants increased as a proportion of those moving to the city in particular, as did the proportion of foreign-born nationals (Table 11.3).

Town and Rural Change

Approximately 40 per cent of the population of County Galway (including the city) was classified as living in 'aggregate town' areas in 1996 (CSO, 1997a) (the 'aggregate town' population is the population residing in settlements of 1500 or over; the 'aggregate rural' population is that proportion residing outside such settlements). The town population is further sub-divided into

Galway City, other towns with a population of 1500 or over, and towns with a population of less than 1500 (which include very small settlements with at least 50 inhabited houses). Rural areas account for the remainder. According to this definition, Galway City has increased its share of the total population of the county over the past 30 years, and towns with 1500 population or over (Ballinasloe, Tuam, Loughrea and, since 1986 when its population exceeded 1500 for the first time, Athenry) increased their share slightly until 1986 but have experienced a relative loss since then (Table 11.5). Some of the growth associated with these towns has probably taken place in rural areas outside their defined boundaries (Figure 11.1a and Figure 11.1c). Nevertheless, all have experienced decline at some time since 1971 and growth has been weak (Table 11.6). Fluctuations have also taken place in manufacturing employment in the towns, although service sector employment has grown continuously (CSO, 1975, 1985, 1993b, 1995, 1998).

Table 11.5 County Galway: shares of total population by type of area, 1971–1996

	% of total population						
Area	1971	1981	1981 *	1986	1986 ^	1991	1996
Galway City	19.1	24.3	25.1	26.4	26.4	28.2	30.3
Towns >1500	8.2	9.3	9.3	9.6	9.6	9.0	8.7
Towns <1500	6.5	6.6	6.1	6.0	6.3	6.1	6.2
Rural areas	64.1	59.8	58.6	57.9	57.6	56.7	54.8
Total pop. (000s)	149.2	172.0		178.6	178.6	180.4	188.8

Source: Central Statistics Office, *Volume 1*, various years.
*1981 data for 1986 boundaries; ^1986 data for 1991 boundaries.

Birth and death rates are not available in published form at the level of individual towns. One-year migration data are available and show that a limited amount of inmigration has taken place to the four towns. The data for 1995–96 are presented for illustrative purposes (Table 11.6). A considerable amount of movement takes place from elsewhere in County Galway accounting, for example, for more than 40 per cent of migrants to Loughrea and Athenry in 1995–96. Movement from other counties in Ireland and from outside the state occurs also. Whilst not growing to any appreciable extent, the composition of the population of these towns is not static.

Table 11.6 Galway County, Galway City and towns with 1,500 population and over: migration 1995–96 by source (%)

	Galway City	Towns >1500 population			
		Ballinasloe	Tuam	Loughrea	Athenry
	Annual average % change in population				
1971–1981	27.7*	0.8	2.2	1.0	
1981–1986	43.2	–0.8	–0.2	–0.1	0.7
1986–1991	47.1	–1.1	–1.8	–0.5	–0.7
1991–1996	50.8	–0.6	0.3	0.4	0.02
Town pop. 1996	57241	5892	5627	3335	1614
	One-year migration 1995–96 (%)				
Resident at same address	81.0	92.0	92.1	89.3	92.1
N who moved and source	10586	435	414	356	128
Same town	46.4	40.9	48.3	33.1	22.7
Same county	10.5	22.5	23.7	41.6	49.2
Other county	27.7	26.9	10.6	14.6	14.8
From outside state	15.3	9.7	17.4	10.7	13.3

Sources: Central Statistics Office, as Tables 11.4 and 11.5.
*Population of former Municipal Borough

Settlements with less than 1500 population registered relative growth during the 1970s but accounted for a more or less similar share of the total population between 1986 and 1996 (Table 11.5). Some of the smaller census towns, with a population of less than 500 and at least 50 inhabited dwellings such as dormitory settlements like Oranmore, Moycullen and Cloonboo gained population between 1991 and 1996. Substantial dormitory housing development has taken place during the past five years in Claregalway and Clarinbridge, which did not qualify as census towns in 1996. The rural areas of the county have recorded continuous decline in population over time. However, it must be remembered that these areas are being depleted continuously as urban expansion takes place, particularly in the environs of the city.

Local Geographies of Population Change

There are 216 District Electoral Divisions (DEDs) in the county and 22 City Wards. Study of population change for these areas provides a good understanding of localised patterns of change. The patterns for the census periods between 1971 and 1991 have been documented previously (Cawley, 1996); the focus here is on the years 1991–1996 and on identifying the distribution of continuous growth and decline over the four census periods. A number of clearly defined spatial patterns emerged in County Galway during the 1970s. Growth took place along the main access routes to the city and in the environs of most other towns and villages. At a distance from towns, in areas with a weak agricultural structure, the population declined; most notably, north-west of the city between Oughterard and Clifden, in the environs of Dunmore and Glenamaddy in the north east and on Slieve Aughty in the south of the county. During the 1980s growth took place west of Oughterard, indicative of the emergence of longer distance commuting. In the first half of the 1990s, the areas of growth corresponded in broad outline with those established in earlier years (Figure 11.1a). However, 46 per cent of the DEDs in the county registered population decline, including districts in the more prosperous agricultural areas between the towns of Tuam and Ballinasloe, which had recorded growth in the 1980s. This points to the increased difficulty that such areas experience in retaining young people (see McDonagh, Chapter 12 and McGrath, Chapter 13). Some rural DEDs contain populations of less than 100 persons. For this reason, minor numerical changes can produce fluctuations between growth and decline between census periods that cannot always be interpreted easily. A longer time perspective provides a more reliable indicator of areas of growth and decline; and it is therefore instructive to study DEDs which experienced either continuous inter-censal increase or decrease from 1971–1996 (Figure 11.1b). The association of continuous growth with the hinterland of Galway City is apparent, although a number of DEDs departed from the general pattern – Killannin, Spiddal, Slieveaneena and Furbogh along the coast, and Carrowbrowne and Galway Rural, east of the city, the latter two of which lost territory and population when the boundary was extended in 1985. Other DEDs which registered continuous growth either contained, or were adjacent to, the settlements of Ballinasloe, Clifden, Loughrea, Monivea, Mountbellew and Tuam. The DEDs that recorded continuous decline between 1971 and 1996 occupied peripheral positions at a distance from large towns (in either County Galway or adjoining counties) and land quality was generally poor, thereby limiting income from farming. Some of these districts are among those eligible for special developmental assistance in the *CLÁR* (Ceantar Leaga Árd-Riachtanais – Weak Areas of Special Need) initiative introduced in 2001 by the Minister of State for Rural Development (Judge, 2001).

Change in Galway City

The dominant trend in population change within the city became established during the 1970s and involved a redistribution of population from the older inner city areas to the newer residential suburbs (Ó Cearbhaill and Cawley, 1984). This general pattern has persisted over time with some exceptions. In the most recent census period (1991–1996), high rates of growth took place in the suburban wards and notably in Ballybrit and Barna where total growth of 90.7 per cent and 57.9 per cent, respectively, was recorded (Table 11.1). A turnaround from decline to growth took place in the inner city ward of Eyre Square in the late 1980s where townhouse and apartment development was stimulated by the government's 1986 Inner City Renewal Scheme. A number of both inner and outer city wards registered decline between 1986 and 1996, through ageing of the population in the Claddagh and Lough Atalia and through the outmigration of young adults from parts of Newcastle and Mervue, where major residential expansion had occurred during the 1970s (CSO, 1997b). Slow growth and decline in city wards means that some scope exists for accommodating population growth in these areas in the future. Nevertheless planning for residential development outside the borough boundary, for a commuting population, was of major concern in the Galway Transportation and Planning Study (GTPS) (Buchanan and Partners, 1999).

A Perspective on a Future Spatial Strategy for Galway City and County

The intensive commuting hinterland of the city, which became established during the 1970s, coincides with the 'inner rural' area (comprising Galway Rural District) classified in the recent GTPS, where growth of 36 per cent is forecast between 1996 and 2016 (from 26,968 to 36,750 persons) (Buchanan and Partners, 1999). The 'outer rural' area, defined in that study, comprises the Rural Districts of Gort, Loughrea, part of Oughterard and Tuam where population growth of 6.8 per cent is forecast (from 42,738 to 45,643). For reasons associated with the costs of providing road, water and sewerage infrastructure, the GTPS favours expansion between Merlin Park and Oranmore in an area designated 'the Ardaun corridor'. Continued development is envisaged elsewhere within the 'inner rural area', particularly in the environs of villages which have been designated for growth already.

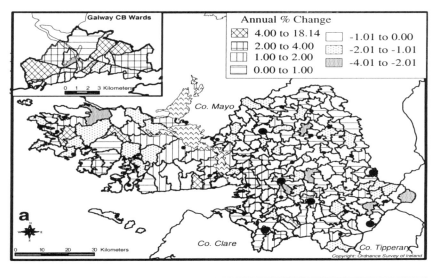

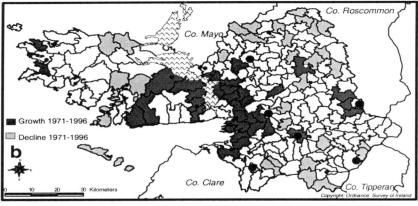

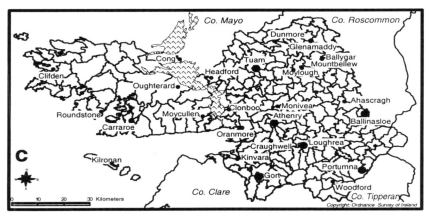

Key for Page 159

Figure 11.1a shows annual % population change 1991–1996
Figure 11.1b shows continuous growth and decline 1971–1996
Figure 11.1c shows the towns in County Galway

'Satellite villages' include Barna, Claregalway, Moycullen, Oranmore, Oughterard and Spiddal, for which specific land use plans were compiled, in the 1970s, as a possible means of relieving pressure on housing, transport and associated infrastructure within the city. It was hoped also that through the adequate development of schools, shops and other basic services and amenities there would be some reduction in the commuter traffic to the city. Another feature of these satellite villages was that a buffer zone (Area of Special Development Control) would be created between them and Galway City; in effect, the retention of a green belt primarily for agricultural use, on which other categories of development would in principle be prohibited. The exception to this was, and continues to be, the provision of housing, under strict conditions, for indigenous farm families, or the replacement of existing substandard dwellings.

The population of the originally rural satellite villages has grown continuously since the 1970s. The population of Oranmore in 1996 (1410 persons), for example, far exceeded that of Clifden which is designated a scheduled town (920 persons in 1996). Reference to the village Land Use Plans indicates that they are essentially residential and local service locations although they have the same classification as urban centres in terms of zoned areas and permitted development densities. Barna and Claregalway have no industrial zone, and industrial zones are relatively undeveloped within Moycullen, Oughterard and Spiddal. Even within Oranmore, which has the largest industrial zone, the level of development in terms of density is low. Commercial uses are mainly concentrated in the village centres, and consist of local shops, pubs and other retail and basic service outlets. The envisaged ongoing development of certain of these villages as primarily residential locations is illustrated in the provisions of the County Galway Housing Strategy (CGHS), 2001–2006 (Galway County Council, 2001) and the Council's estimates of the yet undeveloped residentially zoned land (Table 11.7).

Table 11.7 Estimates of zoned land (ha) in satellite villages of County Galway (April 2001)

Village	Zoned Land	Residentially Zoned Land	Undeveloped Residentially Zoned Land
Barna	619.00	168.00	80.29
Claregalway	151.89	66.13	46.45
Moycullen	239.00	66.36	43.33
Oranmore	657.00	294.00	191.00
Oughterard	–	21.00	–
Spiddal	–	109.00	–

Source: Galway County Council, 2001.

The other locations referred to as having undeveloped residential zones are Athenry (82.73 ha), Clifden (24 ha), Gort (65.7 ha), Loughrea (74.41 ha), and Tuam (166.76 ha). (Ballinasloe has a separate plan). The CGHS report suggests that if this total bank of undeveloped residentially zoned land within the county was developed at a hypothetical density of 15 units per hectare, this would be sufficient to cater for estimated population growth for the period up to 2006. However, this presupposes that population will choose to settle across all of these locations in response to such availability, and it is already apparent that this is not the emergent trend and is unlikely to be so unless adequate local employment opportunities are provided. The report also projects (based on a model developed for the NSS) that the number of households in the county will increase from 44,272 in 2001 to 51,034 in 2006, while the average household size will drop from 3.15 to 2.95. The current maximum housing density generally applied in fully-serviced zoned areas is 25 units per hectare. In 1999, the DoELG issued Residential Density Guidelines for Planning Authorities that made recommendations for increased densities, where feasible, up to a level of 35–50 dwellings per hectare. At densities of this level, an issue for the future is whether the satellite villages will be able to retain aspects of their 'rural' character and identity which essentially preserves the distinction between a separate rural settlement and a suburb of Galway City.

Smaller villages at a distance from centres of employment are less likely to attract or retain a young working population. In areas of open countryside, where farm family members may build homes, the number of such families is unlikely to be of sufficient density to support basic retail and other services. Dependence on towns for such services will therefore continue and, as illustrated in a study commissioned by Area Development Management (Farrell Grant Sparks, 2000), those without adequate public or private transport provision to access basic services will continue to be at a relative disadvantage compared with their counterparts in towns and villages.

Discussion and Conclusions

During the 1970s, Galway City experienced a period of rapid and numerically significant employment growth stimulated by external investment and state regionalisation policy that provided a base for longer term increases in population fuelled by natural increase and by inmigration. The critical mass of employment, skilled labour, expertise and services established in the city enhanced its primacy, and the traditional market towns have barely succeeded in maintaining their shares of the county's population. Remote rural areas have experienced continuous decline. Ex-urban residential expansion into the immediate hinterland of the city accelerated during the 1970s to the extent that the extension of the city boundary became necessary in 1985. Ribbonisation along the main access routes has been a feature of residential development in the countryside since the 1970s. Elements of a key settlement policy were present from an early stage but higher density estate type development was limited in extent until recently. As part of ex-urban expansion, former villages in the 'inner rural' area, identified in the GTPS, have developed as sizable dormitory settlements.

Much emphasis is placed on ex-urban expansion currently. However, other issues require specific attention from a range of state agencies, in parallel with physical planning by the local authorities, if balanced development is to be achieved. The employment base of the market towns needs to be expanded to form local 'hubs'. The service deficits in the more rural peripheral areas of continuous population loss should be met in part at least through the CLÁR initiative. There are also interstitial, primarily agricultural, areas where the population fluctuates between growth and decline and where residents incur additional expense and inconvenience in accessing basic services. It is clear that the distribution of employment opportunities and service provision need to be linked more effectively to physical planning than has hitherto been the case. Herein lies one of the main challenges for the NSS in providing for the future development of Galway County and City.

Acknowledgements

Thanks are offered to Dr. Siubhán Comer, Department of Geography, NUI, Galway and Colm McLoughlin for assistance in preparing Figure 11.1. The digitised map base is used with the permission of the Ordnance Survey of Ireland to whom the copyright belongs.

References

Buchanan, C. and Partners (1999) *Galway Transportation and Planning Study, Recommended Strategy*, Galway Corporation and Galway County Council, Galway.

Cawley, M. (1992) 'Population change in the Republic of Ireland 1981–1986', *Area*, 22, pp.67–74.

Cawley, M. (1996) 'Trends in population and settlement in County Galway 1971–1991', in Moran, G. and Gillespie, R. (eds.) *Galway, History and Society*, Geography Publications, Dublin, pp. 681–702.

Central Statistics Office (1975) *Volume 5, Occupations and Industries*, Government Publications, Dublin.

Central Statistics Office (1978) *Census of Population of Ireland, 1981, Volume 11, Usual Residence and Migration, Birthplaces*, Government Publications, Dublin.

Central Statistics Office (1982) *Census of Population of Ireland, 1981, Volume 1*, Government Publications, Dublin.

Central Statistics Office (1985) *Volume 4, Principal Economic Status and Industries*, Government Publications, Dublin.

Central Statistics Office (1986a) *Census of Population of Ireland 1981, Volume 9, Usual Residence and Migration, Birthplaces*, Government Publications, Dublin.

Central Statistics Office (1986b) *Census 96, Volume 4, Usual Residence and Migration, Birthplaces*, Government Publications, Dublin.

Central Statistics Office (1988) *Census 86, Volume 1, Population Classified by Area*, Government Publications, Dublin.

Central Statistics Office (1993a) *Census 91, Volume 1, Population Classified by Area*, Government Publications, Dublin.

Central Statistics Office (1993b) *Census 91, Volume 6, Principal Economic Status and Industries*, Government Publications, Dublin.

Central Statistics Office (1993c) *Census 86, Volume 8, Usual Residence and Migration, Birthplaces*, Government Publications, Dublin.

Central Statistics Office (1995) *Volume 4, Principal Economic Status and Industries*, Government Publications, Dublin.

Central Statistics Office (1996) *Census 91, Volume 8, Usual Residence and Migration, Birthplaces*, Government Publications, Dublin.

Central Statistics Office (1997a) *Census 96, Volume 1, Population Classified by Area*, Government Publications, Dublin.

Central Statistics Office (1997b) *Census 96, Volume 2, Ages and Marital Status*, Government Publications, Dublin.

Central Statistics Office (1997c) *Census 96, Volume 4, Usual Residence and Migration, Birthplaces*, Government Publications, Dublin.

Central Statistics Office (1998) *Census 96, Volume 5, Principal Economic Status and Industries*, Government Publications, Dublin.

Department of the Environment and Local Government (2001) *The National Spatial Strategy: Indications for the Way Ahead*, DoELG, Dublin.

Farrell, Grant, Sparks (2000) *Rural Transport: a national study from a community perspective*, Commissioned by Area Development Management, Farrell Grant Sparks, Dublin.

Galway Chamber of Commerce (1999) *Economic Development Review 1999*, Galway Chamber of Commerce, Galway.

Galway County Council (2001) *Galway Housing Strategy 2000–2006*, Galway County Council, Galway.

Haughton, J. (2000) 'The historical background', in O'Hagan, J.W. (ed.) *The Economy of Ireland, policy and performance of a European Region*, Gill and Macmillan, Dublin, pp.2–49.

Judge, T. (2001) '£20m project unveiled for 16 depopulated areas', *The Irish Times*, 6 October, p.3.

Matthews, A. (2000) 'Agriculture, food safety and rural development', in O'Hagan, J.W. (ed.) *The Economy of Ireland, policy and performance of a European Region*, Gill and Macmillan, Dublin, pp.232–59.

Ó Cearbhaill, D. and Cawley, M. (1984) 'Galway City, a changing regional capital: employment and population since 1966', in Ó Cearbhaill, D. (ed.) *Galway Town and Gown 1484–1984*, Gill and Macmillan, Dublin, pp.258–82.

O'Farrell, P.N. and Crouchley, R. (1983) 'Industrial closures in Ireland 1973–1981', *Regional Studies*, 17, pp.411–29.

O'Hagan, J.W. (ed.) (1995, 1st edition) *The Economy of Ireland, policy and performance of a European Region*, Gill and Macmillan, pp.228–264.

OECD (1999) *OECD Economic Surveys: Ireland*. OECD Paris.

chapter twelve

PERIPHERAL LOCATION, HUMAN RESOURCE DEFICITS AND
SUSTAINABLE RURAL COMMUNITIES

John McDonagh

Introduction

The sustainability of the Irish rural economy and community is intrinsically linked to a mix of occupations, services and infrastructure. The relentless decline of employment in agriculture and other traditional rural industries however, has increased the motivation of government and community to identify or create new sources of employment for those living in rural areas (see for example North and Smallborne, 1996). Indeed rural development policy in Ireland has, it could be argued, largely concerned itself with demographic issues, unemployment, underemployment and access to resources (McDonagh, 2001). Within this milieu, an important question often overlooked concerns the part geographic location plays in determining the survival or sustainability of rural communities. There is an inevitable link between remote rural areas and their inability to attract people, industries, tourists and skilled personnel. It can also be argued, that there is increased emphasis being placed on positioning in the structure of opportunity rather than in geographical location (see Mernagh and Commins, 1997). So what part does peripheral location play, how is this linked to human resource deficits and what implications is this likely to have for the future sustainability of rural communities? These are the main questions on which this chapter will concentrate. Using case study evidence, the argument here is that there is now greater importance on the functionality of rural areas (in the provision of services, schools, entertainment, access etc.) and this functionality will be crucial in ensuring the future sustainability of rural communities in Ireland. This chapter argues that the aim of rural development should not only relate to issues of geographic location and job creation, but also to the attraction and retention of human resources to rural areas. The probability of this occurring will be a determining factor in the future sustainability of rural Ireland. To explore this likelihood further the main components on which this chapter draws are the operation of the labour market in rural areas, the human resource deficit experienced in rural areas and case study evidence based on two geographically different towns in County Galway.

The Contextual Setting

In terms of sustainability, the European Commission in its seminal paper, *The Future of Rural Society* (1988) laid down a sound strategic policy thrust for the sustainable development of rural areas. The delivery of sustainable development however, ultimately depends on the capacity of human resources in the rural areas concerned. Any limitations with respect to human resources are likely to adversely affect the competitiveness of rural areas and stunt the full exploitation of local potentials to the detriment of the quality of life and the sustainability of rural communities. The deployment of new production technologies, increased productivity and large labour surpluses has lead to out-migration and population decline becoming common features of rural areas in all developed countries. Against this background the creation of new employment opportunities in rural areas has become a major focus of rural policy initiatives.

In European social policy a key emphasis is on employability and maximising labour resources through early and systematic intervention programmes to provide unemployed people with the necessary skills to improve their employability. The Amsterdam Treaty is a case in point as it includes an employment chapter relating to the condition of Member States' employment policies. For this purpose the European Commission draws up annual guidelines and the National Development Plans, prepared by each Member State, must take account of these guidelines. The Guidelines agreed for 1999 at the Vienna European Council in December 1998 included such things as improving employability through improving youth unemployment and preventing long-term unemployment; encouraging a partnership approach; easing the transition from school to work and, promoting a labour market open to all. The development of entrepreneurship was also promoted through making it easier to start up and run businesses; helping companies exploit new opportunities for job creation and making the taxation system more employment friendly. Other important guidelines encouraged adaptability of businesses and their employees through modernising work organisation and supporting adaptability in enterprises; strengthening equal opportunity policies for women and men through a gender mainstreaming approach; reconciling work and family life and, facilitating reintegration into the labour market. The European Commission's White Paper on Education and Training, *Teaching and Learning: Towards the Learning Society*, also identified three factors of upheaval in modern European Society namely:

> the internationalisation of trade, the dawning of the information society and the relentless march of science and technology (1995, p.5),

all of which emphasise the challenge of providing skills, ensuring employability and, promoting economic growth in rural areas. In Ireland, employment policy (particularly that of the Industrial Development Authority (IDA)) has predominantly focused on creating jobs and encouraging multi-national investment. This policy has to a large extent been successful in dealing with chronic unemployment rates. This policy has, however, failed to reproduce and/or retain the range of skills, professions and services needed in rural areas and thereby has contributed to the decline of rural areas and to the human resource deficit which now exists. Indeed McGreil (1999) has argued that this 'laissez faire' policy has consolidated the growth of strong population centres while simultaneously undermining vulnerable rural areas. An attempt to counteract this is the example of the *National Employment Plan for Ireland* (Department of Enterprise, Trade and Employment, 1998) that includes policies and actions to promote a framework for lifelong learning which encourages individuals to access quality education and training on an ongoing basis and enterprises to invest in human resource development, to meet new and rapidly changing needs. These are just a sample of the policies currently being pursued. They do however indicate that rural societies are continually being challenged. The emergence of new needs, the reduced influence of agriculture and the development of a range of technologies in the areas of communication and transportation are all explicitly linked with development, employment opportunities and people's residential choices.

What are the implications?

In the Department of Education's Green Paper (1998) it was suggested that:

the well-educated and flexible workforce which has been a central part of Ireland's current economic growth is itself a wasting asset, unless renewed on an ongoing basis through a continuous drive to upgrade and re-skill.

An OECD report published in 1995, emphasised the intrinsic link between job creation and the enhancement of human resources and that:

> from a social standpoint, rural areas face a dual problem: how to ensure at least some minimum standard of living and associated employment prospects so that the younger segment of the population in particular can be retrained and, how to create conditions that will attract outside people seeking a social life of high quality (OECD, 1995 p.28).

As such the human resource skills deficit has implications at a number of levels from local to national, with obvious implications for education and training both at policy and implementation levels. Finnegan (1994) recognised this in relation to the difficulties faced by rural communities, and suggested that in Ireland the young graduates between the ages of 18–25 were highly mobile and, as a result, were unlikely to contribute to their native community in the short-term. It is for this reason that the:

> approach to enhancing human resources – much more in rural areas – must take a broad view of human resources that encompasses job conditions and life style considerations for the individual and family unit (OECD, 1995, p.28).

According to Ireland's *Employment Action Plan* (Department of Enterprise, Trade and Employment, 1998), 'evidence has already emerged of potential labour/skills bottlenecks in particular fields'. In 1998 the Irish government established a partnership to develop national strategies to tackle the issue of skill deficits, future needs and education and training for business. The issue of labour shortages was also acknowledged in the *Green Paper for Adult Education* as 'a persisting problem (with) serious mismatches between the available skill pool and the demand'. A 1996 Forfás Study showed that 30 per cent of companies saw skill deficiencies as a problem and 60 per cent saw a need for increasing skill levels in technology, quality and customer service. The issue of skills shortages also featured prominently in the 1998 IBEC survey of labour and skills in the services sector. Two-thirds of organisations stated that the main reason they had problems filling vacancies was the shortage of applicants with the right practical skills. Just under half of the participants (47 per cent) stated that they had difficulties retaining existing staff. The *White Paper on Human Resource Development* (Department of Enterprise, Trade and Employment, 1997) also identified a skills gap in the areas of job specific skills; management skills; general flexibility and communication skills. Increasingly coming to the fore also was what O'Sullivan (1999) described as a 'new and critical problem (of) increasing evidence of labour supply shortages'. In fact the SFA National Employment Survey of 1999 showed that of the 57 per cent of companies recruiting at that time, 97 per cent of those companies indicated recruitment difficulties. These difficulties were cross-sectoral – services 100 per cent; manufacturing 94 per cent; distribution 100 per cent and retail 88 per cent. Companies also reported that recruitment difficulties were due to one or a combination of the following factors (Table 12.1)

Table 12.1 National Employment Survey, 1999 (SFA, 1999)

	1999	1998
Lack of Skills	68%	50%
Attitude to Work	06%	14%
Better off on Social Welfare	26%	36%

While these figures do not contain a spatial breakdown, in comparing the 1999 and 1998 survey results, the *Lack of Skills* seems to be the fastest growing barrier to recruiting employers.

The Argument!

The economy of the West of Ireland is not unique. This region, like many other peripheral rural areas, faces a number of well-documented problems. These include lack of employment opportunities, unemployment, low incomes, poverty, inadequate levels of amenity and service provision, and geographic peripherality (see McDonagh, Chapter 7) to name but a few (for a more comprehensive view see NESC, 1994). The interrelationship between many of these problems is often overlooked however. For example, an area with poor service provision generally experiences population outmigration. The lack of adequate infrastructure in the Western Region has been shown to be a limiting factor in the amount and type of development that has taken place particularly in those areas away from the economic centres such as Galway city (see O'Hara, Chapter 10; McGrath, Chapter 13; Western Development Commission, 2001). Indeed one of the current challenges facing the Irish government is determining which areas will receive investment to develop their local economy and infrastructure through the National Spatial Strategy (NSS) (see McCafferty, Chapter 4 and Walsh, Chapter 5). This will have a major impact in attracting and retaining suitably skilled personnel to different areas and indeed will have far reaching consequences for many rural towns and villages. The issue of retaining and attracting suitably qualified personnel to rural areas holds the key to the long-term sustainable development of rural areas. Subsequently, the main thrust of rural development policies and programmes toward the creation of new and varied businesses and employment opportunities in rural areas is rendered void unless people want to live and work in rural areas. With Irish unemployment rates having fallen to under 5 per cent, the lowest since records began, and with increased participation in the labour market the question remains as to how/why there are skills shortages, and why do these skills shortages exist in rural areas (or particular types of rural areas)? For much of the latter half of the 1990s Ireland has experienced growing concerns in creating new employment opportunities and also an increased recognition, by employers and government agencies, of the problem of 'skill shortages' and the effects this has on the economy and viability/sustainability of many rural communities. While this imbalance can be recognised in urban Ireland this chapter argues that in terms of rural, and particularly Western Ireland, not only is the issue of job creation problematic but the attraction and retention of human resources to some rural areas is becoming a key determinant in combating rural decline. Further, this 'problem' is a widespread, multi-disciplinary, cross-sectoral phenomenon affecting a range of skilled, semi-skilled and non-skilled occupations in rural areas; a fact that is poorly recognised in policies and operational programmes designed to promote rural and regional development (see McDonagh, 2000, 1999).

Little empirical study, either in support or contradiction, has been carried out on the human resource deficit in rural Ireland. There is however a significant amount of anecdotal evidence – be it a lack of farm labourers for harvesting silage in the midlands; a lack of hotel staff in Clifden, or an inability to attract nurses to Carraroe, or doctors in Roundstone – which give credence to this argument (see Fig. 12.1). Significantly skill shortages in rural areas range from low skilled to highly skilled and are experienced across all sectors from farm labourers, manufacturing operatives, services or other professionals (like doctors, teachers, nurses, engineers and managers). The Director of the SFA suggested that skill shortages not only affected the well-publicised areas such as construction, tourism and information technology, but that it was virtually impossible to recruit graduate engineers in Ireland because of intense recruitment drives by global operators who pay better than Irish employers. Likewise there was also a problem at a lower skill level (e.g. clerical posts) because young people found these jobs less exciting with fewer promotional opportunities than elsewhere. Keeble *et al.* (1992) in their study on rural England were among the first to show that there were significant shortages of skilled and technical workers, managers and professionals, in many rural firms in comparison to their urban counterparts. Skilled worker shortages were a serious problem for approximately 25 per cent of all remote rural firms with over 33 per cent also having problems recruiting managers and professionals. These shortages resulted in rural firms recruiting their skilled workers from outside the local areas and thereby raising problems of housing availability and such like. Indeed such is the growing recognition of this problem in Ireland that attempts to place more emphasis on the supply of skills to some sectors of the economy has been acknowledged by developments such as the Forfás Skills Group, the Business Education Partnership Forum and the 310m euro (approx. £250m) Education Technology Fund. Further examples of strategies being employed include that of Údarás na Gaeltachta, who are specifically targeting Gaeltacht graduates based overseas in an attempt to get these graduates to return to positions in the Gaeltacht region. A major problem in many of the Údarás factories is the inability to find suitably qualified candidates for skilled jobs (particularly managers) who also have knowledge of the Irish language. There are also other examples of where local community groups (the South Sligo Resource Development Co-operative, for example) send their newsletters abroad to their former residents to try and entice them back to jobs or to act as potential investors in their own areas.

The Case Study Evidence – Tuam and Clifden

To place the anecdotal and reported evidence in a more empirical setting, two areas were chosen for a brief case study analysis. These areas were the towns of Tuam in the north of County Galway and Clifden in the west of County Galway (see Figure 12.2). The reason for choosing these locations were:

Figure 12.1 Newspaper headlines depicting the skills shortage problems experienced throughout rural Ireland.

(a) their proximity and peripheral location, respectively, to Galway city;
(b) their range of employment services from light engineering in Tuam to more tourist industries in Clifden, and
(c) their predominantly rural hinterlands.

A survey was carried out in both these areas encompassing the main employers (hotels, restaurants, retail shops, supermarkets, professional services, manufacturers etc.) in the towns as well as the recruitment agencies dealing with supplying potential employees for vacancies in these areas.

Clifden

Regarded as the capital of Connemara, Clifden is situated approximately 50 miles north-west of Galway city. The backdrop to the town features a landscape of rich variety from the Beanna Beola Mountains, the Atlantic coastline and the Derrygimlagh bogs (with its historic connections to the flight of Alcock and Brown in 1919). This landscape and historic legacy are ably supported by a large number of hotels, guesthouses and restaurants, making Clifden a popular tourist centre. While the main focus is on tourism and tourist activities there are also a number of other industries/businesses in the vicinity of the town. These include a variety of outlets from retail shops to seafood companies. Agriculture is reflective of much of the rest of Western Ireland in that it is small scale but nevertheless important in the local economy.

Tuam

Tuam, situated approximately 20 miles north of Galway, is one of the most historic towns in the West of Ireland. The town has a population of just over 6,000 people and it has a strong industrial and commercial base that supports its surrounding hinterland. Tuam also has a strong agricultural background and the contribution of the farming population to the local economy is still quite significant. Its closeness to Galway somewhat hampers its development in terms of tourism and tourist activities but nevertheless Tuam boasts a large range of activities of interest to visitors and locals alike. These, along with Tuam's historic legacies, in the form of its two cathedrals and early monastic settlements, help in generating income for the area.

Some findings

In the West of Ireland, opportunities for employment are limited, (by accessibility, infrastructure and comparative advantage for example). With this in mind the findings of the surveys yielded some important insights to the workings of the labour market in Western Ireland and to the perceived or actual problems associated with peripheral location. Taking the example of Clifden first, a number of businesses were surveyed including hotels, restaurants, guesthouses, retail units, Small & Medium-sized Enterprises (SMEs) etc. These businesses varied in size from one-person operations to larger hotels and businesses employing in excess of fifty people. The survey itself (due to the constraints of the chapter only a limited amount of the detail of the surveys is been used) dealt with a range of issues: these included respondent details; businesses and employment characteristics; recruitment; retention; attraction of staff and training programmes (the same survey layout was used in the Tuam study). The key insights that this survey provided, and those which are been used in this chapter specifically, relate to attracting and retaining people in the Clifden/Tuam areas, and those aspects of the survey relating to the perceived/actual impact of peripheral location on these areas.

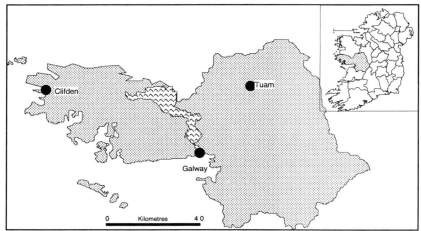

Figure 12.2 The study area

The first notable feature of the Clifden study, particularly in the hotel and services industry, was that the majority of staff employed in this sector were recruited from within a five mile radius of the particular business with as much as 70 per cent of those recruited remaining in the employment for less than twelve months. This turnaround was described as having an adverse affect on continuity within the business concerned and also led to increased time and money being spent on advertising, interviewing and training new recruits. A number of respondents highlighted this situation and suggested that in many cases they felt they were merely investing time and money in training employees only for another company or hotel to benefit:

> *there is no guarantee of employees remaining after training ...*
> *the quick turnover of staff is expensive in time and money ...*
> *and then you have to start all over again* (quotes from interviewees or written comments from survey questionnaires are given in italics).

The next insight was that in a number of instances, even when there were jobs available in the tourism industry (particularly seasonally) these were difficult to fill due to various combinations of unsuitable applicants, lack of experience or indeed no applicants at all. In many cases respondents felt that these types of positions (for example bar work, waitress etc.) were associated with low pay, long hours and were looked upon by many potential recruits as being *'only suited to either the young (15–18 year olds) or married women'*. In contrast to this seasonal workforce with its difficulty in both attraction and retention, a large section of the managerial/specialist staff employed in Clifden showed a different set of characteristics. Generally these group of employees were not recruited locally but were brought in from other areas. The main reasons for this were listed as being the result of a lack of local applicants with the necessary qualifications, experience and practical skills. Paradoxically, the vast majority of those businesses surveyed expressed a desire to recruit locally as this had advantages in terms of what was described as employees *'knowing their customers; being available at short notice'* [and indeed being] *'more likely to remain with the business'*. Another significant feature that emerged was that of Clifden's peripheral location. Employers suggested that Clifden's geographical location and difficulties in terms of access due to its poor public transport, poor road infrastructure and long distance from an international airport, was a deterrent not only in attracting tourists and visitors to the region, but also a barrier in attracting potential candidates for more senior professional and managerial posts.

In the Tuam study many of the same issues were highlighted. These included the majority of staff employed in Tuam businesses being recruited from within a five mile radius; the lack of applicants with the necessary qualifications, experience and practical skills in the local area; the difficulty in retaining staff for any length of time (although this was not as problematic as in Clifden) and, an added dimension, the increased competition with other companies from the large urban area of Galway City. Many companies expressed concern with this latter situation and their inability to compete with salaries, training and prospects for career progression on offer from the larger companies situated in Galway City. Other notable aspects of the survey indicated that there were difficulties in attracting and retaining staff across a broad range of occupational categories from managers, engineering/computer professionals to those of clerical, secretarial, production operatives and skilled/unskilled labourers. This was supported by the findings of the recruitment agencies where there was general difficulties in finding suitably qualified and experienced candidates to fill vacant posts particularly in managerial, professional (architects, accountants) and engineering (electrical, electronic) positions. One aspect that also came through from the Tuam study, particularly in the light-engineering and skilled-maintenance and production sector, was the feeling that *'young people are not interested in the trade skills anymore'*. The lack of appeal currently being experienced in these sectors will undoubtedly have profound effects on the longer-term development of the region. Interestingly the issue of peripheral location was also seen to be a limiting barrier in terms of development within the Tuam area. Whereas the geographic location of Clifden was a more obvious impediment to development, many of the Tuam respondents felt that the lack of a good public transport system linking the town with Galway, and the lack of a more easily accessible major airport in Galway, was increasing the peripherality of Tuam and as a result curtailing its development.

Finally, three further aspects arose during the case studies (in a more general sense and not exclusive to either area). The first is related to sustainable development. While much of the respondents related problems associated with the curtailing of physical development and the absence of skilled personnel, this is mirrored in terms of community development where the skill shortage and human resource deficit being experienced in both study areas is likely to have major adverse effects on the success of local development strategies currently being pursued. In this way it seems illogical that local development plans are being encouraged by government and state agencies yet the skills/abilities to implement these plans may be seriously lacking in local communities due to a failure of government policy to sufficiently address the needs for the future sustainability of rural areas.

The second issue is more associated with creating agglomeration or deglomeration economies and recognising that:

> the labour force is less mobile than is normally assumed
> in economic theory (with) greater wage differentials
> between agglomerations experiencing growth and rural
> areas with population stagnation or declining population
> (Teigen, 1995 p.8)

and moves beyond the notion of creating jobs, to one of suggesting that there is employment available but it is not being accessed. An example which illustrated this situation, of vacant jobs not being accessed, that is, a human resource deficit that is depicted in a lack of suitably skilled personnel willing to take up vacant positions in rural areas, was the year-long search for a doctor to fill a General Practitioner (GP) post in Roundstone, Connemara. In this case finding a suitably qualified candidate was never a problem but convincing such a candidate to take up the post proved to be a major obstacle. The demanding nature of such a position in a peripheral and widely dispersed rural population area and the difficulty of getting locums to fill in during the GP's break were the main reasons cited.

The third aspect, that of the 'black economy', is not something new in either rural or urban Ireland. Opportunities associated with the informal or 'black' economy appear to exacerbate recruitment difficulties even where people with required skills reside in the rural areas in question. In the SFA 5th National Employment Survey (1999) as much as 41 per cent of prospective employees sought to be paid 'off the books'. The Director of the SFA suggested that:

> the pervasiveness of the 'black economy' (was) such that employers often find it difficult to match the take-home pay of someone claiming social welfare and doing occasional work at the same time.

However, the Irish National Organisation of the Unemployed (INOU) disputed this perspective by suggesting that the myth of unemployed people not wanting to work is dispelled by the fact that 90 per cent of the 72,000 jobs created in 1998 were taken up by the jobless. As such, the INOU argued that employers who were having problems filling vacancies should be investigating what they are doing wrong, rather than what is wrong with the unemployed (O'Sullivan, 1999).

What Conclusions can be Drawn?

However valid the arguments presented in this chapter, from the provisional findings of this research, the problem of skill shortages appear to be acute in rural areas. The recruitment and retention difficulties experienced are not uniformly spread throughout rural space and the problem intensifies, particularly in the service/tourism sector, with increased distance from the main urban centres. The functionality of rural areas therefore appears to be a critical determinant of the incidence of this problem. Further, as this brief study illustrates, this shortage of skills is clearly not confined to a limited number of sectors and occupations. It is a widespread multi-disciplinary, cross-sectoral phenomenon. In this regard the role of the NSS and its goal of promoting balanced regional development; improving people's quality of life; maintaining economic competitiveness and ensuring development that is sustainable, will be put to the test (see Walsh, Chapter 5).

It is inevitable that people will move in and out of rural areas no matter what the social or economic circumstances. Some people are undoubtedly attracted to rural areas, like Western Ireland, by the perceived idyll of rural living. An idyll which is bound up with community, kinship, family, safeness, values and mores, a particular way of life, culture and closeness to nature (McDonagh, 2001). It is also clear however, that many others are deterred by factors such as the limited range and quality of services and amenities that can be readily accessed by dispersed rural communities; limited employment opportunities for one's spouse; restricted opportunities for career advancement; the often small networks/community of peers that can lead to isolation and associated difficulties in making suitable substitution arrangements during periods of absence (for example, holidays, illness). In this way not only are there limitations relating in part to the restricted variety and size of many local labour markets in rural areas, there are other added impacts that combine to determine the 'attractiveness' of moving into any given rural area. Perceived peripherality (spatial and aspatial: see McDonagh, Chapter 7) can make an area unattractive to a potential recruit because of geographic isolation from people with similar and/or supportive skills. It can often be the case that it is difficult for the spouse of an employee to obtain suitable employment in a rural locality and thereby make it unattractive to the person that has obtained employment. Out-migration from rural areas also is problematic and in many instances can emanate from attachments to other (mainly urban) places developed during periods of extended stay, as for example, while undergoing training or third level education. Other potentially influential factors in the decision to leave rural areas relate to the relative anonymity afforded by large urban centres and to the desire to join friends (and family) who may have already emigrated. This suggests considerations, other than a dearth of employment opportunities or other economic measures will be a panacea in combating this outflow.

What is clear then from this chapter is that the deep reaching changes and the fate of rural communities in Ireland is at a crossroads. This crossroads does provide new opportunities for rural areas. Significantly, employment in a particular career is only one element of people's choice on where they live. More important elements (and ones that can be addressed) are more closely linked to the functionality of rural space. These include such things as 'quality of life' factors that may exert adverse effects on the attraction and retention of skilled labour in rural areas; deficiencies in recreational provision (e.g. multi-channel television, omniplexes, theatre, libraries, restaurants etc.); difficulties in accessing various public services (e.g. schools, colleges, universities, health care facilities etc.); inaccessibility to facilities such as a variety of retail shopping outlets, banking and personal services. These can all adversely effect the desirability of living and working in rural areas and thereby undermine the sustainability of any rural community. In this way the NSS, due to be published in 2002, will have a crucial effect on assessing how important a determinant geographical location is. The inevitable link between geographic location and remote rural areas and their ability to attract key skilled personnel seems obvious. Equally however, positioning in the structure of opportunity (rather than geographical location) (see Mernagh and Commins, 1997) is becoming increasingly important. In fact government, policy-makers and community alike, have it would appear, reached a point where a major re-think on the future functionality of rural areas is required. Decisions must be taken on determining:

> what people want from rural areas; what people want to do with rural areas; whether everybody can expect to have similar standards and expectations when it comes to access to services and quality of life; whether people will accept trade-offs between rural and urban living and, crucially, whether problems in rural areas can be dealt with exclusively through some specifically regional or rural-oriented planning (McDonagh, 2001, p.209–210).

The political will and speed at which this 're-think' occurs and how the functionality of rural areas (in the provision of services, schools, entertainment, access etc.) is developed will therefore be crucial in ensuring sustainable rural communities in Ireland for the future.

References

Department of Education (1998) *Adult Education in an Era of Learning: Green Paper*, Government Publications, Stationery Office, Dublin.

Department of Enterprise, Trade and Employment (1998) *Employment Action Plan for Ireland*, Stationery Office Dublin.

Department of Enterprise, Trade and Employment (1997) *Human Resource Development*, Dublin: Stationery Office.

European Commission (1995), *Teaching and Learning: Towards the Learning Society White Paper on Education and Training*, Luxembourg.

European Commission (1988) *The Future of Rural Society*, COM (88), 501.

Finnegan, T. (1994) 'Developing the West Together', in N. Collins (ed.) *Unemployment North & South: The major social ill*, pp. 129–140.

Forfás (1996) *Shaping Our Future: A Strategy for Enterprise in Ireland in the Twenty First Century*, Forfás, Dublin.

Fox, W. (1995) 'Designing Infrastructure Policy to Create Jobs in Rural areas', in OECD, *Creating Employment for Rural Development: New Policy Approaches*.

IBEC (1998) *National Survey of Labour and Skills Needs in the Services Sector*, IBEC, Dublin.

Keeble, D., Tyler, P., Brown, G. and Lewis, J. (1992) *Business Success in the Countryside: The Performance of Rural Enterprise*, HMSO, London.

McDonagh, J. (2001) *Renegotiating Rural Development in Ireland*, Ashgate.

McDonagh, J. (2000) 'The hidden challenge for rural Ireland: the growing concern of a human resource deficit'. Paper presented to the Hungarian Visiting Research Group, NUI, Galway, 6 December.

McDonagh, J. (1999) 'Skill shortages in rural areas - a cause for concern in rural Ireland'. Paper presented at the Conference of Irish Geographers, St. Patrick's College, Dublin, 15–16 May.

McGreil, J. (1999) *Quo Vadimus, cá bhfuil ár dtriall? Where are we going?* Report on the Pastoral Needs and Resources of the Archdiocese of Tuam. Unpubl.

Mernagh, M. and Commins, P. (1997) *In from the Margins*, Research and Development Unit, SICCDA, Dublin.

North, D. and Smallborne, D. (1996) 'Small Business Development in Remote Rural Areas: the example of mature manufacturing firms in Northern England', *Journal of Rural Studies*, Vol. 12, (2), pp.151–167.

O'Sullivan, J. (1999) 'Employment reaches record 1.5m plus', *The Irish Times*, 14 May.

OECD (1995) *Creating Employment for Rural Development – New Policy Approaches*, OECD, Paris.

SFA (1999) *Fifth National Employment Survey*, SFA, Dublin.

Teigen, H. (1995) 'Creating Agglomeration or Deglomeration Economies: Development Strategies in Rural Areas'. Paper presented at the XIII International Seminar on Marginal Regions, Maynooth/Kerry, 15–22 July.

chapter thirteen

ENCOUNTERS AT THE PERIPHERY:
RURAL YOUTH AND LABOUR MARKET EXCLUSION IN
NORTH-WEST CONNEMARA

Brian McGrath

Introduction

It is generally accepted that rural dwellers in advanced capitalist societies now reside in a countryside where 'post-productivism' has become the defining feature of agricultural change (Ilberry and Bowler, 1998; O'Hara and Commins, 1998). At the same time new interests – based primarily on consumption and lifestyle – are being continually asserted, often contentiously, within rural space. While the idea of 'rural restructuring' is a slippery one in documenting such changes (Hoggart and Paniagua, 2001), what is particularly evident within empirical analyses is the considerable uneven development that characterises much of contemporary rural society. In this context, rural employment as problematic terrain has been a *leitmotif* of academic, policy and lay discourse for quite some time. Of critical importance, much of the literature in the Irish case has focused on the strategies of response towards this uneven development through agricultural readjustment, rural industrialisation, natural resources development, community economic endeavor (see especially Curtin *et al.* 1996) and, undoubtedly in the future, local governance. Outside of agriculture, the substantive differential implications of uneven development for many rural dwellers are largely undocumented, particularly among those who face not only spatial exclusion but social differentiation based on age, gender, socio-economic position, sexuality and disability.

Recent accounts of rural poverty and social exclusion throughout Europe have highlighted not only the social and economic differentiation of rural areas but also the redistribution of life chances and prospects among rural households in significantly unequal terms. A feature of contemporary rural society is the marginalisation of particular groups who face not only spatial exclusion but also social differentiation based on age, gender, socio-economic position, sexuality and disability. Furthermore, the substantive concerns of marginalized groups have been largely neglected in both policy and research terms. Using empirical evidence from a recent study of rural youth and policy this chapter explores aspects of young people's labour market exclusion in North-West Connemara, a peripheral region along the western seaboard of Ireland. It endeavours to give voice to young people's problematic experiences and encounters in employment in the region by illustrating the types of social practices and relations that serve to reinforce their exclusion. It highlights their attitudes towards development and concludes with a discussion of how public and social policy can become more enabling for young rural dwellers. Overall the objective is threefold: first, to give voice to young people's problematic experiences and encounters in employment in the region by highlighting the types of social processes and encounters that serve to reinforce their labour market exclusion; second, to highlight some young people's perspectives on economic development and policy; and third, to assess how public and social policy can work towards labour market inclusion of young rural dwellers. Before attending to these questions the chapter first presents a brief overview of the research study from which the empirical findings presented here are based in addition to a profile of the case study region, North-West Connemara.

Rural Youth, Labour Market Exclusion and North-West Connemara

The area of North-West Connemara has particular socio-economic and demographic dynamics in terms of high incidences of poverty, poor service provision, high dependency ratios, poor employment structures/options and some counter-urbanization effects (such as 'holiday home' developments). The population of 8,722 persons (Central Statistics Office (CSO) 1996) occupy an area of 780 km^2, which comprises a number of scattered settlements dotted throughout the landscape, the largest being Clifden (920 persons).

Consideration of the region's Economic Dependency Ratio, Age Dependency Percentage and Unemployment Rate demonstrates a picture of economic marginalisation and demographic imbalance when compared with Ireland as a whole (Economic Dependency Ratio is the ratio of those 'inactive' (first job seekers, unemployed, students, home duties, unable to work, 'other', 0–14 age group) to those at work; Percentage Age Dependency are those in the 0–14 and 65+ age cohorts, expressed as a percentage of the 15 to 64 age cohort; Unemployment Rate are those out of work and first regular job, as a percentage of the labour force). Closer inspection of the data reveals that the area, when compared with the national average, experienced considerable decline in agriculture between 1986 and 1996 (see McGrath and Canavan, 2001; McGrath, 2001). Nevertheless, the numbers at work in farming in 1996 constituted 17 per cent of the entire population at work in the area compared with a national level of 10 per cent. While agriculture has lessened in importance as an employment outlet there has been substantial growth in non-agricultural activity (between 1991 and 1996, for every decrease of 100 persons in agriculture in the area there was a gain of 640 persons in non-farm employment, giving a 'Replacement Rate' of 6.4. In the period 1986 to 1991 this rate was 0.8, which meant that non-agricultural employment growth could not match the level of agricultural decline), particularly in commercial, building and professional services but principally in economic activity involving personal (hotels, restaurants, cafes, lodging and boarding houses) and recreational services. Given its poor infrastructure manufacturing has never featured as a significant economic outlet in the area.

Young people between the age of 15 and 24 years (this corresponds to the age categories which the CSO have devised for analysis: 0–14; 15–24; 25–34; 45–54; 55–64 and 65+ and therefore the data here refers to the 15 to 24 year age cohort and not the 16 to 25 year age cohort at the centre of the research project), in the region make up 16 per cent (1,492 persons) of the entire population, with a slightly higher proportion of females to males (770 and 712 respectively). The labour force characteristics of young people in this age cohort reveals several significant gender differences, particularly with regard to their labour force and education characteristics although given the immense change in the Irish economy since 1996, the official statistics may not reflect as accurately as one would wish the changing employment routes and pathways of young people. Some of these include:

> (i) The proportion of males in- and out-of-employment is higher compared with both females in the area and the corresponding national averages;

(ii) The female population is considerably higher than the number of males in education.

The employment outlet typical for young people in the area (the nearest age cohort for which employment data is available from the CSO is the 15–34 age category and is indicative only of the age group at the centre of this discussion), is found in personal and recreational services; the proportion of males and females at work in this category are 25 and 43 per cent respectively. For males, work activities with the highest uptake apart from this source are commerce (18 per cent); agriculture (17 per cent); building (14 per cent) and manufacturing (14 per cent). The major employment sources for the female workforce are commerce (24 per cent) and professional services (18 per cent). The high incidence of part-time employment is also a distinguishing feature of the region.

In the context of these particular characteristics this chapter is based primarily on qualitative data from a recent international study on rural youth and policy entitled *Policies and Young People in Rural Development*. Similar in its objectives to other studies of rural youth transitions (namely those of Shucksmith *et al.*, 1996; Pavis *et al.*, 2000; Cartmel and Furlong, 2000), the overall purpose is to analyse in a bottom-up way the impact of policies on young people's transitions from school to work in rural areas. In addition to a comprehensive policy audit and documentary analysis of official statistics a qualitative methodology was employed and included semi-structured interviews with forty-one young people (22 females and 19 males) living in the area as well as focus groups with young people (in unemployment, third level education and the Youthreach programme) and local policy actors (statutory and community representatives). A 'non-probability purposive' sampling strategy was adopted given its emphasis on qualitative *processes* and *experiences* rather than trends and patterns. The recorded and transcribed interviews ranged in duration from twenty five minutes to one-and-a-half hours in which young people's perceptions of the social relations and practices involved in moving from school to employment, higher/further education and training were explored. Of the forty-one individuals interviewed, nineteen were at work; nine were unemployed; six were participating in trainee programmes and seven were still at school. In educational attainment terms sixteen had successfully completed the Leaving Certificate examination while a relatively high number (20 respondents) had failed to complete their education to this level (the remainder were still at school). The average age of respondent was 19.5 years.

What are the Typical Dimensions of Labour Market Exclusion?

Labour market attachment offers one, albeit critical, dimension of social inclusion in contemporary society. Such attachment concerns not just economic reward but regard for conditions and prospects within work. Indeed several studies have highlighted the predominance of 'secondary' labour markets within rural areas (Monk and Hodge, 1995; Cartmel and Furlong, 2000; Pavis *et al.*, 2000), characterised as poorly paid, low-skilled, offering little security or fringe benefits and providing few prospects. This is particularly the case where tourism and manufacturing are important employment sectors (Chapman *et al.*, 1998). So, what are the typical dimensions of labour market exclusion among young people in North-West Connemara as evidenced in this study? and what are the main barriers encountered in attempts to improve their prospects?

Low pay

The tourism industry plays a predominant role in the local economy of North-West Connemara. Restaurant work, chambermaiding, bar work, cleaning, Bed and Breakfast activity are outlets where most young people tend to find work, often from a young age. Most of this work also tends to be undertaken by young women. Strong criticism was levelled against local businesses that refused to pay staff a reasonable wage level. As a result it was suggested that local employers were finding it increasingly difficult to recruit staff (see also McDonagh, Chapter 12). One young male chef commented:

> nobody wants to go into catering because the hours are too long and the young ones are the only ones they could get in to do the hours for practically next to nothing money [Interview 13; Male].

However, opportunities to earn higher wages were identified by young males working in the construction and the (limited) manufacturing industries in the area. Both industries are physically demanding and typically dominated by a male workforce. In a region where housing development has been pronounced over the last number of years the opportunities available to young males to earn higher incomes than their female counterparts in manual work are more evident. It was suggested that when labourers were needed the possibility of earning 51 to 64 euro (£40 to £50) per day could be expected. One young male in a manufacturing job worked 'piece-rate' and could earn 152.40

euro (£120) per day when demand existed. This is not to suggest that conditions of employment are that better off in such sectors as the next section will illustrate.

Working conditions

The working conditions associated with particular occupations were a source of concern for many young people. Those with experience of tourism work were highly dissatisfied with the long hours while several males described the working conditions associated with construction as particularly problematic. The evidence suggests that working conditions have a considerable impact on the quality of life of many young people. Considerable dissatisfaction was expressed with regard to working long hours and receiving poor rates of return in tourism employment outlets. While tourism tends to be dominated by females, a number of males had similar experiences in relation to the physical demands that work in this sector placed on them. One young male commented:

> I have worked on 3 or 4 building sites in my life and it was a hell of a lot easier to work on a building site carrying around blocks and cement all day than it was in that hotel [University Focus Group; Male 2].

In relation to the construction sector, some of the work is intermittent and dependent on whether the employer has sufficient work available. Much of the work takes place during the summer months when the weather is more suitable for building activity. However, the working conditions associated with building activity meant that this type of employment was considered unsuitable by some young people. A number of males felt that labouring activity was physically demanding and could have significant negative impact on their physical well-being. While building work was viewed as being readily available, some males felt it did not reflect what they believed was a reasonable means of earning a living. One young male described his feelings about labouring in the construction sector as follows:

> I don't want to work on building sites. It's not really the wages; it's the job. It's heavy and hard work; labouring is anyhow. I definitely wouldn't want to do it. You could get to do anything and my back is fairly bad from working on buildings already. So if I'm working on them for the rest of my life I'll have a lot of trouble [Interview 14; Male].

The dominance of males in sectors of the local economy, such as manufacturing, was viewed by one young woman as having negative consequences for the rights of female workers. She described feelings of powerlessness dealing with management because women constituted a minority in the workplace and therefore had less bargaining power. Many young people expressed disillusionment with the unskilled and monotonous quality of the work they were engaged in. Several interviewees identified lack of job satisfaction with the nature of employment available to them on the factory floor or in hospitality outlets.

Limited choice & availability of work

Young people felt constrained by the lack of opportunities and the gendered nature of work available in the local economy of the Western Region. Primarily females who had the most experience working in this sector described the difficulties associated with the seasonal nature of tourism employment. The work options available to males were identified as construction, manufacturing, bar work or fish farming, while the opportunities available to females were suggested as restaurant and hotel work, childminding and secretarial positions. The limitations that local economic opportunities place on young people's career advancement was highlighted by a young male who felt he would never realise his ambition in the area:

> I always wanted to do something like sound engineering or the likes of television or music. Living around here it's not the easiest job to go at because there is no place that you could apply to do it. The only job you could get around here is bar tending, building sites. There are other jobs but they are the main areas [Interview 14; Male].

Another male emphasised the restricted choice of employment, particularly for those who would like to have a trade occupation. He described the situation of a cousin who wanted to train as an electrician but experienced difficulties in finding a sponsor for his apprenticeship; a typical problem also identified by the Youthreach coordinator in the focus group discussion. A number of young males also felt that there were better choices for males in terms of the work that they could undertake. There was a stereotypical perception among some that women were compelled to move away from the area to find suitable female-type employment. The seasonal nature of employment was a frequently mentioned problematic feature of the local economy. The strong dependence on tourism means that having work all year round in

North-West Connemara is an impossibility for many young people. The tourism season generally begins in March and ends around October, with some additional busy weeks over the Christmas period when many people return to the area. A number of young people had experience of working all year round; a possibility that exists in some retail outlets, in the limited number of factories and in outlets such as garages. Several businesses in the area are family run establishments and, according to one former employee of a retail outlet, this created its own set of difficulties:

> It's like any job here; they are all family run businesses and you work for about 3 or 4 members of the one family, and you have 3 or 4 bosses. When you are working in the place you are told 3 or 4 times to do something. Family run businesses are difficult [Interview 18; Female].

Competition within a limited jobs pool was also identified as a difficulty of the local labour market. A number of females who were undertaking or had completed secretarial courses described the limited number of employment outlets available to them once they had completed their training. They viewed this as a significant constraint and felt they would have to travel elsewhere to enhance their job prospects.

Career prospects

One of the most disillusioning aspects for 'qualified' rural youth is the mismatch between their qualifications and the type of employment available in the area. Considerable frustration could be identified among people who expressed their wish to remain in the region but yet face poor prospects within the local labour market. In terms of the mismatch that exists around qualifications and employment prospects, the focus group with university students highlighted significant problems faced by this cohort of young people who had left the area for educational reasons. The students expressed their wish to return to the region in the future but the impracticality of finding suitable employment in the local labour market was a source of considerable concern:

> It's the working that's the problem. What can we do. If I graduate as a biotechnologist I don't foresee any biotechnology companies setting up anywhere in Connemara ... I'd like to go into the medical side of biotechnology so it's going to be fairly hard [University Focus Group; Female 1].

The prospects of finding employment among those with higher education credentials were also highlighted by a number of local males who had lower educational attainment levels. They suggested that it was only those with higher qualifications, such as teachers or IT professionals, who needed to move outside the area to find work while the rest of the population would have no difficulties. The absence of promotional prospects was identified by a young woman in the bar trade as a disconcerting feature of the local employment market. She felt that the hard work she had contributed to the business over the years was taken for granted and believed that she would be accorded a higher position if she worked in a similar capacity outside the area:

> I know how to run a bar now at this stage – I have enough experience of it ... Like it's not that I want the name 'manager' but it's nice to be saying other than I work in a bar ... if you were working somewhere else for six or seven years and you done that, you done the orders, you done the stock, you know what you're doing, you wouldn't be classed as just a barperson. [Interview 20; Female]

What are the Main Barriers to Employment?

Analysis of interviews with young people reveals a host of constraints encountered in making the transition to work or finding a better job. These barriers include: (i) limited work experience, (ii) eligibility criteria among agencies, (iii) availability of childcare, (iv) limited transport and (v) labelling.

Work experience

Having sufficient work experience to access employment was identified as a significant barrier by some young people. A distinctly rural dimension of this is the limited opportunities available in remote areas for gaining experience and knowledge that might lead to better prospects. Gaining work experience through training centres such as Youthreach (a 'second chance' education/training programme for young people) was viewed by some 'unqualified' young people as an important way of providing more options for employment. Learning skills in this way was viewed favourably by an ex-Youthreach trainee:

> Only for this place [Youthreach] God knows where I would be ... with the experience it was great. I know a lot

about bar work now so if I was ever fed up with the petrol pumps I could fall back on that [Interview 3; Male].

On the other hand, work experience alone can prove problematic for those who seek occupational mobility outside the area. In one particular case where a young chef had developed considerable experience working in the family business, the barrier that proved most difficult for him was accreditation and recognition of his experience. Having applied for a position in a large city centre hotel, he was refused a job on the grounds that his qualifications were insufficiently accredited. Training and accreditation are important policy considerations that are taken up later in the chapter.

Eligibility criteria among agencies

One young female who had attained diploma qualifications from a third level institution identified the experience of returning and finding work in the area as frustrating. Her experience suggested that many of the opportunities available to her when she returned could only be accessed through FÁS, the National Training Authority. However, in order to be registered with this agency she needed to claim unemployment payments. She felt this limited her chances of finding jobs that may have sufficiently suited her:

> So you have to go 'sign on' until you can be on FÁS and then you can go and get a job. It's ridiculous. I mean when I finished up [college] I said I'd look up some jobs and everything was FÁS, FÁS, FÁS ... Unless you were on FÁS you couldn't apply [Interview 16; Female].

She described applying for a job for which she was suitably qualified but discovered that, as a FÁS scheme, it was only applicable to people claiming unemployment payments or the one parent family payment.

Availability of childcare

The role of childcare in undermining rural women's ability to enter the labour market has been documented by a number of authors in the UK (Stone, 1990; Little *et al.*, 1991). For a number of young mothers in this study, childminding was identified as a particular concern in facilitating their transition to work. They mentioned reliance on family, grandparents and other networks to look after their offspring. One lone parent held particularly strong feelings about the need for a crèche in the area since it was becoming especially difficult to find a childminder in the current economic climate when work can be more readily available elsewhere.

Lack of transport

The availability of transport is especially critical for accessing employment in rural areas since much of the work is available at a considerable distance away (Pavis *et al.*, 2000). Poor public transport and lack of private means of travel have significant implications for the uptake of work. Overcoming the transport barriers in accessing work was easier for some than others, particularly where a car had been given to a person by a parent or relative. Two young males who were given cars by their family found it allowed them greater freedom, particularly for finding work. Some young people expressed difficulty in overcoming the transport barrier while others relied on transport provision through family or the goodwill of people in the area willing to offer a lift. Some young people saw transport as a necessity for their work despite the large expense incurred. For instance, a young apprentice felt that he could not undertake his training without access to a car, which he found particularly expensive on a limited training allowance.

Labelling

In a small community where people and their histories are very often known to each other, certain contacts can work to young people's advantage while the obverse can also be the case, i.e. where one's reputation can be used against their interests. Networks can provide young people with information regarding the record of the employer while employers themselves can use existing staff to vouch for the character of potential employees. University students in the focus group discussion suggested that young people could be unfairly treated on the basis of gossip and perceptions of one's family, and highlighted the negative aspects of small community life:

> Well if there was anything against your family it would never be forgotten. They would go into every aspect of your life. You wouldn't be able to find any place to live or get a job. If your reputation precedes you at all, that's it [University Focus Group; Female 1].

Young People's Perspectives on Economic Development

Young people advanced a variety of perspectives regarding the overall development of the West Region and the role of young people as stakeholders in the process. This related to their perceptions of how development was achieved; who the most powerful actors in the community were and what position young people had in influencing decision-making. Throughout the interviews, there were few references to the development needs of the region and how prospects for people there could be improved. A number of young males felt that the population of the area was too small to warrant any significant developments and felt it would be uneconomical to develop its infrastructure on these grounds. However, the focus group with university students generated considerable discussion regarding the type of development that existed in the region – reflecting perhaps a hardening of opinion on the area once outside it. According to a number of students, the over-dependence on tourism would, in time, have detrimental effects. One male compared the situation with more favourable economic developments taking place in the Irish-speaking part of Connemara:

> We are overly dependent on tourism and in a way it is ruining our identity and culture. If you look at south Connemara Gaeltacht, they have major internet businesses, they have modern businesses, they have fishing industries ... Basically, tourism is keeping us alive and has done a lot for our area, but we are just dependent on it and in the end it could end up destroying us [University Focus Group; Male 2].

Those considered the most powerful actors in the community were identified as business owners and commercial interest groups, such as the Chamber of Commerce. Many young people suggested that the interests of these groups dominated community life. Local politicians were also seen as significant actors with a certain degree of power and interestingly few references were made to the capacity of development organisations and community groups in influencing change. Young people described the influence of business people in the following terms:

> There's a clique here, certainly. And you know they'd be business owners and that kind of stuff. And they'd say what goes on and what doesn't [Interview 16; Female];

The priest, the hotel owners, the shop owners, mainly the people who own the establishments and doing business, they are the people who are listened to ... Then the people who live here, they wouldn't really be listened to. Their point of view wouldn't be taken into account [Interview 14; Male];

Everybody knows somebody who'd be in the Chamber of Commerce or who'd be involved in local politics. I used to go to them, voice my opinion to them. Whether they take notice of you or not is up to them, but you know you're doing something about it [Interview 17; Male].

A female, who suggested that developing facilities for younger people was undermined by an over-emphasis on the tourism sector, expressed criticism of those who were preoccupied with business interests:

They are [powerful] if it's for a cause they feel is important. They wouldn't call getting young kids off the street and into some place, they wouldn't think that important. They would be more inclined to think of how to bring the tourists in; it's just tourists, tourists, tourists [Interview 12; Female].

The perceived lack of attention paid to the region by development bodies such as the Industrial Development Authority (IDA) was a source of concern to one male participant of the university focus group. He believed that the area was continually ignored in official economic development policy:

The IDA has a great reputation for these past few years. We have seen all the stats everywhere, but I don't see much happening. That's their job, bringing in foreign multi-nationals that demand a high tech, highly educated work force but there is none of that coming into Connemara [University Focus Group; Male 1].

Overall, the interviews provide little evidence that young people take an active interest in political affairs, particularly with regard to the role of local politics in influencing development. The most articulated criticism of local politicians took place during the focus group discussion with university students. They criticised the inaction of local councillors and lack of funding and campaigning for the region. In addition, other parts of Ireland were seen as gaining disproportionately compared to the West Region. An example of one criticism expressed about local councillors and TDs is as follows:

There is nowhere near enough political movement for the West. There is no where near enough money coming out ... Because of lack of political representation a lot of funding is going to places like Tipperary [University Focus Group; Male 2].

Regarding the political nature of development, it was also felt that the Irish-speaking region of Connemara received more favourable treatment with regard to funding and grant-assistance. A resident of Inishbofin, an island on the coast of North-West Connemara, expressed his dissatisfaction with the unfavourable position of islanders in the non-Irish speaking parts compared with their counterparts in the Gaeltacht. He was highly critical of politicians who he perceived as making tokenistic gestures when visiting the island but had no real interest in its development since it was a non-Irish speaking area:

> I know lads on the Aran islands, they're getting a boat and they're getting a massive grant whereas I would like to get a boat for myself for the season and I'd like to see more grants being pushed this way ... Different TDs, that spend half their life living in the Gaeltacht and they come out here once a year they say they will call to every house and they only call to one or two houses ... If they apply for a grant, they put them on the bottom of the pile: 'never mind them, they don't speak Irish so don't give them anything' [Interview 15; Male].

In terms of the availability of facilities for young people within North-West Connemara, a geographical distinction was also made by a male participant of the university focus group. He felt that young people south of the main town in the region, Clifden, did not have access to the type of facilities available in other parts of the area. He felt that more funding and balanced development of the region was necessary:

> I think it is fair to say if you drew a line through Clifden, for a lot of us below Clifden there isn't a huge amount of facilities, say in the likes of Ballyconneelly, Roundstone and Cashel areas ... What it boils down to is you need funding. You can't do anything without money [University Focus Group; Male 1].

In this regard, within North-West Connemara some young people identified Letterfrack as an area of the region where most activity was concentrated, particularly in social and cultural development. Some young people suggested the presence of development organisations as the main reason the area had more opportunities and activities than other parts of the region. During the interviews and the university students' focus group, this was seen as a good example of what could be achieved through community effort.

What are the Implications of the Findings for Public and Social Policy?

While many of the problems which rural economic restructuring has created may be global in origin, the role of the Irish state in exacerbating the more negative consequences of structural change cannot be downplayed. It has been argued that state policy-makers in Ireland have traditionally adopted development policies that favour exogenous type operations, in which support for large economies of scale producers and businesses are dominant. In the context of areas such as North-West Connemara, where tourism and aquaculture are important natural resources, the ownership and control of resources by large capital-intensive operations creates few employment opportunities for young people in sustainable terms. In this approach to development, invariably the needs of capital for profit take precedence over the quality of jobs provided to young people. In contrast, efforts to redress this form of development trajectory by supporting petty commodity production systems, whether individual, familial or co-operative activity, have been undertaken by development agencies such as FORUM. Despite being under-resourced these forms of production offer better possibilities for rural youth to earn livelihoods that may be less exploitative and more financially rewarding.

In spite of the fact that some people who work in the area live in Galway city, there is no strong pattern of commuting in the other direction. Neither is such a pattern likely to emerge according to a number of policy actors interviewed. The longer-term future in relation to income for those remaining is seen to be in combining various forms of employment and sources of income. Small numbers of jobs which have the potential to provide a good income were forecast for the shellfish and furniture sectors, both of which have developed through the efforts of community based organisations, over long periods of time. While the overall economic base is significantly weak, young people should be encouraged, through institutional support, to develop a range of skills that meet local economic requirements. Support for initiatives that encourage multiple-income earning strategies, for instance through the combination of farming and aquaculture activity, should be widened and strengthened. For these types of resource developments to take place effectively, explicit state support will be needed on a long-term basis. However, as Tovey (1996) reminds us, careful monitoring of policy supports needs to be undertaken to ensure that class and gender equality are adequately addressed. This latter dimension becomes an issue in endogenous developments such as shellfish cultivation that are heavily male-dominated; an issue that reflects more the nature of economic potential than the design of interventions. In addition, given the unique spatial and social processes of exclusion in the area, policy-makers need to ensure that more flexible arrangements are available to young people in terms of training requirements. Acknowledging this as a complex issue, it is necessary to recognise how local specificity is not always explicitly catered for in nationally formulated policy. A clear example of this is the non-recognition by FÁS of the qualifications of many skilled trades people who have returned to the area but yet are unable to provide apprenticeship training to young people because they do not meet national criteria.

The capacity of young people to initiate micro-enterprise formations should be encouraged and supported from an early age. This mobilising of natural and human resources, in sustainable terms, is not only an economic issue but a cultural and educational one. In some parts of Ireland, school programmes in entrepreneurship have been initiated to allow young people explore how local resources may be harnessed in economic ways. In North-West Connemara, there exists strong potential for young people to develop micro-enterprise initiatives given the strength and quality of local natural resource endowment. In addition, identifying and initiating social economy developments warrants serious consideration in local policy formulation. This form of economic activity is becoming increasingly recognised for its income-generating capacity, in addition to providing much needed services, in disadvantaged communities. The creation of a new social economy scheme under the National Development Plan 2000–2006 (Department of Finance, 1999), indicates the recognition such activities are receiving at official policy level. However, eligibility criteria laid down by FÁS precludes people below the age of 35 years which means that in rural areas, where it is not possible to draw on a large population, such criteria are damaging to rural development.

Finally, the formulation of the County Development Strategy presents considerable potential in harnessing the activity of all agencies at county and regional level, including LEADER, Partnership Companies, County Enterprise Boards, to ensure that employment creation and support for enterprise formation is sufficiently inclusive of areas throughout North-West Connemara. This would require an extensive county-wide audit of project development and employment creation to identify where activity is currently dispersed and supported.

Conclusion

There are many complex aspects to understanding the nature of the local economy, against which it is difficult to provide an overarching framework for resolving the many problems that persist. Although policies will not eliminate the structurally embedded causes that give rise to the weak economic base in the region, they can address the more negative consequences of rural restructuring and challenge the economic processes that serve to exclude young people's integration into employment.

Although employment has increased dramatically in Ireland in recent years, regions such as North-West Connemara continue to suffer the worst aspects of rural economic restructuring. The result is that many rural areas are emptied of young people, attracted by the prospects of employment and opportunities elsewhere. As the findings suggest, for those who remain in the local labour market, much of the employment can be characterised as low paid, seasonal and providing few prospects for career advancement. Much of the employment takes place in the tourism sector where these features predominate. In addition, traditional sectors such as agriculture and fishing have become increasingly marginalised, so that for many young people, the opportunity to earn a livelihood in these activities is a formidable challenge. The demise of traditional routes to employment and the limited job opportunities and life chances that certain rural areas can provide for young people underscores the urgent need for social and public policy providers to recognise and proactively engage with restructuring processes at many levels.

References

Cartmel, F. & Furlong, A. (2000) *Youth unemployment in rural areas*, Joseph Rowntree Foundation, York.

Central Statistics Office (1996) *Census of Population*, Government Publications, Dublin.

Chapman, P., Phimister, E., Shucksmith, M., Upward, R. and Vera-Toscano, E. (1998) *Poverty and Exclusion in Rural Britian: The Dynamics of Low Income and Employment*, Joseph Rowntree Foundation, York.

Curtin, C., Haase, T. & Tovey, H. (1996) (eds.) *Poverty in Rural Ireland: A Political Economy Perspective*, Oak Tree Press, Dublin.

Department of Finance (1999) *The National Development Plan 2000–2006*, Government Publications, Stationary Office, Dublin.

Hoggart, K. and A. Paniagua (2001) 'What rural restructuring?', *Journal of Rural Studies*, 14, (1) pp.41–62.

Ilberry, B. and Bowler, I. (1998) 'From agricultural productivism to post-productivism', in Ilberry, B. (ed.), *The Geography of Rural Change*, Longman, Essex.

Little, J., Ross, K. and Collins, I. (1991) *Women and employment in rural areas*, Rural Development Commission, London.

McGrath, B. (2001) 'A problem of resources: defining rural youth encounters in education, work and housing', *Journal of Rural Studies*, Vol 17, No. 4, pp. 481–495.

McGrath, B. and Canavan, J. (2001) *Researching Rural Youth in the West of Ireland – A Mixed-Methods Approach*, SSRC Research Series Report, 9, Social Sciences Research Centre, Galway.

Monk, S. and Hodge, I. (1995) 'Labour markets and employment opportunities in rural Britain', *Sociologia Ruralis*, 25,(2), pp.153–172.

O'Hara, P. and Commins, P. (1998) 'Rural Development: Towards the New Century', in Healy, S. and Reynolds, B. (eds.) *Social Policy in Ireland: Principles, Practice and Problems*, Oak Tree Press, Dublin.

Pavis, S., Platt, S. & Hubbard, G. (2000) *Young People in Rural Scotland: Pathways to Social Inclusion and Exclusion*, Joseph Rowntree Foundation, York.

Shucksmith, M., Chapman, P., Clark, G., Black, S. and Conway, E. (1996) *Rural Scotland today; the best of both worlds?*, Avebury, Aldershot.

Stone, M. (1990) *Rural Childcare: A Study for the Rural Development Commission*, Rural Development Commission, London.

Tovey, H. (1996), 'Natural Resource Development and Rural Poverty' in Curtin, C., Haase, T. and Tovey, H. (eds.), *Poverty in Rural Ireland: A Political Economy Perspective*, Oak Tree, Dublin.

chapter fourteen

INFORMATION ECONOMY ACTIVITY IN GALWAY CITY
AND REGION

Séamus Grimes

Introduction

Information and communications technologies (ICTs) have
made a major contribution to Irish economic development in
recent years. While much of this contribution has been a direct
result of the attraction of significant inward investment in sectors
like electronics, software and internationally traded services, there
have also been important developments in indigenous enterprise,
particularly in the software sector. Although the contribution at
the national level has been impressive, the impact in terms of
regional development has been somewhat disappointing, with
almost 80 per cent of employment in ICT-related sectors being
concentrated in the greater Dublin region. The challenge that this
presents to regions like the West of Ireland will be explored in this
chapter. Firstly the chapter will contextualise Ireland's ICT sector
in an international perspective, paying particular attention to the
successful attraction of increasingly sophisticated investment in
ICT sectors. The policy background underlying attempts, both to
embed foreign investment within the local economy, and at the
same time to promote the indigenous high technology sector will
be explored. With the over-concentration of inward and other
investment in the Dublin region, the policy objective of
regionalising ICT activity has been given increasing priority.
Attempts to bring about a greater level of regionalisation will
clearly depend on the capacity to ensure that the necessary social
and physical infrastructures are in place to support such
investment, particularly the regional supply of IT skills and of high
quality broadband infrastructure. This chapter will analyse the
extent to which Galway city and region have already been
successful in stimulating information economy activity, both
resulting from foreign and indigenous investment. It will also seek

to identify some of the key barriers, which appear to be preventing further growth in this activity in the region.

Ireland's Emerging Information Economy

In order to understand the ICT sector in the West it is useful to consider the emergence of information economy activity in Ireland in an international context. Attention will be focused in particular on inward investment and indigenous activity in internationally traded services sectors such as software, financial services, and teleservices of various types including shared services. An important part of this explanation is related to how new information and communication technologies have been transforming the geography of economic activity in recent years, as the process of globalisation has deepened. Scholars like Castells (2000) have identified the connection between the development of the new technologies and a fundamental restructuring of capitalism, with transnational corporations decentralising non-core production and services activities. This process of outsourcing has presented relatively peripheral European regions like Ireland with new opportunities to attract increasingly sophisticated inward investment, to seek to promote a greater level of embeddedness of such investment within the local economy, and to encourage indigenous enterprise to exploit niche areas in an increasingly global market. This process of outsourcing has not only impacted on the changing profile of inward investment, but it has also been reflected in important changes within multinational branches already established in the country, as companies undergo a continuous process of re-inventing their activities in order to remain innovative and competitive.

Despite a continuing debate among economists about their contribution to productivity, policymakers have increasingly regarded ICTs as being key determinants of competitiveness and economic growth. This is obvious in the policy formulation of the EU, which places increasing emphasis on promoting the 'Information Society' throughout Europe. The contribution of the new technologies relate not only to the significance of the ICT sector within the economy, but also to their exploitation as the move towards e-commerce gathers pace. Having identified the significance of the IT sector more than 25 years ago, Irish policymakers have sought to ensure that Ireland would have low cost capacity and high speed access to ICT infrastructure to establish a 'first mover advantage'. With the necessary infrastructure in place, regions like Ireland enhance their attractiveness for foreign investment, and they can also improve their capacity to build connections to centres of excellence such as Silicon Valley, enabling indigenous enterprise to become world class.

These developments have also been associated with a new international division of labour, as companies seek to exploit comparative advantages of particular locations to fulfil certain aspects of their production process, which have become spatially separated (Daniels *et al.*, 2001). The new communications technologies also allow companies the flexibility of undertaking back office functions at locations remote from their operating businesses. The decisions of multinational companies to locate in semiperipheral countries like Ireland, and in peripheral regions like the West of Ireland, is not simply a question of cost factors, but can also be related to the relative ease of access to scarce IT skills, such as software engineers. Increasingly, Ireland is facing more intense competition for ICT and other such investment from regions in Eastern Europe, particularly Poland, Hungary and the Czech Republic. It should also be pointed out that the new international division of labour has been associated with new labour practices and with the emergence of a distinction between multi-skilled core workers and flexible peripheral workers. Among the more important core workers are those involved in R&D activities, much of which tends to be located in the home region of multinational companies.

Despite the increasing impact of global forces at work, local regions in some countries are succeeding in developing some dimensions of 'innovative milieu', such as knowledge-based continuous innovation and learning-based competitiveness. Successful regions are characterised by mechanisms of knowledge transmission and learning, arising from inter-relationships between suppliers and customers, informal collaborative links between firms, inter-firm mobility of workers and spin-off of new firms from universities. Recent Irish policy developments suggest a commitment to foster the development of clusters of new knowledge-intensive enterprise in regional centres (Enterprise Ireland, 2000). It might be argued, however, that while the Dublin region reflects some of these processes of change, developments in smaller regional centres like Galway city are much more embryonic. It is also encouraging to note that within the new more innovative form of economy, it has frequently been small start-ups, rather than the larger established companies which have introduced 'subversive' technological products and services (Cohen *et al.*, 2000). The Irish economy's dependence on Foreign Direct Investment (FDI), however, has encouraged the use of imported rather than locally generated technologies. Ireland's traditionally low R&D intensity, is indicated by low levels of business expenditure on R&D as a proportion of GDP (at 1.5 per cent) and a low government share of R&D spending of 5.5 per cent compared with an OECD average of eight per cent. It is only in the most recent phase of ICT expansion that this problem is being addressed, with significant support from EU programmes targeted at Research, Technological Development and Innovation (RTDI) (Grimes, 1999). R&D business spending as a proportion of GDP has more than doubled over the 1990s, with ICT industries contributing a third of the total (OECD, 2000).

The Irish economy in general, and the Dublin region in particular, have benefited from the increasingly globalised nature of economic activity, and from the restructuring of operations controlled by multinational companies. Ireland has one of the highest concentrations of information and communications technology activity and employment in the OECD (OECD, 1999). In 1997, one quarter of a million more people were in the labour force than in 1990. This jobs boom has been fuelled to some extent by an influx of ICT companies together with impressive growth in indigenous companies in areas like software, computing and communications skills. Ireland, with 34 per cent of the global market, is the biggest exporter of software products in the world, having overtaken the US in 1998. Export growth between 1996 and 1999 was almost double the growth of Ireland's export markets, which was attributable to the economy's specialisation in foreign-owned high-growth, high technology sectors. Perhaps the single most important factor in attracting investment has been the low rate of corporation tax, which at 10 per cent compares well with other regions in the developed world, but loses its edge when compared with zero tax rates in Hungary's industrial zones. Other factors, however, such as many years of wage restraint have also contributed to rates of profitability for MNCs, which are among the highest in Europe. Despite the on-going and understandable criticisms of Ireland's high level of dependence on foreign direct investment, in a world where the pace of technological change is accelerating, attracting FDI is essential to replace the inevitable decrease in employment in declining sectors. In 1997, with only one per cent of the EU population, Ireland gained 23 per cent of all FDI projects in Europe, covering manufacturing, software, teleservices and shared services projects. The loss of almost 5,000 jobs in the ICT sector in 2001 alone, alongside the creation of around 2,500 new jobs in the sector, has resulted from the exposure of some of the least innovative and most mature technologies from the serious downturn in the US economy. Despite these worrying developments, it is acknowledged that foreign-owned firms are much more deeply embedded in the economy than in the past, because the pool of available skills, work practices, back-up services and external agglomeration economies are much more important (Barry and Bradley, 1997).

Non-Metropolitan High-Tech

Encouraging high technology development outside the Dublin metropolitan area has proven to be a particularly difficult challenge to date. This is true, not only in the case of the Industrial Development Authority's (IDA) efforts to encourage inward investors to locate in the regions, but also in relation to a highly centralised and urbanised pattern which characterises indigenous internationally traded services, with around 80 per cent of that sector located in the greater Dublin region (Enterprise Ireland, 2000). High-tech activity in the urban metropolitan area has spilled over to outliers in places like Leixlip, with a considerable amount of the activity increasingly being located in new large campus facilities such as IBM in Mulhuddart, or in the newly developed business parks like the National Digital Park in Citywest, on the outskirts of the city.

While there is a growing dispersal of internationally traded services operations establishing in the other main urban centres like Cork, Limerick, Galway and Waterford, these developments are still small scale relative to the significant cluster of high technology activity in the Dublin region. Although there have been important developments in upgrading telecommunications infrastructure, both nationally and regionally in the past year, the relative position of Dublin *vis-à-vis* other centres is significantly superior. In addition to the large concentration of internationally traded service activity in the International Financial Services Centre (IFSC) in Dublin, other significant developments such as the MIT Lab and the National Digital Park have also been located in the city. It would appear that in the early stages of these developments, such activities require the many services associated with the country's largest urban centre. The National Digital Park in the Citywest Business Campus has already attracted very significant e-commerce hub activities from companies like

Microsoft, Oracle and Netscape. The Park has been designed to meet the needs of companies with very heavy data transfer. Broadband data transmission facilities will be available to all occupants of the Park with an initial capacity of 155 megabits/s rising to 622 megabits/s in the near future.

A number of reasons would suggest, however, that a greater spread of high technology activity to the provinces make take place in the future, and indeed, there are some positive signs to suggest that a trend in that direction is already underway. One significant factor, which has diminished the attractiveness of Dublin, is the rapid pace of development that has affected the city in recent years. This has resulted in significant overloading of the transport infrastructure with resulting high levels of congestion, thereby having an increasing negative impact on the quality of life of urban commuters. The overheating of the housing market has resulted in a situation where many young middle class individuals and couples find it increasingly problematic to obtain a foothold in the housing market. These factors make it quite difficult for high tech companies to expand their staff numbers and there is some evidence of provincial branches of companies opening up to overcome some of these problems.

Two important factors are likely to lead to a greater diffusion of IT-related activity towards the regions, and particularly to the West, North-West and Border regions, which now constitute the only remaining Objective 1 part of the state. The development agencies, therefore, can offer much more attractive incentives to companies willing to locate their operations in these regions. The IDA has been given a clear directive to focus their attention on regionalising further inward investment. Variations in the quality of telecommunications and other infrastructures, such as roads and electricity supply, not to mention access to regular airline connections, will clearly affect the ability of the agencies to operationalise this mandate. The North-West region, which is only beginning to see a small level of development in this sector, has been relatively neglected in terms of broadband infrastructure until recently, while more basic requirements such as electricity supply also need further development.

Ireland's Internationally Traded Services Sector

In 1997, internationally traded services accounted for more than two thirds of net employment growth with rapid growth in software, financial services, telemarketing and shared services. In

1998, 44.2 per cent of new jobs created in companies supported by the IDA were in international services as compared with 14.2 per cent of the gross number of jobs lost (O'Sullivan, 2000). Of the 50,000 jobs in internationally traded services, around 36,000 were located in Dublin and the South-West, while the region with the next largest concentration had less than 4,000 jobs in this sector (Table 14.1). Around 71 per cent of companies and 76 per cent of employment in foreign-owned internationally traded services are in the Dublin region, compared with 60 per cent of indigenous companies and 70 per cent of related employment (Enterprise Ireland, 2000). Despite the recent significant policy shift towards seeking a greater regionalisation of investment in Ireland, 65.7 per cent of FDI in 1999 went to the International Financial Services Centre in Dublin alone (Fórfás, 2000).

Table 14.1 Internationally traded services companies by sector

Sector	No of companies	% US owned	% in East region	% in West region	1995 or after	% Temporary
S.Ser/DP	42	69.0	40.4	11.9	57.0	6.4
Other	19	52.6	63.0	0.0	26.3	30.2
Tele - marketing	34	59.0	61.0	5.9	79.0	12.1
Software Contr	36	58.0	77.0	2.7	55.5	13.4
Software	89	41.6	78.6	9.0	64.0	5.2
Total	220	53.2	67.3	7.7	60.4	11.0

Source: IDA Ireland, 2001

Table 14.1 shows the breakdown of the 220 companies by sector, the largest being 89 software companies and the smallest 19 'Other' companies. Overall, 53.2 per cent of these companies were US-owned, with 69.0 per cent in Software Services/Data Processing, and 41.6 per cent in the Software category. The second most significant country of ownership was the UK (18 per cent) and the third was Germany with 11 per cent. In Software Services/Data Processing, the other main countries represented were Germany and the UK (both 10 per cent) and Canada (7 per cent). Other key countries with software companies in Ireland apart from the US were the UK (23.6 per cent) and Germany (12.3 per cent). In telemarketing the UK with 23.5 per cent of companies was the other main non-US country involved. The main non-US countries involved in software contractor companies were the UK (11 per cent), the Netherlands and Germany (both 8 per cent), and Canada and Japan (both 6 per cent). Overall 70 per cent of internationally traded services companies were found in the East, while not surprisingly the South-West region with the second largest city in the State had 12 per cent of these companies (Table 14.2). Software services/data processing with 40.4 per cent in the East region was the only sector with less than 60 per cent of companies in that region. Other regions that were relatively successful within this category were the South-West and South-East (both at 14 per cent), the West at 12 per cent and the Mid-West at 7 per cent. Software was the most highly concentrated sector with 78.6 per cent in the East, while Software Contractors were next with 77 per cent located in the East.

ICT in the Galway Region

The number of industrial jobs generally has doubled in the past seven years to 10,000 and some projections suggest that this number could expand to 20,000 by 2010, with the ICT sector expected to play a significant role in that expansion. It should also be remembered that other sectors, including construction, tourism, health and education also contributed significantly to employment growth in recent years, with indigenous enterprises making an important contribution. The 1999 IDA Annual Report indicated that because of the Objective One status of the West Region, Galway City and County Mayo had a target of doubling jobs from Greenfield projects by the end of 2002. High technology and other companies, which insist on locating in Dublin, will receive only token grant aid from IDA Ireland. The IDA has toughened its stance on grant aid in order to drive investment in the Objective One regions. Unless they are deemed 'strategic industries', where expansion is seen as necessary to continue consolidation and where the company is seen as strategically important for the economy, foreign companies locating in Dublin normally do not receive any grants at all. In contrast, large-scale investments in the regions can secure incentive grants of as much as 38,000 euro (£30,000) per employee. Taking the Galway, Mayo and the Midlands regions together (IDA region), the number of IDA supported companies increased from 116 to only 124 between 1994 and 1999. Permanent employment in these companies increased by 24 per cent during this period, from 13,689 to 16,978. In 1999 in the West Region, six of the ten new projects were Greenfield investments, while four were expansions of existing companies. It is interesting to note that while the West Region had only 67 of the 124 IDA-assisted companies in the larger region, around 11,000 of the 16,978 workforce were employed in the West Region, indicating the larger average size of investment particularly in Galway City. The IDA strategy is to encourage subsidiaries to progress their operations up the value chain in order to become more independent within their corporate structures. Not only has expansion taken place in software and internationally traded services, but also in the healthcare sector, which is one of the major regional specialisations.

Foreign-Owned Companies

With the recent merger of Hewlett Packard and Compaq, one of Galway's major foreign-owned ICT companies has been affected by its second major restructuring since the opening of Digital Equipment, the first major ICT investment in 1971. This initial investment was a relatively unsophisticated manufacturing plant, which by 1977 employed 1,000 people. Further expansion in the 1980s, and in particular the important development of Digital's first European Software Centre, increased employment to 1,800. At this stage, Digital had become the major employer in the local economy, with an estimated 'net worth' to local business and the community of 127 million euro (£100 million) a year. The company also provided advanced training for its workforce, employed large numbers of graduates and had significant research linkages with NUI, Galway, particularly in the area of computer integrated manufacturing.

Partly because of Digital's dominant role in Galway's ICT sector, its closure in 1993 was a devastating blow to the local economy, and particularly to approximately 40 supplier companies such as Pulse Engineering in Tuam and Cable Products in Castlebar. The closure resulted in 760 redundancies. The continued operation of Digital's European Software Centre played an important role in subsequent developments, as Compaq later absorbed this activity together with some engineering activities when it took over Digital. In retrospect the response to the closure has been positive, with quite a few small high technology companies, particularly in software, emerging through the initiative of former workers. Among the important outcomes was the establishment of the Galway Technology Centre, which recently housed 33 small indigenous enterprises, employing around 300 people. The centre underwent considerable expansion recently. Despite the continued criticism of dependence on FDI in Irish industrial policy, the restructuring of Digital's operation in Galway revealed a significant transfer of high technology and high quality business skills to the local workforce, which proved to be an important basis for a sizeable number of indigenous start-ups, particularly in software (Green *et al.*, 2001). Compaq's existing operation in Galway employs around 500 people in four separate units: they include R&D, software publishing, a European business and technology support operation. With a total workforce of 2,200 in Ireland, most of whom are based in its Dublin operations, Compaq Ireland is a major employer in Ireland. When Compaq acquired Digital in 1998, it already was the top international PC manufacturer, and adding Digital increased its involvement in software, giving it a large share of the systems market. Its European Software Centre is involved in software research and development, software business generally, and sales and marketing support for Europe, the Middle East and Africa. In its R&D section, Compaq employs 25 high performance technical computing engineers, who recently designed Europe's largest supercomputer, and are currently designing the world's most powerful computer. However, while it is too early to predict what the outcome of the new merger with Hewlett Packard will be for Galway, the history of mergers in the ICT sector has not always been positive.

Table 14.2 Foreign-owned ICT companies in Galway

Company	Origin	Activity	No employed	Year began
Nortel	Canada	Telecommunication. hardware/software	450	1973
Siebel Systems	US	Localisation/technical support	120	1999
ADC*	US	Communications billing system	200	1994 /99
3Com	US		20	
PMC Sierra*	US	Circuit design	35	2000
Start Amadeus	Germany	Software development	100	1999
Compaq*	US	Firewall software/ software marketing	500	1998
Silicon & Software Systems	Holland	Circuit design		1998
Data Dimensions		IT systems	51–200	1996
Graham Technology	UK	Software development	15	1997
Baurer GmbH	Germany	Software & Consultancy	16–50	1998
Telelogic Ltd*	Sweden	Software		
AND Data Ireland		Digitised mapping	51–200	1997
Asita		Network software	16–50	
Fotonation		Software development	16–50	1999

Source: IDA Ireland, 2001; ADC: formerly Saville Systems (Canada) 1994; PMC; Sierra: formerly Toucon Technologies (Ireland) 1994; Compaq: formerly Digital (US) 1971; *Closed

Nortel's Galway plant was originally established as a manufacturing and assembly plant in 1973, and as recently as 1994 it was still predominantly involved in manufacturing. In recent years it has doubled its workforce while at the same time concentrating on R&D, customized solutions and customer support activities. Like other major ICT companies in Ireland, Nortel also have a major investment in Northern Ireland, which until recent cutbacks employed 2,400, and the Galway operation over the years has had to compete with this plant and with sister plants in Wales and France. In 1999, the Galway facility's circuit pack manufacturing activities were transferred to Nortel's facility in Cwmcarn, Wales, resulting in a loss of 65 jobs, while the outsourcing of the facility's logistics and distribution function resulted in a further loss of 50 jobs. A more positive development was the emergence of the indigenous start-up, CT Solutions, which was established by former Nortel R&D employees. The company supported this new start-up by agreeing to bundle its product on its call centre platform. In 1999, Nortel in Galway had a wages bill of 38 million euro (£30 million) per annum, and provided an estimated 32 million euro (£25 million) per annum in business to local suppliers. Since the first draft of this chapter, Nortel reduced their Galway operation by a further 150 employees, in the most recent round of retrenchment, retaining those who are mainly involved in R&D activities.

As can be seen from Table 14.2, the remaining foreign-owned ICT companies in Galway were established much more recently and were much smaller operations. ADC Software Systems, a US company, is a global provider of broadband solutions for the telecommunications industry, and its Galway operation, employing 200, looks after the European and Middle East/Africa regions. ADC Software Systems took over the Canadian company Saville Systems in 1999, which had established an operation in Galway in 1994. It has two R&D groups, one dealing with integrated technology and the second with service level assurance and network performance tools. The Galway site fits into a global network of ADC outlets, providing technical support, software consultancy and product implementation services. Following the world's time zones, ADC in Galway begins to provide back-up and technical support to customers once its Australian counterpart in Brisbane closes for business.

Many multinational and some leading indigenous ICT companies have established multi-site operations in a number of cities in Ireland, with Dublin, Cork and Galway being among the more common choices. Silicon and Software Systems, which was established in Dublin by a Trinity College academic, and which was since taken over by Philips, is the largest independent software design company in Europe. In 1996 it opened a division in Cork and in 1998, it established units in Galway and the Czech Republic. In 1999 its European and US operations merged and at that stage it employed 300 engineers. It also opened a division in 1999 in Poland. Much of this expansion, including the Galway unit, has resulted from the on-going challenge of finding suitable IT skills (for further insight to the human resource deficit experienced in many parts of Western Ireland see McDonagh, Chapter 12).

One of the smaller and more recently established foreign-owned companies is PMC-Sierra, which acquired the Irish-owned company, Toucon (established in 1994 by former Digital employees) in 2000 for 33 million euro (£26 million). This company is involved in high-speed Internet-working semi-conductor solutions, developing Internet infrastructure equipment. Its 35 Galway employees form an R&D group within PMC-Sierra, offering integrated circuit design services to companies like Hewlett Packard. Using Digital Galway equipment, its first project was with Digital Reading. Digital was very supportive of this start-up and compensated for a lack of venture capital at this early stage of development. Toucon operated as an independent design house specialising in the R&D of next generation chips for broadband technologies, and had been doing design work for PMC-Sierra since 1998. In addition to the significant focus on software development within the ICT sector in Galway, another important area of activity within Galway's internationally traded services sector was teleservices (Table 14.3). In addition to Compaq's technical and business support division, a number of other companies, including insurance, publishing and even a water purification company, had data processing and other forms of back office activities located in Galway city and county.

Indigenous ICT Enterprises

For the past 25 years there has been a strong tradition of links between indigenous start-up companies and foreign-owned multinationals in the ICT sector. The growth of the indigenous high tech sector, and particularly that part of it specialising in software, has been one of the most positive Irish economic developments.

Table 14.3 Teleservices Companies in Galway city and county

Company	Origin	Activity	No employed	Year began
McGraw-Hill	US	Software/DP	51–200	1987
PH Brink Int		Tech language translation	16–50	1998
DER Irl	German	Invoice control	51–200	1997
Compaq	US	Business & technical support	200+	1998
Cigna	US	Claims processing	51–200	1988
Ionics	US	Telesales	60	1999
Biomedical Research	Ireland	Multilingual telemarketing	25–50	1997
Irish Response	Ireland	Call centre	<25	1999
Inter Group Insurance Services		Claims Processing	16–50	1998

Source: Enterprise Ireland, 2000 and IDA Ireland, 2001

The role of Enterprise Ireland in promoting indigenous enterprise has been very important, with the agency not only providing badly needed funding during the start-up phases of companies, but also taking equity participation in the companies. Table 14.4 indicates that three quarters of these companies were established since 1995, and around the same proportion had fewer than 30 employees. Many of these companies have grown out of MNCs, and they have brought the certification standards of those companies with them. Companies like Digital and Nortel have provided an important training ground for indigenous companies seeking to compete in a global economy. A number of these companies, including Toucon Technologies, are located in the IDA business park on the university campus in Dangan. A former Digital employee established Aimware, which employs 43 people, in 1996. It was set up with a Business Expansion Scheme loan from a local investor, which was backed by investment by other former Digital employees. It developed a software system that manages the software development process efficiently, and has been delivered via the Internet since the beginning of its operation. Another former Digital employee, who left the company before they closed their operation in Galway, established Storm Technology, which employs 40 people, in 1995. The founder of this company recognises the significant contribution which Digital has made through the powerful international network it created in the ICT sector, which gave easy access to many people in senior positions in the sector in the US. This company is now one of the largest independent suppliers of software consultancy, e-business and web integration services. Its 35 highly skilled consultants, analysts, architects and engineers provide services to major ICT companies in Ireland and abroad. While the majority of these companies are located in a few business parks in Galway city, a small number of companies, supported by Údarás na Gaeltachta, form a cluster of activity in Furbo (Tables 14.4 and 14.5).

Table 14.4 Indigenous ICT companies in Galway City and environs

Company	Activity	No employed	Year began
CT Solutions	Software	3 +	1996
AIMware	Software development	30	1996
Storm Technology	Software	40	1995
Big-back	Software	18	2000
Sybernet		25	1995
Qset	Software consultancy	33	1992
BSM Ireland	Software prod. & services	17	
Distributed Software Consultancy	Software development	40	1996
Infopoint Systems	Multimedia software	<25	1996
Infoscience Software	Software	35	1980
IntegrityData Associates	Software	7	1999
Marine Computation Services	Software	25–30	1991
S&P Media	Software development	<25	
Unisoft systems	Software development	<25	1999
Am-Beo	Software systems	50	2000
Direct Marketing Technologies	Software	20	1994
FKM Ltd	Software localization	150	1997
Global Eng Systems	Software systems	25	1992
ICE Comp. services	Software development	10	1990
PlanNet21 Communications	Networking systems	<25	2000
Yac.Com Ltd	Software	25–50	2000
DBA Irl		6	1996
Galaxy Software		7	1998
Gold Fish Electronics		6	1996
Blue Tree Systems		12	1996
Kennys Book Export Co Ltd	Books	20	1999
Aveoen	Software	8	2001
Aqua fact Intl	Marine consultancy	10	1994
Menlo Park Tech	Software	20	2000

Source: Enterprise Ireland, 2000; * Closed

Table 14.5 Indigenous ICT companies in County Galway

Company	Activity	No employed	Year began	Town
Orbitel Telecommunications	Software	15	2000	Ballinasloe
Clearview Solutions	Software Services	25	2000	Oughterard
Omac Laboratories	Geochemical Analysis	25	1980	Loughrea

Source: Enterprise Ireland, 2000

Conclusion

The transformation of the geography of economic activity in recent decades associated with the restructuring of capitalism and the exploitation of new information and communications technology, has provided peripheral regions like Ireland with new opportunities to attract more sophisticated inward investment, and to foster indigenous high technology enterprise capable of competing in global markets. An important dimension of this economic restructuring has involved the trend among multinational companies to outsource non-core activities to semi-peripheral regions, a process which has been associated with a new international division of labour. Both the consequent attraction of ICT-related inward investment and the growth of relatively new indigenous sectors such as software, have made a major contribution towards Ireland's impressive economic performance in recent years.

The fact remains, however, that a significant proportion of this activity continues to be concentrated in the greater Dublin region, a region that has experienced significant levels of over-development in the past twenty years. More peripheral and less urbanised regions like the West have only participated in this development to a modest extent, and much of the ICT activity in the West Region is in fact concentrated in Galway city. The major downturn which is currently affecting the ICT sector in the US and throughout the developed world, will clearly add to the challenges facing Irish development agencies in seeking to bring about a greater level of regionalisation of such investment in the future.

This preliminary analysis of the nature and extent of Galway's ICT sector reveals a cluster of activity with a significant multinational presence together with a growing cluster of indigenous enterprises, involved particularly in software. The history of Galway's ICT sector to date has been relatively traumatic with two changes of ownership in one of the first major foreign-owned companies to invest in the city. Linkages between the multinational and indigenous sectors to date suggest many positive indications for building a more sustainable high technology sector in the region in the future.

References

Barry F. and Bradley J. (1997) 'FDI and Trade: the Irish host country experience', *Economic Journal* (107), pp.1798–1811.

Castells M. (2000) *The Rise of the Network Society*, Blackwell, Oxford.

Cohen S.S., Bradford De Long J. & Zysman J. (2000) *Tools for Thought: What is new and important about the 'e-conomy'?*. BRIE Working Paper #138, University of Berkeley.

Daniels P., Bradshaw M., Shaw D. & Sidaway J. (2001) *Human Geography - Issues for the 21st Century.* Pearson Education, Harlow

Enterprise Ireland (2000) *Opportunities for Ireland's High-Technology Internationally Traded Services (ITS) Sector to 2007*, Dublin.

Forfás (2000) *International Trade and Investment Report, 2000*, Dublin.

Green, R., Cunningham, J., Duggan, I., Giblin, M., Morooney, M., and Smyth, L. (2001) 'Boundaryless Cluster: Information and Communications Technology in Ireland', in Bergman, E.M., den Herteg, P., Charles, D.R. and Remoe, S. (eds.) *Innovative clusters: drivers of national innovation systems*, OECD, Paris.

Grimes, S. (1999) 'Information Society Technology Programmes, Structural Funds and European Cohesion: the case of Ireland'. Paper presented to Royal Geographical Society/Institute of British Geographers Annual Conference, University of Sussex, January.

IDA Ireland (2001) Unpublished data provided by IDA Ireland.

OECD (1999) *The Knowledge-Based Economy*, Meeting of the Committee for Scientific & Technological Policy at Ministerial Level, June, OECD, Paris.

OECD (2000) *IT Outlook 2000*, OECD, Paris.

O'Sullivan M. (2000) 'The sustainability of industrial development in Ireland', *Regional Studies*, 34(3), pp.277–290.

chapter fifteen

IMAGES OF THE WEST OF IRELAND IN PRODUCT PROMOTION

Sheila Gaffey

Introduction

This chapter utilises the promotional materials of Small & Medium Enterprises (SMEs) in two regions in the West of Ireland to examine the use of imagery, particularly images of place, for the purpose of promotion and marketing quality hand crafts and rural tourism. The chapter is contextualised within the academic literature relating to the formation and evolution of particular images of the West of Ireland and highlights the role of place (particularly, rural) imagery in the promotion of individual products and services. Further, the chapter analyses some of the possible meanings that may be connotated through the use of such imagery in the West of Ireland.

Studies of Regional Imagery

Regional images may be defined as representations of places (Gold and Ward, 1994; Ilbery and Kneafsey, 1997) which consist of one or more of a variety of elements (e.g. people, animals, landscapes including land, water and sky, folklore, legends) which are designed to convey regional characteristics. Studies of the use of regional imagery have been undertaken internationally at varying geographical scales and in different contexts. These range from place promotion of towns and cities for industry, to representations of place for tourism consumption, to associations between product and place of production, to the changing representations of rurality (Hughes, 1992; Bunce, 1994; Gold and Ward, 1994; Urry, 1995; Hopkins, 1998). In relation to Ireland, the evolution of regional images in literature, tradition and Irish tourism promotion has received some attention, particularly in the case of the West of Ireland (Nash, 1993; Brett, 1994; Kiberd, 1995; Kneafsey, 1995; Kockel, 1995; Gibbons, 1996; Leerssen, 1996;

Graham, 1997). Academic study of the use of regional images as marketing devices is of relatively recent origin and readily available studies relate in particular to links with the promotion of Ireland as a tourism destination (O'Connor, 1993; Quinn, 1994; Bell, 1995; Kneafsey, 1995; Kneafsey, 1997). Few, if any, studies of the use of imagery in the promotion of sub-national levels have been undertaken. The use of regional imagery in the promotion of individual tourism SMEs has received little attention and its association with crafts is underexplored. This study seeks to address, to some degree, this gap that exists.

The Myth of the 'West'

Kockel (1995) sees the predominant regional images of Ireland today as being those of the North and the West. The West's image is one of a place apart, a haven from modern industrialised society. The Northern image is one of conflict and war, with questions of identity bound up in the Catholic/Protestant, Nationalist/ Unionist dichotomy (Connolly, 1997; Poole, 1997). The West of Ireland, including the south-west and north-west, retains a romantic image of a magical place apart, a place in sharp contrast to urbanised, industrial life where the traditional Irish culture and way of life survives (Byrne *et al.*, 1993; Kockel, 1995; Gibbons, 1996; Duffy, 1997; Kneafsey, 1997). The West as the site of true Irishness was constructed historically in two ways: by English colonists in the 17th and 18th centuries to whom it represented the 'primitive other' (Kneafsey, 1997), and by the early 20th century literary revivalists and the Irish-Ireland movement who saw the West of Ireland as the last remaining outpost of true Irishness (Nash, 1993).

'National memory is an important aspect of national identity' (Azaryahu and Kellerman 1999, p.109) and revivalism as a cultural convention played an important part in defining Irish identity in the late 19th century. Within nationalist ideology, the rock-strewn, barren landscape of the West of Ireland came to symbolise Ireland as a whole in opposition to the 18th century estate landscapes which were seen to represent English exploitation of Ireland (Graham, 1997). The establishment of the West of Ireland landscape as the cultural heartland of the country played a fundamental role in the formation of Irish nationalism. The idealised, unspoilt landscape of the West, untouched by modernity, came to represent Ireland before suppression by England. Identity is often defined in distinction from a hostile 'Other' (Said, 1993) and the West's 'Otherness' from England and the estate landscapes elsewhere in Ireland contributed to its elevation to the quintessential Irish landscape. Images of the West were further elaborated in the era of film with:

> Robert O'Flaherty's *Man of Aran* (1934) … a cinematic reflection of the theme of wild beauty in the western isle. In *The Quiet Man* (1952) John Ford celebrates the West as a passionate, patriarchal, violent society, while David Lean's *Ryan's Daughter* (1970) and Jim Sheridan's *The Field* (1992) can be seen as more recent manifestations of this self-same mythology (Duffy 1997, p.68).

The 'real' Ireland of the revivalists was a rural Ireland, a myth created by artists, intellectuals and political leaders, such as William Butler and Jack Yeats, Paul Henry, Sean Keating, George Russell, Michael Collins and Eamon de Valera, who themselves were the urban based descendants of country people (Gibbons, 1996; Kiberd, 1996). Revivalist literature and opinion portrayed the rural as a romantic idyll where the traditions of true Ireland persisted, with the farmer as the moral and economic backbone of the country. The idealisation of the West and the equation of rurality with true Irishness has also been a dominant theme in 20th century Irish art (Gibbons, 1996). In fact, as Duffy (1997) notes, Paul Henry's depictions of 20th century Achill's 'desolate landscapes of thatched houses and blue mountains became part of the nationalist iconography of the Free State' (p.67). Even prior to this, rural Ireland was portrayed by most artists in terms of wild, romantic, picturesque landscapes, with little reference to the reality of social and economic conditions of the time (Brett, 1994; Duffy, 1994). As early as 1841, travel writers described the romanticised landscape of the West of Ireland with the peasant as a 'valuable accessory to the landscape' (Hall and Hall, 1841 quoted in Brett 1994, p.123).

O'Connor (1993) contends that images used by tourist organisations tap into pre-existing stereotypes, selecting some of the more benign supposed characteristics of Ireland and Irish people to promote the country abroad. The evolution of Irish tourism promotion is grounded in the fact that historically Ireland has been dependent on the British and the US tourist markets. Whilst tourist images are created to combine the needs of the tourist with what the host country has to offer, they are also selected from a range of images already in existence in the market countries. These images evolved, in Britain, from colonial rule (an unpopulated landscape; virgin territory to be claimed by the tourist) and, in the US, from the vast numbers of Irish émigrés

(Ireland is a fictional land where time has stood still and the landscape is unchanged and unspoiled; it is a Tír na nÓg, where tourists can come to rejuvenate themselves) (O'Connor, 1993). Johnson (2000) uses the terms 'empty space' and 'empty time' to describe these representations of Ireland. In Britain and the US there is extensive imagery to tap into, but in other markets, e.g. Italy, the images of Ireland are more limited. However, O'Connor (1993) identifies a number of common themes that continue to be reproduced for tourist consumption. These include the image of Ireland as a picturesque, unspoiled, timeless country with a friendly and quaint people, a place where past traditions and ways of life still exist, a pre-modern society. Nash (1993) observes that images of the West of Ireland continue to be used today in tourism promotion as a representation of the landscape of Ireland as a whole. The image of the West has been constructed 'as both representative and different, its difference lying in its offer to the tourist of unique access to true Irishness' (Nash 1993, p.87). Kneafsey (1997) supports this contention in her examination of promotional materials relating to County Mayo, with brochures asserting that 'Mayo is the most Irish part of Ireland' (p.150). The overall themes emerging from all the representations and texts of Mayo examined include coastal scenery, mountains/wilderness/ rural scenery, historical ruins, holiday activities, traditions/music, and people/history/legend. These themes broadly match those identified by Quinn (1994) in her content analysis of verbal and visual presentations in brochures produced to promote Ireland as a tourist destination in Continental Europe. She identified a number of broad concepts: a world apart from modern society, an attractive, unspoiled environment, friendly people, a relaxed pace of life, a vast cultural heritage, and a large selection of sporting opportunities. She notes that '(a)ny semblance of "modern life", instantly familiar to the predominantly urbanised Europeans targeted by the brochures is carefully disguised' (Quinn 1994, p.65). In looking at images of Connemara in the West of Ireland, Byrne *et al.* (1993) state that:

> Connemara as perceived from one social vantage point or another is a construct which is assembled out of different components, depending partly on the requirements of the viewer (p.236).

Different images of the area that are identified include: a magical, peripheral area, the last outpost of true Irishness, a refuge or contrast from modern urbanised life. Connemara has long been described as authentic, yet various versions of authenticity can be identified, from its depiction as the location of unpolluted Irishness postulated by the revivalists, to its designation as a place of escape from modernisation, the last frontier identified by Synge (*ibid.*, 1993). Having identified past and contemporary images of the West of Ireland and their use in national tourism promotion, the next section examines the use of imagery by a sample of crafts and rural tourism SMEs in two Western regions, the Northwest (comprising counties Leitrim, Roscommon and Sligo) and the Southwest (Kerry and West Cork).

Using Imagery in Western Ireland

A sample of 99 rural tourism and craft SMEs were purposively chosen for the study, based on size (less than 50 full-time employees) and certain quality criteria pertaining to quality certification, association with the region and more subjective dimensions of attractiveness and use of value added techniques of production. An interview survey was carried out to identify the types of promotion and marketing activities currently carried out by these producers and to ascertain if, and how, place imagery was used in these activities. Relevant promotional materials used by respondents were collected for investigation and a socio-semiotic analysis of the content of the text and images communicated in these materials was conducted to supplement the interview data. Content analysis allows us to understand:

> the form and substance of messages, and the choices made by speakers and writers ... to discern the strategies of messengers, compare different types of messages (Schrott and Lanoue 1994, p.327).

In this instance, an analysis of 168 pieces of promotional literature used by the selected producers is described in order to understand the content, or 'form and substance', of these messages to potential consumers. The most frequently occurring type of promotional material was the brochure, followed by business cards, web pages and swing tags or labels. In terms of their format, the various media contained a variety of different types or units of content, including approval symbols, logos, maps, photographs, sketches, slogans and text.

Recurring themes in imagery used

Apart from providing practical information about the product, what emerges from the content of the promotional materials studied is a range of recurring motifs, which were used in a variety of ways to promote products. The most frequently occurring of these motifs were categorised as 'connection to place/use of regional imagery', 'people', 'landscape/natural environment', 'craftsmanship/tradition' and 'connecting with the past'. It is clear that these themes correlate with those identified previously in the literature, i.e. the image of Ireland as picturesque, unspoiled, timeless, with a friendly and quaint people, a relaxing pace of life, a place where past traditions and ways of life still exist (O'Connor, 1993). To a large extent the actual images identified by Kneafsey (1997) and Quinn (1994) were found in the research sample of both crafts and tourism respondents' literature. Certainly, Ireland as picturesque and attractive was evident in photographs, sketches and written text. The various scenic images identified by Kneafsey (1997) were present in large quantities in the sample. The unspoilt environment was implicit in many logos which used flowers, vegetation, greenery and animals, and in landscape photographs and those illustrating various outdoor activities. Numerous textual references were made to the unspoiled natural environment, particularly in the promotional literature of tourism respondents. The image of friendly people was apparent in photographs of hospitable owners and enthusiastic staff, with smiling, welcoming faces denoting 'homeliness' and a quality service. The quaintness identified by O'Connor (1993) and the people in traditional attire highlighted by Quinn (1994) were not in evidence. People were shown in modern clothes and emphasis was placed on a friendly, efficient, quality service with personal attention. The relaxing pace of life was evident in numerous references to tranquillity and getting away from the stresses of modern life. The themes of timelessness and a world apart from modern society were recurrent in the sample. Historical photographs and sketches showed how the product used to be and the people who inhabited that landscape of the past. Slogans invoked a mythical past of splendour and elegance ('*Formal magnificence, from past to present*', '*Gracious elegance since 1897*'). Textual descriptions invited readers to rediscover that past time ('… offers the opportunity of going back in time to an era when leisure, grace and beauty symbolised the good life') and to enjoy the relaxed, tranquil setting ('absorb the tranquil silence broken only by the song of the thrush'). Frequent textual references to the 'craic' to be had and traditional Irish music in pubs, as well as invitations to '(s)tep over the threshold and take a step back in time' to 'the old fashioned comfort of ', portrayed an image of a place where past traditions and ways of life exist. These themes were also evident in craft producers' literature where an emphasis was placed on traditional, handmade methods of production, handed down from generation to generation or the 'the age-old tradition of the Celt'. In relation to O'Connor's (1993) assertion that, where work was represented, it was romanticised, in the tourism literature of this study, there were very few images of work. In crafts, however, work was idealised, with craftspeople shown in solitary work, working with their hands and so engrossed in their work that they are oblivious of the camera.

Having identified the themes occurring in the images used by producers in their promotional materials, the next step is to examine the ways in which certain images of place tap into, and expound, particular myths. A number of practical examples are used to highlight this process. A simple socio-semiotic analysis of these images highlights some of these ideologies and place myths. As with all interpretative deconstructions of material culture, there are no definitive readings of these texts (Gottdiener, 1995). What follows is one interpretation grounded in semiotic analysis. This study of signs and socio-semiotics is a branch of semiotics which examines both signs and their social context of the images used and this does not exclude other possible meanings (Gottdiener, 1995).

Connotated Myths and Ideologies

A good example of a logo which falls into the 'connection to place/use of regional imagery' category is that used by a craftworker in the Southwest of Ireland. The logo consists of a sketch of a white-washed, thatched cottage with a wooden, traditional style half-door and stone path, set in a rural landscape with mountains in the background (Figure 15.1). The by-line *'Home-made in West Cork, Ireland'* was used in conjunction with the logo (as distinct from 'homemade' which may have pejorative connotations, e.g. homemade clothes). At a denotative level, this sketch purports to be an icon of the workshop or home where the craft item was produced. Some of the product is sourced from outworkers who work from home and this is also invoked. However, the sign is loaded with secondary meanings that symbolise a variety of connotated myths. First of all (the order is unimportant as these signs are not linear), the connection to place is made explicit in the by-line, where the consumer is informed of the place of production. The thatched cottage also connotes a certain image of 'Ireland' and 'Irishness', one aimed particularly at an American market. This is the Ireland of *The Quiet Man* where white-washed, thatched cottages with red, wooden doors, donkeys and carts and red-haired colleens exist in an idealised landscape outside of time. This particular sign achieved its referential role metonymically. Metonymy works by making a part of reality stand for the whole, in other words they work indexically, e.g. smoke, is an index of, or indicates fire. In this instance, one sign (the thatched cottage) motivates the receiver to construct the rest of the chain of conceptions (*The Quiet Man* imagery) that comprise the myth (an idyllic, timeless, rural Ireland).

Figure 15.1 Traditional cottage logo

Another myth made explicit in the by-line is the notion of the product being 'home-made'. Again, the sign supports this image through connoting cottage industry, which in turn signifies authenticity, tradition and quality. This particular craft product is largely intended for a tourist and/or export (primarily American) market. The image of a craft product, home-made in a cottage in rural Ireland, works on two levels in these markets. On one level, it has been suggested that consumers' search for authenticity, not just in the product, but in the unusual (for them) conditions under which it was produced, is an effort to bring an element of distinctiveness or uniqueness to their own lives (Spooner, 1986). MacCannell's (1976) argument in relation to tourism echoes this contention: that tourists seek the authentic as a means of escaping from their everyday, meaningless lives and that 'authentic' crafts may link the tourist/consumer with a place that evokes a more primitive life, untouched by modernity and rich in meaning. Littrell *et al.* (1993), in a study of US holiday-makers, identified 'cultural and historical integrity' and 'craftsperson and materials' as major themes in the tourists' descriptions of authenticity. Authentic products were identified as those being genuinely from the area and hand-made in the traditional way using the original methods handed down for generations. On another level, for Irish-Americans in particular, the image is a nostalgic reminder of their roots, both real and imagined, harking back to the cottages where their grandparents lived simpler, more natural, self-provisioning lifestyles. This links into the third major myth connoted in this logo, that of the link between crafts and rurality. Fisher (1997) contends that:

> associations of rurality and craft production converge, reinforce and compound each other … [and] pivots on the idea of 'self provisioning and family enterprise' (p.232).

The traditional thatched cottage of the logo is very much associated with rural Ireland at a connotative level, but this association is made manifest in the sketch which is quite obviously set in a rural, mountainous landscape. The significance of the rural/crafts production symbol lies in its paradigmatic choice that sets it up in binary opposition to modern, industrial/urban based production. The latent meaning is that the traditional craftworker works in harmony with nature and society producing only that which is needed, using non-invasive methods and natural materials as opposed to modern industry which is artificial, inauthentic and goes against nature. This in turn feeds into the myth of the rural idyll. An increasingly urbanised Western society has constructed a myth of rurality and the countryside based on a combination of abstract values and real images, symbolising community, harmony with nature, wholesomeness, purity and a collection of cultural and landscape images which stand out against urban and industrial imagery (Bunce, 1994; Cosgrove, 1998; Hopkins, 1998).

'Connection to place' is often invoked, in slogan and in written text more generally, through the use of the Irish language. An example of this is the slogan, 'Bréagtar bean le seod súirí', which is unquestionably an invocation of 'Irishness', the literal meaning being almost entirely unimportant (as the vast majority of readers are likely to have very little or no knowledge of the Irish language). For the slogan to work, readers need only recognise it as being Irish. In some cases this was used as a general sign of Irishness and, in other instances, as a marker of location within the Gaeltacht specifically. For craftworkers, much of the text relating to 'connection to place/use of regional imagery' consisted of descriptions of particular place features and historical figures and events, which had been used as inspiration or as the subject in product design. West of Ireland examples include, 'dark, brooding clouds draped over solid but distant mountains', '(i)nspired by the soft tones and greenness of Ireland', '(s)he lives … in West Cork, where the natural beauty around her home inspires her designs', '(h)is work … evokes all that is the West of Ireland'. This 'inspiration' evolves from a desire to tap into the perceived pool of positive images already established in consumers' minds about the region, as well as an attempt to market products to tourists by utilising the rhetoric of place promotion.

For craftworkers, descriptions of craftsmanship and skill and a long tradition of craftwork are a recurring theme. This is especially so in relation to handmade production of products, connoting authenticity and quality. The 'craftsmanship and tradition' theme shows pictorially, the majority of craftspeople at work, the craftsperson's tools or the craftsperson with the product or alone. These images seek to provide evidence that the products are handmade by a real person. For example, the constituent elements in the photograph in Figure 15.2 include a person sitting or standing at a workbench not directly facing the reader; casual, work-like clothing (sometimes an apron); small objects which can be identified as various types of tools either in the hands of, or next to, the person; the product in an unfinished state (usually being handled by the person); a room containing other unfinished products, raw materials and work benches. The iconographic code at work in this composition combines all of these signified elements to depict a craftsperson creating a product by hand, so engrossed in their work that they are oblivious of the camera.

Figure 15.2 Craftsperson at work (craftsperson's face blurred)

Similar motifs can be identified in the textual imagery relating to the theme of 'craftsmanship and tradition'. Descriptions of products as being handmade are the most frequently occurring motif in the West Region:

> because all the [product] produced is absolutely hand made, the spirit of the crafts man is liberated, unencumbered by machines of mass production.

Here, the secondary meaning plainly connotes the myth of the handmade craft as authentic and binarily opposed to modern (artificial), industrial based production.

Tourism respondents use various images of people, ranging from depictions of members of the target market enjoying relevant activities, to proprietors and employees of the business, signifying hospitality and a friendly service. Figure 15.3 illustrates a typical example of a photograph used to promote angling businesses.

Figure 15.3 Photograph of a fisherman

The myth of the photograph as proof of an event (Sontag, 1977) comes into play here using some simple iconic codes. The elements included in this composition include a smiling man posing for the camera with a fish held in his hands in a gesture of display; a net full of similar fish; plastic containers and various pieces of half unseen equipment; and a body of water surrounded by green vegetation. These various signifiers combine to produce a syntagmatic composition of a seasoned (well-equipped) angler, satisfied (smiling) and proud (displaying his catch for the camera) after a highly successful fishing trip (numerous fish in the net positioned at his feet, implying the entire catch is his). The green vegetation in the background symbolises an unspoiled and fertile environment, a theme reflected in the multitude of clean fish in the net. Photographs are most successful in tourism marketing when they show people having fun or partaking of appropriate activities, particularly if they look like the target market (Briggs, 1997). This principle has been adhered to in the majority of the photographs present in the sample, as it has been in this example, as the target consumer for angling businesses in Ireland is generally male, aged over 35 years (the man in the picture) and in the ABC1 social class, that is, managerial/professional/white collar, and so could afford the expensive equipment shown (Bord Fáilte, 1997). The intended reader is expected to identify with the angler and believe that he too can be this successful if he visits this area. This is a good example of the denoted message (a smiling man with fishing equipment displaying a fish and a full net) naturalising the symbolic message (satisfaction and success guaranteed).

Images of nature and the environment, as well as evocations of the past, tapped into myths of the countryside idyll, harmony with nature and the pleasures and simplicity of past times. For example, several photographs of craft products showed the product displayed on a natural stone or wood surface, sometimes with other natural materials such as fern fronds and shamrocks framing the edges of the composition. There are several layers of meaning operating in such photographs. The association of the product with natural materials is an attempt to naturalise the product itself and disassociate it from modern, artificial mechanised processes. The message is: this object is not machine-made, it is something of nature, using natural materials and it is authentic (the framing of the products 'within nature' emphasises this point). This in turn relates back to the craft/rural/traditional/authentic versus industrial/urban/modern/artificial myth as discussed above. Another reading of the use of natural materials is to highlight nature and environment as inspiration in product design. The colours and shapes of the products mirror those of the natural materials shown. The choice of the particular surfaces (stone; wood which appears old and preserved) is also significant. They connote an ancient landscape, enduring through time against elemental forces. The juxtaposition of such ancient materials with the craft being promoted, imbues the product with the same characteristics of longevity, antiquity and a timeless, natural beauty. The use of leafy, green vegetation again represents environmental consciousness and the signification of the shamrock evokes Irishness.

Another motif evident in the 'landscape/natural environment' category is the use of one photograph, or a collage of photographs, of a product, superimposed against a landscape scene. Although often not specifically named, these are usually either a generic landscape of a type generally associated with the Atlantic south-west coast of Ireland, or are of a recognisable, real place, which in this case was a view of the Blasket Islands from the Kerry coast (Figure 15.4).

Figure 15.4 Photograph of the Blasket Islands (product name removed)

Such photographs attempt to signify similar meanings to those just discussed (naturalising the product; ancient landscapes; environmentalism) as well as identifying the product with real places which are already embedded in the public awareness as desirable and beautiful locations. In Figure 15.4, the movement of the tides and the setting of the sun also signify natural cycles and the passing of time, which is reflected in the textual description accompanying this photograph which refers to 'a [product] collection with a timeless beauty...'. The punctuation here also indicates that, like nature, the product will last eternally. The use of the word 'forged', which is usually associated with the blacksmith trade and crafts such as metalwork, equates the land with the product. It implies that, like the land, the craft was also 'forged by nature's artistry'. This metaphor further serves to naturalise the product and the production process.

Conclusion

In his analysis of television advertisements of the Australian Tourist Commission, Waitt (1997) states that:

> these advertisements are an integral part of generating abroad the imagined geographies of Australia and inventing the imagined community that holds Australian society together (p.48).

He goes on to alert us to the fact that all national tourism promotion bodies have the authority to advocate landscapes that are part of the 'iconography of nationhood' both in terms of their promotion abroad and their part in the self-identity that connects people in an imagined community (p.57). Gold and Gold (1995) agree that 'tourism is one of the main ways in which a nation is represented to outsiders' (p.202) and express concern that conventional tourism promotional policy, at least in Scotland, portrays only a partial picture of the country. This may limit a nation's ability to expand its tourist base, as well as develop other economic opportunities. In addition Hughes (1998) argues that:

> (t)ourism is important to geographers ... not simply as a result of its acknowledged global economic importance, but more significantly for its semiotic realization (*sic*) of the spaces that are nurtured in the tourist's imagination (p.30).

It is evident that the use of connection to place and specific regional imagery is prevalent in promotional materials used in Western Ireland. Overall, images portrayed are of a natural, unspoiled, rural environment, where traditional methods of production survive in an idealised landscape out of time. Readers are invited to experience the tranquillity of a countryside which is worlds away from the modern, urban experience through consumption of its products (that is, crafts) and through consumption of the place itself (that is, rural tourism). The results of this study lead to the conclusion that it is not only tourism that semiotically produces spaces in people's imaginations, but also any promotional device that utilises, and therefore propagates, place images. Therefore, it is important to critically assess the specific place images used in the promotion and marketing activities of individual businesses as well as those used by national promotional bodies in any attempt to establish how we portray ourselves.

Acknowledgements

This paper is partly based on research conducted as part of an EU-funded project on Regional Images and the Promotion of Quality Products and Services in the Lagging Regions of the EU (RIPPLE) by laboratories in France (University of Caen; CEMAGREF, Aubiére; ENITA, Clermont Ferrand), Finland (University of Helsinki), Greece (University of Patras), Ireland (National University of Ireland, Galway; Teagasc Rural Research Centre; Teagasc National Food Centre), Spain (University of Valencia), and the United Kingdom (Coventry University; Scottish Agricultural College, Aberdeen; University of Wales, Aberystwyth). The overall co-ordinator of the research was Professor Brian Ilbery of Coventry University.

This research was supported by the Irish Research Council for the Humanities and Social Sciences Government of Ireland Scheme.

References

Azaryahu, M. and Kellerman, A. (1999) 'Symbolic places of national history and revival: a study in Zionist mythical geography', *Transactions of the Institute of British Geographers*, 24 (1), pp.109–123.

Bell, D. (1995) 'Picturing the landscape: *Die Grune Insel*: tourist images of Ireland', *European Journal of Communication*, 10 (1), pp.41–62.

Bord Fáilte (1997) *Perspectives on Irish tourism, 1991–1995, the product*, Bord Fáilte, Dublin.

Brett, D. (1994) 'The representation of culture' in Kockel, U. (ed) *Culture, tourism and development: the case of Ireland*, Liverpool University Press, Liverpool, pp.117–28.

Briggs, S. (1997) *Successful tourism marketing: a practical handbook*, Kogan Page, London.

Bunce, M. (1994) *The countryside ideal: Anglo-American images of landscape*, Routledge, London.

Byrne, A., Edmondson, R. and Fahy, K. (1993) 'Rural tourism and cultural identity in the West of Ireland' in O'Connor, B. and Cronin, M. (eds) *Tourism in Ireland: a critical analysis*, Cork University Press, Cork, pp.233–57.

Connolly, S. J. (1997) 'Culture, identity and tradition: changing definitions of Irishness', in Graham, B. (ed) *In search of Ireland: a cultural geography*, Routledge, London, pp.43–63.

Cosgrove, D. (1998) 'Cultural landscapes' in Unwin, T. (ed) *A European geography*, Longman, United Kingdom, pp.65–81.

Duffy, P. J. (1994) 'The changing rural landscape 1750–1850: pictorial evidence', in Gillespie, R. and Kennedy, B. P. (eds) *Ireland: art into history*, Town House, Dublin, pp.26–42.

Duffy, P. J. (1997) 'Writing Ireland: literature and art in the representation of Irish place', in Graham, B. (ed) *In search of Ireland: a cultural geography,* Routledge, London, pp.64–83.

Fisher, C. (1997) "I bought my first saw with my maternity benefit': craft production in west Wales and the home as the space of (re)production', in Cloke, P. and Little, J. (eds) *Contested countryside cultures: otherness, marginalisation and rurality,* Routledge, London, pp.232–51.

Gibbons, L. (1996) *Transformations in Irish culture*, Cork University Press, Cork.

Gold, J. R. and Gold, M. M. (1995) *Imagining Scotland: tradition, representation and promotion in Scottish tourism since 1750*, Scolar Press, Aldershot.

Gold, J. R. and Ward, S. V. (eds) (1994) *Place promotion: the use of publicity and marketing to sell towns and regions*, John Wiley and Sons, Chichester.

Gottdiener, M. (1995) *Postmodern semiotics: material culture and the forms of postmodern life*, Basil Blackwell, Cambridge.

Graham, B. (1997) 'Ireland and Irishness: place, culture and identity', in Graham, B. (ed) *In search of Ireland: a cultural geography*, Routledge, London, pp.1–15.

Hall and Hall, S. (1841) *Ireland: its scenery and character*, Jeremiah Howe, London.

Hopkins, J. (1998) 'Signs of the post-rural: marketing myths of a symbolic countryside', *Geografiska Annaler*, 80 B (2), pp.65–81.

Hughes, G. (1992) 'Tourism and the geographical imagination', *Leisure Studies*, 11, pp.31–42.

Hughes, G. (1998) 'The semiological realization of space', in Ringer, G. (ed) *Destinations: cultural landscapes of tourism*, Routledge, London, pp.17–32.

Ilbery, B. and Kneafsey, M. (1997) 'Regional images and the promotion of quality products and services in the lagging regions of the European Union', Paper presented to the Third Anglo-French Rural Geography Symposium, Nantes, September.

Johnson, N. C. (2000) 'Historical geographies of the present', in Graham, B. and Nash, C. (eds) *Modern historical geographies*, Pearson Education, Essex, pp.251–72.

Kiberd, D. (1996) 'The periphery and the center', Waters, J. P. (special issue editor) *Ireland and Irish Cultural Studies, The South Atlantic Quarterly*, 95 (1), Winter, pp.5–21.

Kneafsey, M. (1995) 'A landscape of memories: heritage and tourism in Mayo' in Kockel, U. (ed) *Landscape, heritage and identity: case studies in Irish ethnography*, Liverpool University Press, Liverpool, pp.135–53.

Kneafsey, M. (1997) *Tourism and place identity: change and resistance in the European Celtic periphery*, PhD thesis in Geography, University of Liverpool.

Kockel, U. (1995) ''The West is learning, the North is war': Reflections on Irish identity' in Kockel, U. (ed) *Landscape, heritage and identity: case studies in Irish ethnography*, Liverpool University Press, Liverpool, pp.237–58.

Leerssen, J. (1996) *Remembrance and imagination*, Cork University Press, Cork.

Littrell, M. A., Anderson, L. F. and Brown, P. J. (1993) 'What makes a craft souvenir authentic?', *Annals of Tourism Research*, Vol. 20 (1), pp.197–215.

MacCannell, D. (1976) *The tourist: a new theory of the leisure class*, MacMillan, London.

Nash, C. (1993) ''Embodying the nation' – the West of Ireland landscape and Irish identity' in O'Connor, B. and Cronin, M. (eds) *Tourism in Ireland: a critical analysis*, Cork University Press, Cork, pp.86–111.

O'Connor, B. (1993) 'Myths and mirrors: tourist images and national identity' in O'Connor, B. and Cronin, M. (eds) *Tourism in Ireland: a critical analysis*, Cork University Press, Cork, pp.68–85.

Poole, M. A. (1997) 'In search of ethnicity in Ireland', in Graham, B. (ed) *In search of Ireland: a cultural geography*, Routledge, London, pp.128–47.

Quinn, B. (1994) 'Images of Ireland in Europe: a tourism perspective' in Kockel, U. (ed) *Culture, tourism and development: the case of Ireland*, Liverpool University Press, Liverpool, pp.61–73.

Said, E. (1993) *Culture and imperialism*, Chatto and Windus, London.

Schrott, P. R. and Lanoue, D. J. (1994) 'Trends and perspectives in content analysis', in Borg, I. and Mohler, P. Ph. (eds) *Trends and perspectives in empirical social research*, Walter de Gruyter, Berlin, pp.327–45.

Sontag, S. (1977) *On photography*, Allen Lane, London.

Spooner, B. (1986) 'Weavers and dealers: the authenticity of an oriental carpet', in Appadurai, A. (ed) *The social life of things: commodities in cultural perspective*, Cambridge University Press, Cambridge, pp.195–235.

Urry, J. (1995) *Consuming places*, Routledge, London.

Waitt, G. (1997) 'Selling paradise and adventure: representations of landscape in the tourist advertising of Australia, *Australian Geographical Studies*, 35 (1), pp.47–60.

chapter sixteen

Sustainable Waste Management

Máire Ní Chionna

Introduction

The general cry in recent years has been that current waste management systems are 'unsustainable'. The subtext to these remarks is often along the lines of 'this can't be allowed to continue' or 'the system must be altered before it collapses'. Other comments refer to ever increasing quantities of waste, or the folly of perfectly good items being thrown out as rubbish. So why is sustainability important? Moreover, what aspects of sustainability might be important? In this chapter, these significant questions will be addressed through exploring aspects of sustainability encompassing environmental, economic and social elements all bound togther under the banner of sustainable development.

Sustainable Development

The earth's resources are finite. The rapid increase in human population and the development of an economic system based on high resource use per capita has brought this fact very much to the fore in the global agenda. This realisation of the finite nature of material resources and the recognition of a moral responsibility to hand on a clean and healthy environment to future generations, has given rise to that much used concept – sustainable development. The concept of sustainable development originated in the early 1970s, and was used by Ward in documentation prepared for the 1972 Stockholm Conference on the Human Environment (Ward and Dubos, 1972). The concept was publicised in *Our Common Future* or 'The Brundtland Report' in 1987 (WCED, 1987) and since then has been a much used and contentious concept since the Brundtland Report defined it as:

> Development which meets the needs of the present without compromising the ability of future generations to meet their own needs (WCED, 1987), [and] Sustainable

development is a process in which the exploitation of resources, the direction of investments, the orientation of technological development and institutional change are all in harmony, and enhance both current and future potential to meet human needs and aspirations (*ibid.*).

Sustainable development is a process, a way of approaching the economic and social development of society. Three aspects are often explicitly referred to, namely, environmental protection, social equity and economic development. However, the environmental aspect is the fundamental upon which the other two rest, as it provides clean air and clean water and a stable climate within which social and economic development can take place. Any development process that continuously degrades the environment cannot be considered sustainable. Following this reasoning, societies which consider themselves developed due to their high economic standing, may not be highly developed when measured against the wider criteria of sustainable development. Consequently any waste management system that is promoted as sustainable has to be examined in terms of how it complies with sustainable development criteria. In particular this includes the minimisation of detrimental environmental effects and its place in the economic and social development of the community.

Waste – A Material Resource

Waste conjures up different images for different people. Some equate it with 'rubbish' or 'refuse' (typically a mixed bag of domestic waste) or any dirty contaminated material that has been discarded by industry. However, the term waste has a very broad meaning in both Irish and European Union (EU) legislation. The legal definition of waste is:

> any substance or object which the holder discards or intends to or is required to discard (Waste Management Act, 1996)

This definition means that *any* material can be classified as 'waste' depending on the intention of the previous holder of that material. This is a very wide definition that may yet be challenged in the courts. Under this definition a material may be classified as waste under one circumstance, and not under another. For example, in road construction design, one of the objectives is to match 'cut' and 'fill' where possible. *Cut* is the excavated material where there is a local high area and *fill* is material used to make up low-lying areas.

However, material which was perfectly useful as the *fill*, becomes *waste* if there is too much and the surplus has to be disposed of off site. Even where the surplus material is sold on, it is still regarded as waste under the above definition. Table 16.1 sets out the annual tonnages of waste produced in Connacht. The waste produced in the largest quantities by far is animal waste in the form of manure and slurries. Excluding agricultural waste (which also includes mushroom compost and farm plastic wrap), domestic refuse accounts for 25 per cent of total non-agricultural wastes produced in Connacht. Looking at these various 'wastes', it is clear that waste is, or discarded material is, in actual fact a material resource.

Table 16.1 Quantities of waste in Connacht

Waste type	Amount (tonnes/year)
Household	139,116
Commercial	53,162
Industrial	121,063
Construction/demolition	201,510
Litter/street sweepings	8,345
Water treatment sludges	1,263
Wastewaster treatment sludges	13,540
Mining & quarrying	46,672
Healthcare	1,384
Agricultural animal waste	6,188,707
Mushroom compost	28,418
Farm plastic wrap	2,555
Total	**6,815,734**

Source: *Waste Management Plan for the Connaught Region 1999–2004* (Galway, Mayo Sligo, Leitrim, Roscommon County Councils and Galway Corporation)

Pursuing further this notion of waste as a material resource, where materials are dirty and mixed together, there is a high energy required (labour and money) in separating them into their constituent components. This material is dumped in a landfill, or burnt in incinerators so that some energy is recovered. However, if the constituents are kept separate and kept clean, then the resource becomes far more amenable to recycling and reuse, and the energy embodied in extracting or forming those raw materials is not lost. Although waste can be described as a material or commodity, it is subject to rigorous legislation because it is a commodity that the holder no longer wants. Yet one person's waste could be another company's raw material being used to make profit in adding value.

The well-known waste hierarchy explicitly states an order of preference in managing waste. The hierarchy goes from the best option, which is the prevention of waste occurring (*Reduction*), through *Reuse; Recycling* and *Thermal Treatment* to the least favoured disposal option, which is *Landfill*. This hierarchy is based on the principles of least environmental risk and the minimal use of natural resources (individual cases in restricted circumstances may throw up some reversals within the preferred hierarchy). A society moving towards sustainable development will be seeking to move waste management from the bottom half of the hierarchy towards the top half, with 'Reduce, Reuse, Recycle' playing the major part in waste management. In order to understand some of the constraints in moving up this hierarchy, it is useful to look at the different aspects concerned.

Reduction

Reduction is at the top of the waste hierarchy. Explicitly, this implies that the primary objective in any waste management plan should be to reduce the production of discarded or contaminated material in the first place. An important starting point is to apply the view that most 'waste' is a potential resource that can be reused or recycled. In addition the production of that waste required inputs of resources and so reducing waste will reduce the use of resources. The reduction of waste and resource input can be achieved by:

> decreasing consumption, i.e. purchase second hand or lease items;

> designing products that last longer, that produce less waste when in use and that produce less waste and pollution during manufacture;

> designing for less packaging, and

> designing packaging for reuse.

Reuse

Reuse seems self-explanatory. The product is used again after cleaning and sometimes after repair. The product may be used for the same purpose or for a different purpose. In many cases reuse occurs on a continuous or regular basis and the product remains in one place. However, in some cases, products can be transported long distances to where there is more demand for them. Examples of reuse include second hand items, refillable drink containers and reusable packing containers. Reuse causes little pollution and uses little energy compared to recycling as long as the transport distances are of the same order in both cases.

Recycling

In terms of preferred options, recycling is in the middle of the waste hierarchy. This option has a lot of positives but also some limitations. In theory, practically all solid waste can be recycled, but in practice most products in Ireland are not. Recycling means taking a discarded product, cleaning it, processing it (with water, heat or chemicals) and turning it into a raw material. Energy is required to process the product and to transport the discarded products to the reprocessing plant. There are four stages in recycling: Segregation, Collection, Reprocessing; and Market

Segregation refers to keeping discarded materials separate so not to contaminate each other. Obviously, if the discarded material is going to be processed into a new raw material, 'clean' batches of waste have more value. Segregation requires the understanding and co-operation of those discarding the material. Where it is proposed to introduce recycling of significant amounts of household waste, a major public education and reinforcement campaign is required to bring the general public along in this new habit. This is a significant cost that must not be underestimated.

Collection refers to getting the material from the discard location (household, shop, factory, office, building site) to the plant where the material will undergo cleaning and processing. This could involve at a minimum three, and often more, transfers of the material. Transportation costs can be a significant part of the economic cost of recycling. Indeed transportation will impact in terms of the environmental costs. Where the collection costs are high for rural areas and small villages, then the collection of segregated waste may be replaced by provision of Bring Centres or Recycling Centres – depots with containers for all the different types of recyclable wastes, into which the householder (or small business in some cases) can deposit their waste segregated by type.

Reprocessing may take place in Ireland (glass, demolition waste, some plastic) but most likely somewhere else for many common materials. The processing costs per tonne reduce as the quantities increase and economies of scale set in, so large plants are favoured.

The final product, a raw material, is placed on the *Market* like any other raw material. This is a global market in many cases and the demand for these raw materials goes up and down, being affected by any variations in the supply of virgin material or alternative materials. As the market price for recycled material fluctuates, it has a knock-on effect on the economics of a recycling system.

Moving up the Waste Hierarchy

So what are the various obstacles to moving up the waste hierarchy? Are they related to social factors or inadequate legislation or do they spring from the economic system? Initial explorations indicate that all factors contribute and social, legal and economic solutions will be required to overcome these obstacles.

Social obstacles or the 'people factor' includes a weak sense of civic duty or civic pride. People often do not see how their actions contribute to the overall degradation of the environment and can feel their efforts will not make a major difference to the overall problem of waste management. Further, people in general are busy and want convenience and think that they pay enough taxes already. They do not want to pay for the transition to a low waste society if, in the meantime, the cost of waste disposal gets higher and higher. People also have more disposable income and so there is less financial incentive to reduce consumption or reuse. Finally people have a preference for new products rather than a second-hand alternative. They want the 'good feeling' associated with having new cars, clothes, tools etc.

Markets and fiscal instruments are also contributory factors. The tax system makes no distinction between using virgin resources and recycled material. In some cases the tax on a second-hand product is higher, and subsidies, in some cases, favour the purchase rather than the leasing of goods. The recent introduction of environmental levies, the plastic bag levy introduced in March 2002 and the landfill levy to be implemented in June 2002, marks a welcome shift towards the use of fiscal instruments.

Design is also an important factor. Designers and specifiers do not seem to be fully aware of their role in the ecological loop, often designing mixed plastic products that are difficult to disassemble for recycling. Material engineers and scientists need to look more systematically at the reuse and recycling implications of new materials. Ultimately the company employing the researchers may not see any commercial benefit to researching the reuse and recycling implications of new materials in the absence of relevant market and fiscal instruments.

EU Policy Development

Policy is now being developed at EU level, which looks at Producer Responsibility themes. *A Green Paper on Integrated*

Product Policy (COM, 2001) sets out how the design of products need to take into account the full life cycle costs of that product, and in the design parameters, the ease of reuse or recycling of the product after it has completed its primary use. An Integrated Product Policy approach aims to ensure that environmental problems are not shifted from one stage of the product life cycle to another. The policy will relate to the whole life-cycle of a product, from the initial mining of raw materials through to the production, distribution, use, recycling and final disposal. Designing a product with a view to its final disassembly, reuse or potential for easy recycling will open up a whole new aspect of design for material scientists, production engineers and manufacturers. How the environmental cost of long-distance transport is factored in, might ultimately point towards designing for a regional (or local) market rather than a global one in specific cases. Geographic location and the economics of transport will be crucial in determining which forms of waste management flourish. It would seem that one way of increasing the economic benefit of the inflow of material goods to a region is to derive secondary benefit from the materials after the first use is completed. Thus the discard from one sector of the economy becomes the raw material for another. This source of materials has not been seriously developed and should become more significant in the future as the quantities of clean, segregated waste in this region increase.

In some EU Countries, 'Product-Panels' have already been set up to look at possible solutions and full life cycle costs for particular products (in Denmark, there are product panels on electronics, textiles, the transportation of goods, and building and construction). There is an enormous challenge in this endeavour. It seems that the current economic system favours use of materials and energy rather than use of labour. In the final analysis a move into sustainable resource management will need participation by all stakeholders – consumers, producers, governments and the EU institutions.

Local Developments

Local authorities are beginning to invest substantial resources in environmental awareness and in promoting 'Reduce, Reuse, and Recycle'. All local authorities in Connacht have a long-term environmental awareness programme in place, and are setting up recycling centres, composting centres, bring banks, etc. As the cost of disposal to landfill goes up, the private sector is also coming forward with significant investment in this sector. There are collection services for cardboard and glass, with private companies in specific locations collecting household recyclables. Galway City Council has reduced domestic waste going to landfill by 50 per cent from 2000 to 2002 due to the transformation to segregated collection of food waste, recyclable waste and residual waste for landfill. A similar scheme is in operation in Ballinasloe and is about to be implemented in the Aran Islands. Galway County Council operates two recycling centres for the general public with two more at the advanced planning stage. All waste collectors will be required to move into segregated waste collection of domestic waste by a target date under the new Waste Collector Permits just recently issued.

Change in attitudes to waste management however is only in its infancy. There is still a lack of knowledge of what a local recycling centre, composting facility or anaerobic digester plant looks like and how it might impact on a locality. This feeds into past experience of unresourced small local dumps and general suspicion about effective enforcement of regulations in Ireland. This, together with the Not In My Back Yard (NIMBY) factor produces opposition to proposals to build this infrastructure. This is causing delay in the provision of recycling centres, as some landowners are not willing to sell land if it is to be used for some form of waste mangement facility.

Ultimately, if we wish to have a society in which waste is managed in a sustainable way, then individuals, communities, interest groups, business interests, local authorities and central government will have to engage with an integrated system of waste management that takes into account environmental, social and economic concerns.

References
Ward, B. & Dubos, R. (1972) *Only One Earth*, Penguin, UK.

World Commission on Environment & Development (1987) *Our Common Future* (report of the Brundtland Commission), OUP.

Irish Government (1996) *Waste Management Act, 1996*, Govt Publ, Dublin.

Mayo County Council and others (2001) *Waste Management Plan for Connaught Region*.

COM (2001) Green Paper on Integrated Product Policy http:// europa.eu.int/comm/environment/home/ipp.htm accessed 23 Nov 2001.

chapter seventeen

WATER QUALITY ISSUES IN THE WEST OF IRELAND

Kieran R. Hickey

Introduction

Ireland boasts one of the highest availability of fresh water per capita in Europe. With over 6,000 lakes of surface areas greater than one hectare (some exceeding 1,000 hectares), numerous rivers and aquifers, water, particularly for domestic, industrial, agricultural and human consumption represents one of the key economic resources of the state (Stapleton *et al.* 2000). Recognising this position, why is there a significant problem in relation to water quality in Ireland? Further, what are the main threats to water quality in Ireland; how much knowledge do we have about these threats and, should Irish people be more concerned about this issue than currently appears to be the case? This chapter will explore some of these issues and examine the current water quality issues facing the West of Ireland. This will be achieved through identifying changes in groundwater, river, lake and coastal water quality and attempting to determine the causal factors of these changes. This in turn will feed into discussion on two key issues currently facing the West of Ireland, those of contaminated group water schemes and nitrate control zones.

Why Should we be Concerned about Water Quality?

Issues relating to the environment, water quality and growing waste management problems throughout Ireland are increasingly being pushed to the top of the agenda both socially and politically. This debate has been spurred on not only by the realisation of the populace that the availability of clean drinking and bathing water is increasingly being threatened but also by heightened media awareness of such incidents as the discovery of large-scale illegal dumps in a number of sites throughout the country; revelations of previous dumping of radioactive material in the Irish Sea and emerging evidence on the possibility of similar dumping in one landfill site in Ireland. Furthermore, the European Union (EU) 'watchdog' has raised awareness of Ireland's rather tardy response to environmental directives with the country currently facing 111 prosecutions for failing to implement substantial numbers of EU environmental legislation and directives. Among the most serious of these, if it is possible to determine levels of seriousness in relation to damaging the environment, include issues of water quality and waste management. In particular there are 17 specific cases of infringement of the EU's waste directive alone (McNally and O'Doherty, 2002). Further dissatisfaction, of particular relevance to the West of Ireland, has been expressed with regard to the rural group water schemes which show significant contamination, and the implementation of nitrate control zones.

All however is not totally negative, with the Environmental Protection Agency (EPA) (2002) reporting that for the first time in nearly 30 years there has been an overall improvement in Irish river water quality. Up until this latest survey there had been a general decline in the number of stretches of rivers classified as unpolluted with a consequent rise in the number of stretches of rivers being designated as slightly or moderately polluted (there has been no change in the number of stretches of rivers designated as seriously polluted). This survey also showed that 400km of previously polluted river channels are now in 'satisfactory condition'. Most of the improvements have occurred in catchments where new anti-pollution measures have been put in place. These measures have included the installation of phosphorous removal in sewage treatment works, nutrient management plans on farms and improved slurry storage (EPA, 2002). The positive improvements indicated in the report are however tempered somewhat by the inclusion that 30 per cent of Irish river channels are still polluted (EPA, 2002).

Causes of Pollution and Implications for Western Ireland

The principal causes of pollution are sewage and agricultural and industrial discharges. Increased development pressures, the intensification of agriculture, runoff of excessive fertiliser use, non-existent and outdated sewage treatment plants and industrial contamination all play a contributory part in polluting the environment. Lake water throughout Ireland and the West of

Ireland is considered good as approximately 80 per cent of the 124 largest waterbodies were considered to be in satisfactory condition when they were surveyed between 1995 and 1998 (Stapleton *et al.,* 2000). The main attributed cause of poor lake water quality in the West of Ireland has been the runoff of nitrates and phosphates in the form of fertilisers, slurry, poorly treated municipal sewage and occasional industrial spills (Stapleton *et al.,* 2000). This has led to a decline in oxygen levels in water and eutrophication occurring (Anon, 2002d). Despite considerable effort in improving lakes like Lough Derg and Lough Ree this is being offset by disimprovements in other lakes such as Lough Sheelin which is primarily affected by agricultural pollution (Stapleton *et al.,* 2000).

The West of Ireland in general has the highest overall water quality in comparison with other regions throughout Ireland. This is due primarily to its low population numbers and little heavy industry. Taking a summary of river quality as determined by the EPA (Table 17.1) an excellent insight into the issue of water quality in the West of Ireland can be gained. The blocks selected in Table 17.1 provide summary data for Co. Donegal, Co. Clare, Co. Galway and a comparative figure for Co. Dublin showing low, moderate and relatively polluted and highly polluted areas. This data is derived from complete coverage of Ireland's water quality by the EPA using interactive maps and attached data tables with each survey site block measuring 22km square. It is interesting to note that none of the three blocks chosen for the West of Ireland had a site with serious pollution (serious pollution levels are more often associated with urban and/or industrial areas). The blocks representing the West of Ireland show slight or moderate pollution affecting a considerable number of survey sites, few sites with severe pollution but a majority of sites remaining unpolluted. The block representing Co. Dublin is included to give an insight into just how far water can become contaminated (worryingly this is by no means the worst block on the grid).

Table 17.1 Summary river water quality of four EPA grid blocks 1995–1997 (www.epa.ie).

Block	No. of Survey Sites	Seriously Polluted	Moderately Polluted	Slightly Polluted	Unpolluted
Low Co. Donegal	24	0	3	1	20
Medium Co. Clare	18	0	7	1	10
Relatively high Co. Galway	25	0	10	2	13
High Co. Dublin	28	2	14	6	6

In terms of coastal and estuarine areas the ongoing causes of poor water quality lie in the discharge of untreated or partially treated sewage; high levels of nitrates and phosphates being washed into the river systems and eventually ending up in the estuaries and bays; and occasional heavy metal and other contaminants. An example of this is the Garavogue Estuary which forms the central and largest of the three estuaries feeding into Sligo Bay. The estuary currently has five outfall points and a disused landfill that affect this estuary. Estimates of the annual input of Biological Oxygen Demand (BOD), over the period 1991–1995, provide a useful measure of organic pollution, nitrogen and phosphorous (Table 17.2).

Table 17.2 Estimates of the annual input budget of BOD and nutrients to the Garavogue Estuary between 1991–1995 (Marine Institute, 1999).

Source	BOD (tonnes/year)	Total Nitrogen (tonnes/year)	Total Phosphorous (tonnes/year)
Riverine inputs	409	145	9
Municipal inputs	828	40	156
Industrial inputs	54	n/a	n/a
Landfill inputs	5	n/a	n/a
Atmospheric inputs	n/a	14	<1

These estimates show the dominant source of BOD and phosphorous for this estuary coming from municipal sources. High levels of BOD also come from riverine inputs, which is also the dominant source for nitrogen inputs. This is an unusual result as in most of the other West coast bays and estuaries the dominant source of all three measures of organic pollution are riverine inputs. This includes the Shannon Estuary, North Inner Galway Bay (the city area) and Lough Foyle. This shows how important the pollution of rivers and lakes is in controlling estuarine and coastal water quality. This will increase in importance as more and more coastal cities and towns get new and/or substantially improved sewage treatment facilities as in the case of Mutton Island in Galway Bay and Sligo Town. This form of contamination is added to by the dumping of dredging or inert material at a number of locations along the West coast. These include Fenit Harbour, the Shannon Estuary and three sites and Burton Port, West Donegal and Tory Island. In the latter case 16,000 tonnes by dry weight of inert material was dumped in 1996 (Marine Institute, 1999). No chemical analysis of this material was carried out. At other sites this type of material was found to contain relatively high levels of heavy metals such as cadmium and arsenic amongst others.

Groundwater contamination is also very variable and depends considerably on local hydro-geological conditions. Many areas are highly vulnerable to groundwater contamination due to the porous nature of the underlying limestone rock that covers nearly half of the island of Ireland (Daly *et al.*, 2000). The poor state of groundwater in many areas has been identified in recent ground water samples taken by the EPA which show 38 per cent (of the samples) having faecal contamination and 20 per cent showing high nitrate levels (Anon, 2002a). A number of causes of this type of groundwater contamination can be identified. These include poorly sited domestic septic tank systems which threaten localised groundwater pollution and can contaminate local wells; excessive fertiliser use, particularly nitrates in predominantly tillage areas which are then carried into the groundwater during winter rainfall events (MacConnell, 2002), and an increase in illegal dumping. The latter pollutes groundwater because they are often located in unsuitable sites with highly porous rocks such as limestone. Further, they are often poorly operated, lack official monitoring and can contain material that can easily contaminate groundwater (O'Brien, 2002). This lack of responsibility is having far reaching impacts for society in general and rural areas in particular with the latter facing increasing problems of water contamination through poorly maintained local group water schemes.

The Issue of Group Water Schemes

Local authorities produce and distribute more than 90 per cent of the drinking water in the country and 91 per cent of samples were found to be within EU safety limits for contaminants (EPA, 2001). In more remote rural areas many people are dependent on group water schemes for their drinking water. These are schemes set up by private individuals and committees and supply about 7% of the country's drinking water. However, the concern here is that only 60 percent of group water schemes were found to be within acceptable safety levels (Table 17.3). In addition to Table 17.3 a serious water contamination incident that occurred in Shanbally, Co. Galway was not responded to by the local authority (EPA, 2001).

Table 17.3 Counties with low compliance levels for faecal coliforms in 2001 in the West of Ireland (EPA, 2001).

	Public Water Supply	**Group Water Schemes**
Faecal coliforms	Co. Sligo	Co. Donegal Co. Galway Co. Mayo Co. Roscommon Co. Sligo

Substantial investment in Group Water Schemes can be anticipated under the National Development Plan 2000–2006 (Department of Finance, 1999) with an allocation of 533 million euro. This may not be sufficient to bring all Group Water Schemes up to minimum safety levels. Some grants are available in 16 designated areas under *Clár*, the rural regeneration scheme. These grants of 6,477 euro (£5,100) while useful in providing running water, do not satisfy the actual cost for many householders in more isolated areas which can be up to 11,430 euro (£9,000) (Siggins, 2002). Further, in response to both EU and local dissatisfaction the Minister for State for Rural Development has indicated that a new water services authority will be set up under legislation which would involve licensing group water schemes or closing them down if they failed to meet EU standards (Siggins, 2002).

Nitrate and Phosphate Pollution

Ireland is the only EU country that has not dealt with the issue of the Nitrates Directive of 1992. As such, the EU is currently preparing to prosecute Ireland as a result of this failure (MacConnell, 2002). This is not surprising, as successive Irish Governments have failed to implement a series of EU environmental directives. The Irish government is faced with two options in relation to the nitrate issue, the first of which is to designate the whole country as a Nitrate Vulnerability Zone (NVZ) or alternatively to designate major catchments as NVZ's (Anon, 2002b). The concern for Ireland as expressed by the various farming organisations is that the imposition of NVZ's would have a heavy impact on Ireland's commercial farmers and would present a major challenge to 40,000 farmers (although, it has been noted that farmers who currently are in the REPS (Rural Environmental Protection Scheme) would in most cases already conform to the Nitrate Directive). The government are however being forced to act as the EU is threatening to withhold 248 billion euro (£1.95 billion) in subsidies unless Ireland complies with the Nitrate directive (among others). The initial stage of this blockage of payments concerns proposed top up of area based payments for farmers in mountain areas. This will continue and get worse until the government makes a formal decision on implementation of the nitrates directive (Ryan, 2002). One further concern, which has not been highlighted in relation to nitrates, is the growing body of evidence that suggests that nitrate rich food has been linked to serious human health problems including colon cancer, as well as animal health problems (Storey, 2002).

The situation with regard to phosphates is not a great deal better. Again Ireland has failed to implement the EU Phosphates Directive. The EPA estimates that between 1979 and 1998 farmers unnecessarily spread more than 0.5 million tonnes of phosphates, wasting in the region of 762 million euro, and causing a drastic decline in water quality. Other directives not implemented (that may also have a significant impact on the farming community) include the Water Framework Directive, Waste Directive and the National Climate Change Strategy. In the latter case the agricultural sector produces almost 33 per cent of the country's greenhouse emissions with the Climate Change Strategy also envisaging a further reduction of 5 per cent in the national herd which is also likely to have serious implications for commercial farming, particularly in relation to stocking levels (Anon 2002b).

Impacts on the West of Ireland

It seems likely that the smaller rural group water schemes may be forced to cease operating, as the cost of complying with the EU water quality regulations will exceed the ability of many of the members of the schemes to pay. It is also possible that the numbers of households relying on their own wells will increase as the smaller group water schemes are abandoned. This will lead to an extension of mains water schemes to many smaller settlements and rural areas not now covered by this service. The larger schemes will have to become stand alone mains systems with their own purification plants in order to meet EU drinking water quality regulations. It is difficult to predict the likely impact of the implementation of these various EU directives and the National Climate Change Strategy in an already marginal agricultural area. However it is possible to suggest a number of strategies that farmers whether commercial or part-time might adopt. The most obvious route would be for farmers to enter the REPS scheme; this would make most farm activities compliant with the various EU directives. It would also provide valuable additional income, which would offset any losses that may result due to the implementation of the various directives. Some farms may cease to exist altogether either being bought out or being converted to forestry. These processes are ongoing at present on marginal land throughout the West, but the rate of change may be increased as a result of these directives. These directives will encourage further farm diversification and a movement to higher quality and less quantity products. This would include a further significant movement into organic farming and activities such as agri-tourism.

Concluding Remarks

EU Environment Commissioner Margaret Wallstrom has argued that it is essential:

> that all Member States adhere fully to these legislative measures if we are to ensure a sustainable management of water quantity and quality throughout Europe (Anon, 2002c).

Ireland, however, has continued to fail to implement a large number of EU directives over the last 10 years or so. This is unacceptable from economic, social and political standpoints and it will 'cost' Ireland in the longer term, not only in terms of potential health hazards, alarming as this is, but also in monetary terms as the country will be forced to implement these directives or face very significant withholding of EU funds. Considerable expenditure will have to be undertaken to implement these various directives and this will require the use of resources that might otherwise have been used to the benefit of rural areas. Ireland it seems, only responds with national legislation after serious problems arise or they are forced to do so by the EU. Essentially Ireland is reactive in terms of environmental legislation and not proactive (Anon, 2002c). For the West of Ireland to achieve any level of sustainable management of water quantity and quality, considerable and possibly painful adjustment to the various directives is inevitable. Unfortunately the indirect cost will most probably fall heaviest on those most vulnerable, namely the small-scale farmers and members of the smaller rural group water schemes.

References

Anon (2002a) 'River water quality shows pollution decrease', *Irish Times*, 24th Jan. 2002.

Anon (2002b) 'Nitrate pollution', *Irish Times*, 7th Jan. 2002.

Anon (2002c) 'Water quality: Commission acts against France, Greece, Germany, Ireland, Luxembourg, Belgium, Spain and the United Kingdom', *Rural Europe,* Spring 2002.

Anon (2002d) 'Awake to the problems of pollution', *Irish Independent*, 23rd Jan. 2002.

Daly D., Drew D., Deakin J., Ball D., Parkes M. and Wright G. (2000) *The karst of Ireland: limestone landscapes, caves and groundwater drainage systems*, Geological Survey of Ireland, Dublin.

Department of Finance (1999) *National Development Plan 2000–2006*, Government Publications, Stationery Office, Dublin.

Environmental Protection Agency (2001) *The quality of drinking water in Ireland, 2000*, Environmental Protection Agency, Wexford.

Environmental Protection Agency (2001) *Water quality in Ireland 1998–2000*, Environmental Protection Agency, Wexford.

MacConnell S. (2002) Cabinet discusses running of nitrate zones, *Irish Times* 17 January 2002.

MacConnell S. (2002) Mustard may become common crop in effort to prevent water pollution, *Irish Times* 31 January 2002.

Marine Institute (1999) *Ireland's marine and coastal areas and adjacent seas, an environmental assessment*, Marine Institute, Dublin.

McNally F. and O'Doherty C. (2002) 'Criminal enquiry will investigate illegal dumps', *Irish Times* 1st Feb. 2002.

O'Brien T. (2002) 'Dump operating beyond planning terms has polluted groundwater', *Irish Times*, 25th Feb. 2002.

Ryan R. (2002) 'EU blocks payment for mountain farmers due to nitrates impasse', *Irish Examiner*, 15th March 2002.

Stapleton L., Lehane M. and Toner P. (2000) *Ireland's Environment: A Millennium Report*, Environmental Protection Agency, Wexford.

Siggins L. (2002) 'Extra funding for rural water schemes', *Irish Times*, 28th Jan. 2002.

Storey D. (2002) 'Beware of nitrogen when it crosses the nitrate barrier', *Irish Examiner Farming Supplement*, 28th March 2002.

Mary Cawley is a Senior Lecturer in the Department of Geography, NUI, Galway. Her research interests relate to the changing nature of rural society and economy on which she has published extensively. One stream of her research relates to population change and migration. She is a former President of the Geographical Society of Ireland.

Gerry Finn has 25 years experience in the Public Service. From 1993 to 1999, he was CEO of Roscommon County Enterprise Board. During the same period he also acted as Chairman of the County Roscommon Partnership Board that had responsibility for socially excluded and disadvantaged people. Appointed Director of Community and Enterprise for County Roscommon in 1999, he has been Director of the BMW Regional Assembly since February 2000.

Sheila Gaffey completed her Ph.D. in the Geography Department, NUI, Galway in 2001. She has an MSc (Agric) in Rural Development from UCD and has worked with international research partners in studying lagging regions of the EU. Her research interests include rural and community development, rural tourism and semiotics. Sheila has also recently been awarded a Government of Ireland Postdoctoral Fellowship.

Séamus Grimes is a Senior Lecturer in the Department of Geography at NUI, Galway. He has achieved international recognition in relation to his academic publications and has been involved in a number of EC funded research projects. His research interests centre mainly on Information and Communications Technology (ICT) and the implications of these new technologies on regional development. His most recent publications include an *Overview of Opportunities Offered by Information Society Technologies (IST) for European Peripheral Areas*, Netcom and Communications Studies NETCOM 14(3/4) 2000; and *Rural Areas and the Information Society* in Roberts and Hall, *Rural Tourism and Recreation*, CAB International, 2001.

Kieran Hickey is a lecturer in the Department of Geography at NUI, Galway. His main interests are in recent environmental change and human impact on the natural environment. Kieran has been involved in a number of international research projects including investigations of Coastal Change funded by the European Commission. He has published extensively in national and international journals and is currently completing a book on *The Natural History of Wolves in Ireland*.

Michael Keane is a Professor in the Economics Department at NUI, Galway. He has published extensively in national and international journals and has made a major contribution both to academic literature and to policy creation in terms of regional and rural development in Ireland. Michael has been involved in numerous EU funded projects and he was responsible (with P. Commins) for publishing a comprehensive document on developing the rural economy as part of the NESC Report on *New Approaches to Rural Development* in 1994.

Marie Mahon, a graduate of the Masters of Rural Development programme at NUI, Galway, is a Ph.D. student in the Department of Geography working on an HEA–funded research project in the Environmental Change Institute.

Des McCafferty is Senior Lecturer and Head of the Department of Geography in Mary Immaculate College, University of Limerick. His research interests are in local and regional development, with current work in this area focusing in particular on the links between territorial development and urbanisation in Ireland, as mediated by the evolving Irish urban system. Publications include the books *Competitiveness, Innovation and Regional Development in Ireland* with James A. Walsh, and *Local Partnerships for Social Inclusion?* with Jim Walsh and Sarah Craig. He is currently President of the Geographical Society of Ireland, and recently completed a three-year term as Chair of the Irish Branch, Regional Studies Association.

John McDonagh is a graduate of NUI, Galway. He obtained his Ph.D. degree from Bristol and was a lecturer at Northampton University before returning to take up a lectureship post at NUI, Galway in 1997. John's main research interests are in rural and regional development and he has a number of publications in national and international journals. John was recently involved with a number of European partners on a EU funded project investigating 'Environment, Transport Policies and Rural Development'. His monograph, *Renegotiating Rural Development in Ireland*, was published by Ashgate (December 2001). John is currently working on a HEA-funded project exploring the issue of common lands in the West of Ireland.

Brian McGrath is a Lecturer/Assistant Director of the Masters in Community Development at the Department of Political Science and Sociology, NUI, Galway. His principal research interests include social exclusion, rural sociology, community development, youth and research methodologies. He is currently pursuing a Ph.D. with the Department of Land Economy, University of Aberdeen and has recently published articles in the *Journal of Rural Studies* and *Administration*.

Máire Ní Chionna, BE MSc DIC, Chartered Engineer, is a water and environmental engineer. Her career includes periods working in Malawi, Nepal, Scotland as well as Ireland, where she has been employed in the private sector, public service and UNICEF. Recently appointed Senior Engineer in Galway County Council, Máire also serves on Comhar – the National Sustainable Development Partnership.

Pádraig Ó hAoláin has a distinguished reputation as a contributor to the development of the Gaeltacht region. He has presented numerous papers on the problems and opportunities facing the Gaeltacht and has published in a number of different fora on this subject. His current position is Leas-Phriomhfheidhmeannach-Forbairt Réigiúnach, Údarás na Gaeltachta.

Patricia O'Hara is Senior Policy Analyst and Manager of the Policy Division in the Western Development Commission. She has written and published extensively on regional and rural development and the farm family. Her most recent work is the *State of the West* report for the Western Development Commission, published in July 2001.

Brendan Smith is one of Galway's longest serving community activists. His leadership involvement in localised issues with a nation-wide urban dimension include neighbourhood recreational facilities for all age groups, eco-friendly waste management systems, legislative standards on private rented accommodation and the construction of non-vehicle transportation networks. He is a member of the Galway City Development Board, chair of its Eco-City sub-structure and secretary of the acclaimed Terryland Forest Park. Initiated by Brendan in the mid-1990s, the latter project is now a flagship of successful community-local authority partnership.

Jim Walsh is Professor and Head of the Department of Geography and Chairman of the Board of the National Institute for Regional and Spatial Analysis (NIRSA) at NUI, Maynooth. He is a member of many advisory bodies including the National Economic and Social Council and the Expert Advisory Group for the National Spatial Strategy. He has published extensively on regional and local development. Recent co-edited or co-authored books include *Regional Planning and Development in Europe; Competitiveness, Innovation and Regional Development in Ireland,* and *Irish Agriculture in Transition – A Census Atlas.* Jim is currently the President of the Geographical Society of Ireland

Barbara Walshe has worked for many years as a voluntary community activist and is currently working for the Community Workers Co-Operative. She supports the community sector in the BMW Region, particularly those who have an anti-poverty focus within the new structures that are emerging as part of the Local Government Reform process. Barbara represents the Community/ Voluntary Pillar on the National Public Transport Forum and the Rural Transport Sub-Group.

READER'S NOTES

READER'S NOTES